TRAVELS WITH
Mary Jane

CONFESSIONS OF A
70-YEAR-OLD STONER

BY THE OLD HEAD

AUTHOR

THE OLD HEAD

Copyright © 2015 by The Old Head

Published by the Corregidor Peace Institute Press (CPIP), 2015
www.cpi-press.com | info@cpi-press.com

ISBN 978-151-77860-5-2

Layout & Design: Juvelin T. Aripal

Available in print and Kindle E-book at www.amazon.com

For Terry

"Dope will get you through times of no money, better than money will get you through times of no dope."

–Freewheelin' Franklin

CONTENTS

PROLOGUE

It turned out to be creeper weed, but even before the THC took hold, I was on a natural high I had never experienced before. It was my first legal toke of marijuana in more than forty years as a cannabis consumer. That alone was enough to provide an unexpected euphoria, a natural high that somehow helped validate a part of me, the thrill of the forbidden in reverse.

I was sitting in a small coffee shop about a five-minute walk from my overpriced hotel in Amsterdam's Canal District. It had been almost three hours since my plane landed at Schipol International Airport, and among friends back home the over-under on how long it would take me to get high once I touched down in Holland was two hours. I was running late.

I felt like an unofficial ambassador for all of the stoners I knew who had never been to Amsterdam, as well as those who had and knew what they were missing. Anybody with a passport and the price of a plane ticket can visit Amsterdam; it's not a big deal. Nevertheless, there was still a certain amount of satisfaction involved. I was finally there after all those years of reading about it in *High Times* and *Cannabis Culture* and listening to other peoples' stories. It was my turn at last.

The coffee shop was a hole-in-the-wall affair just off Rembrandtplein (Rembrandt Square). There was a coffee and cannabis bar in one corner, a couple of tables and chairs, and a window looking out on the alley. At the back of the first floor was a flight of stairs leading up to a couple of rooms where you could sit and smoke. Some god-awful techno pop was circulating through the sound system. Techno is popular in many smoking dens, and I was always happy when I stumbled upon a coffee shop playing reggae.

There was a laminated menu listing different types of weed and the per gram price. The weed itself was displayed in glass containers similar to the ones used by tobacconists and candy stores. The young Moroccan working the counter seemed puzzled when I asked if any of the marijuana was sativa.

"This is good. It will get you really high," he said, ignoring my question and indicating a glass jar three-quarters full of brown buds.

It clearly wasn't sativa, an indicia/sativa hybrid at best. But what was I going to do? I had to start somewhere, so I bought three grams of the recommended weed for 25 Euros, settled into a window seat with a cup of coffee, and began cutting up a nice sticky bud with my Leatherman Squirt. I'd already bought a cheap pipe before deciding which coffee shop to try. The plan was to smoke every bit of marijuana I purchased during my stay and then ditch the pipe before I flew home.

The pot was strong indicia, a nice spacey head without a total draining of physical ambition. Sitting in the window seat writing postcards, I felt like a giant looking down from a distant hilltop, watching my faraway handwriting grow progressively worse and my messages increasingly cryptic.

There was a pretty young backpacker at the counter and a couple of semi-predatory white guys were chatting her up while the Moroccan shopkeeper showed her how to roll a fatty.

"I feel so much closer to God since I started smoking," she gushed with such unabashed naiveté it's quite possible she was sincere. But it wasn't God these guys were trying to get closer to.

My traveling companion, JR, was back at the hotel sleeping. Whenever you check into a hotel with JR, he's in bed sleeping before you can hang up your coat and take a piss. He does it so quickly and furtively, I've never actually seen him pull back the covers and climb in. He's just suddenly there. It's disconcerting in a funny way. And for reasons I can't quite fathom, always reminds me a scene from a Three Stooges movie. Maybe it's because JR often still has his clothes on.

I had swallowed 10 mg of amphetamine about 30 minutes before the plane landed, so I was good to go even though I hadn't slept much during the flight. But I was beginning to feel guilty about leaving JR back at the hotel, and besides, I was starting to get hungry and didn't want to eat alone the first night in town.

Back at the Hotel Nes, JR was still asleep, looking uncomfortably like a corpse with his hands clasped over his chest. Sleep is second only to sex in JR's personal hierarchy of human experiences, so I let him snooze while I scribbled a few notes in my journal and thumbed through some of the guidebooks and maps I had brought with me.

If you look at a map of Europe, you can see that Amsterdam is very close to England, just a few hundred miles to the east of London (the city in which I first got high) and only a few miles more from Bristol (the place of my birth.) Our Amsterdam hotel put me geographically closer to those two awakenings than I had been since 1967. That's when I went back to England for the first time since my family immigrated to Canada when I was a kid.

My return to the old sod was admittedly a callow bid for adventure, the sort that comes from having absolutely no idea what the hell you should be doing. There's nothing unique about it; I was just one of millions of middle-class kids using the "trying to find myself" excuse for bumming around.

I had been attending a fine arts school, a wonderful place full of loonies and misfits—a fair number of whom were actually quite talented. The big deal after three years of studying painting, drawing, sculpture, printmaking, and art history was the opportunity to compete for a traveling scholarship. Every third-year student got a designated portion of a wall in the main public galleries on which to hang or display his or her work. The winners were given enough money to go damned near anywhere in the world they wanted, no strings attached.

I knew three things for sure: I didn't deserve to win, I wasn't going to win, and I could go just as far and stay almost as long by using my final semester's tuition to travel. My alleged career as an artist was over without a second thought or a moment's regret. I haven't used a paintbrush for anything other than house painting since.

Icelandic Airlines was the cheapest way to get from the United States to Europe in the '60s. They flew old propjets that took 16 hours (14 of them in the air) to get from New York to London, with stops in Reykjavik and Glasgow. Deep into the flight, somewhere over the North Atlantic, a longhaired guy came down the aisle asking if anybody had any rolling papers. Looking back, the foreshadowing seems obvious, but at the time it was just one of dozens of new experiences transpiring before my eyes as I watched much like I would a movie.

By then I was already past the metaphysical point of no return. My adventure had already begun and the catalyst was waiting for me when I emerged from customs at Heathrow Airport, still groggy from my transatlantic odyssey and the gin and tonics I'd gulped during a layover in Glasgow.

That was the first time I saw Terry and Susan, the cousins of my art school friend, Miranda, who had agreed to meet me upon my arrival in London. The three of them shared a flat in Kensington where I would be staying, at least for a few nights. They were all on their way to a meal and movie, and I was going with them. Forget that I had not slept in almost two days and was dragging two suitcases. Just like that, I was sucked into their circle and thrilled to be there.

Susan and Terry were tall, thin, and fair-haired; they spoke English with a Mexican accent and exuded a charisma that went beyond their physical beauty, which was considerable. You couldn't help but be smitten by them.

Susan, sweet and kind to virtually everybody she met (even me), was one of the most beautiful women I've ever known. It took me a while to get used to being around her. It's not easy to relax in the company of a goddess, and I was guilty of staring, even though I took pains to hide it. Shit. She affected everybody like that at first. And there I was, still worried about pimples.

After I'd known her longer and we'd spent some time together, I was comfortable in her presence but remained acutely aware of her beauty. I remember how proud I was the day I accompanied her on a shopping trip to buy a new winter coat and how, when sale clerks assumed I was her boyfriend, she was kind enough not to tell them different.

But it wasn't Susan who changed my life; it was Terry, grinning, charming Terry—my guide to a world I barely knew existed, the person most responsible for setting me on a course that had brought me to this moment.

PART

Departure From
The Familiar

MAGIC BEANS

Terry was standing in the doorway of Susan's bedroom, smiling and brushing his lanky hair out of his eyes. "Come in here," he said. "I want to show you something."

I'd been in London a week or so, crashing on the sofa and trying to figure out what to do next. I was also falling under Terry's spell, but that was to be expected. Everybody was mesmerized by Terry, even Susan, though she was more immune than most. She was, after all, his older sister and even more beautiful than he.

I followed him into the bedroom where he stood in front of an open drawer, rummaging through his sisters clothes until he found what he was looking for—a small clay object not much bigger than a large pea. He held it up to his eye like a diamond dealer appraising a stone and then glanced at me.

"Did you ever see one of these before?"

I hadn't, but I could see that it was a tiny pipe bowl, blackened inside from use.

"It's a skuff," he said, grinning devilishly, "the bowl from the pipe that Moroccans use to smoke hashish and kif."

Terry carefully fitted the bottom half of a ballpoint pen barrel into one end of the bowl, raised it to his lips, and pretended to smoke, rolling his eyes in an exaggerated way and laughing.

"Do you have anything to smoke in it?" I asked, trying to hide my eagerness.

"No, I ran out. But you can buy hash on the streets in Morocco just as easily as you can buy vegetables. We should go there, maybe bring some back to London."

And so the seed was planted, and over the coming weeks Terry provided enough manure for it to grow and blossom in my imagination. Not all of the talk was about mind-altering drugs. Terry was overflowing with all sorts of esoteric knowledge, much of which he'd acquired growing up in Mexico.

Susan and he were U.S. citizens but their Anglo-American parents lived near Guadalajara, where the kids had received all of their education prior to coming to the U.K. Their parents were obviously fairly well to do and could afford to finance their childrens' London escapade with eagerly anticipated checks. I, as I was acutely aware, was flying without such a safety net.

Susan attended art school on a fairly regular basis, while Terry's alleged purpose for being in England was to "improve his English."

Actually, there was nothing really wrong with his English, even though it was his second language. He loved to talk and expressed himself admirably; his accent, quaint sentence structure, and occasional use of the wrong tense only added to his charm.

Terry was the flip side of the Latin playboy stereotype—a blue-eyed, blonde-haired dandy who could pass for Peter O'Toole's son but sounded more like Ricardo Montalban's rakish nephew.

Terry taught me so much in such a short period of time; I'm still sorting out some of it today. Among the more sensational bits were his riffs about "Mexican magic," most of which seemed to revolve around seeking success at such frowned-upon activities as gambling and thievery.

These spells weren't from the hocus-pocus school of magic, where you utter a few words and wave a wand. They were complicated, ritualistic procedures that had to be painstakingly followed, step-by-step, and if the supplicant did things in exactly the manner prescribed, it was guaranteed to work. You didn't even have to be Mexican.

Terry said the cook and the gardener back home had taught

him about magic. Although the couple normally wouldn't have admitted to a gringo that magic even existed, they'd helped raise Terry from a young boy and knew that his roots were sunk almost as deep in Mexican soil as their own. The spell I remember best was designed to create a power object that would enable a gambler to always win as long as the object is in his possession.

I'll describe the daunting process of obtaining this ultimate good luck charm strictly for its titillation value, for it is my fervent hope that nobody tries this at home.

The first step is to visit a graveyard at midnight, dig up a fresh corpse, cut off its head, and take it home with you. Always a good start to a spot of magic, don't you think?

Next comes the really gross part, grosser than digging up the body and cutting off its head—you push a bean into the right eye until it disappears. Then you plant the head in a large pot or jar filled with dirt.

Terry never said what type of bean it was, but I always imagined it to be a pinto. In point of fact, I don't think it makes a difference. Regardless, you water the head every day at midnight until a sprout, fertilized by the decaying brain, grows up through the dirt and out the eye socket.

The first branch and the first pod on that branch is marked with a bit of thread, and when the pod is fully mature, the first bean from the first pod is removed and kept, an infallible gambling talisman, purchased with a slice of your soul.

Terry was confident that the magic worked but didn't really think any supernatural power was responsible. Instead, he figured anyone who performed such a grisly rite would brainwash themselves into believing that they were omnipotent when playing games of chance. And as far as Terry was concerned, if you believed strongly enough that something was true, it was, at least for you.

By the time we went to Morocco, enough of this notion had rubbed off on me that I was able to stay relatively calm in several stressful situations. But that trip was a smuggling venture not a gambling junket, so no heads were severed.

THE GATEWAY TO TOMORROW

The same day the check came from his parents, Terry and I took an evening flight out of Heathrow, headed for Tangier. We'd had a couple of weeks to plan while he waited for his monthly stipend to arrive, so there was no point in delaying. We went straight from the bank to the ticket office and then headed back to the flat to pack our bags.

On the way, we stopped at a swank tobacconist and each bought an expensive cigar. They were to be our "victory cigars," not to be taken from their cellophane wrappers and smoked until we were safely back in London, mission accomplished—a juvenile notion perhaps but also a measure of our confidence, a ritual in which we used the cigar as a symbol of future success, a way of influencing our own fate through positive visualization of things to come.

Yeah, I was eating that shit up, and the way things turned out, I'm glad I did. We left a note for the girls and, the next thing I knew, we were on a BOAC jet winging our way to fuckin' Africa.

Our plan was simple: score some hash, smuggle it back to England, and use the profits to finance a series of progressively larger smuggling ventures. Terry figured that after three or four trips to Morocco we would have enough money to go to Hong Kong, where we would have an ocean-going yacht built, complete with hidden smuggling compartments. Then we would sail around the world, buying and selling drugs, living like kings.

Sounded good to me.

Today, I wouldn't dream of such a crazy caper, but this was
1967 and the recreational drug scene was in its adolescence. It
was before organized crime took over the marijuana market, back
when amateurs still did most of the smuggling. Some of them,
like Billy Hayes, the guy who wrote *Midnight Express*, (made into a
riveting movie in 1978) got busted and paid a heavy price.

But Hayes' book hadn't been published by the time Terry
and I took off for Tangier. Besides, it wouldn't have made any
difference anyway. We had the elixir of youth running through
our veins—we were immortal, anything was possible.

What made me different from many youthful drug smugglers
was that when we left for Tangier, I'd never been stoned. On
several occasions, joints had been passed around at art school
parties, but I never even got a buzz from the few puffs that had
come my way.

Terry had grown up smoking Mexican weed and had wide
experience with all sorts of mind-altering substances and spoke
highly of the good weed. For me, the whole smuggling thing was
a way to make money. I didn't want to go back to the States and
although I wouldn't have minded getting a job, when I looked
in the papers and saw the sort of wages people were earning
and compared them to how much everything cost, I quickly
abandoned the notion.

I talked about writing a screenplay, but that was pretentious
bullshit. I was counting on the hashish being as cheap as Terry
said it was. So I went all in and decided to invest most of my
money, just under five hundred dollars, in the caper. If everything
went according to Terry's calculations, we could finance another
hash run and make enough to live on for a while.

The first time Terry suggested the scheme, I happily agreed.
It was a solution to my money problem, a chance to hang out
with Terry and, in my puerile imagination, a cool James Bond-ish
thing to do.

We were so impatient to dive headlong into the outlaw
economy, scant attention was paid to detail in advance and we'd

just jumped on the first available plane. It's a very short flight from England to Morocco, but we had to change planes in Gibraltar, and there was a layover of more than 10 hours. The flight for the final leg of our journey, a short hop across the Straits to Tangier, wouldn't take off until around 9 a.m. the next morning.

Our original solution to this inconvenient dilemma—head for the nearest boozer—was foiled upon arrival at the first pub we came across, where we were greeted by a group of drunken British soldiers staggering noisily out the door. We'd forgotten that Gibraltar was British territory, and as such, the drinking establishments followed the same licensing laws as the U.K. Chucking-out time was 10 p.m., and we suddenly found ourselves alone in the empty streets of this legendary steppingstone between Europe and Africa.

"Let's see if we can find the apes," said Terry.

The Rock of Gibraltar is known for many things besides being an insurance company icon, including, most famously, its apes. Actually, they are not apes; they are monkeys, Barbary Macaques to be precise. Legend has it that there used to be a secret tunnel beneath the Mediterranean between Africa and Gibraltar, and that monkeys used it to travel to The Rock before some sort of seismological event sealed the passage forever.

It's a wonderful story, made all the better by the fact that nobody really knows how they got there. But regardless of their origins, they are the only wild monkeys in Europe, and even that has a back-story.

There is superstition that when the monkeys leave, so will the British, which has resulted in a situation where the British military makes sure the monkeys don't die off or skedaddle.

"Which way do we go?" I asked.

"Up there," said Terry, pointing toward the top of The Rock.

Partway up was the ruin of an old fort, where the Union Jack, lit by a spotlight, fluttered against a black sky. Terry, who seemed to know a lot about the place for somebody who'd never been there before, said it was a Spanish fort from the time before the

Brits took over. For all I knew, he could have been making it up as he went along—hell, he could have been making up most of what he told me—but it didn't really matter. So-called reality was rapidly becoming beside the point.

A different kind of reality was opening up to me, one where nothing was true or false but everything was possible in the space · between the two extremes.

Terry and drugs would be the doorway and key to this new reality, and although I hadn't yet quite stepped over the threshold, old assumptions were beginning to loosen from their moorings, as even older ones, forgotten for generations, were awakening somewhere inside of me. I stood poised, not only between two continents, but also between the straight world and a much wider vision of life.

We never did see any monkeys, but we smelled them all right. The undeniable odor of monkey shit came wafting faintly from somewhere beyond the road, out in the darkness.

Our impromptu primate search came to a sudden conclusion when we reached an "Off Limits" sign at the outskirts of a British Army base. No point fucking with the Army, so we turned around and walked down the hill and out onto the beach, where we found a small overturned boat to sit on. We looked out across the water toward our destination, just 12 miles away.

Eventually, we made our way back to the airport, which was dark and locked for the night. We sat down with our backs to the glass front door and tried to get some sleep. How strange to wake up in a Kensington flat and fall asleep on the doorstep of Africa.

CROSSING OVER

It wasn't very comfortable propped against the door, and after a short, fitful nap, Terry gently rousted me and pointed to a light glowing low in the sky.

"I thought you'd like to see the sun come up over Africa."

Soon figures began hurrying past us, shadow-like against the gray half-light, day workers, mostly domestics and laborers, just off the ferry from Tangier. It was also the start of a new day for your intrepid narrator and his partner in crime, a day so full of wonders that it still stands out, one of a handful of such days among the many, a day that helped shape so many of those that followed.

Terry and I were the only passengers on the small, twin-engine propeller plane that took off from Gibraltar on that clear, sunny morning and carried us across the thin strip of blue water that separates Europe from Africa. We had the pretty stewardess all to ourselves, and she laughed as she lurched around the cabin in high heels, gamely trying to maintain her balance as the small plane banked to the left and followed the beach down the coast toward Tangier.

Below us we could see the curve of Africa gently bending south, a breathtakingly beautiful approach that belied so much of what would greet us once we touched down.

The Moroccan customs officials were only interested in one thing: How much money we had with us. When we told them (nobody told the truth, of course), they wrote the amount on a little card and said we had to spend all of our money before we left Morocco. Moreover, we were supposed to get the card stamped every time we bought something and give the card back when we left.

We could have had our suitcases packed with plastic explosives for all they knew or maybe cared. Perhaps things really were as laissez-faire as Terry claimed. Back in London, while we were waiting for his check to arrive, I had voiced a few trepidations that had snuck past my bravado. Terry shrugged them off and told me that he'd heard that if the Moroccans caught you trying to smuggle drugs out of the country, all they did was take all your drugs and money and not allow you back into the country for a year.

But nobody smuggled drugs into Morocco. Money was different. Tangier was a tax-free international city for much of the first half of the 20th century and the freewheeling business climate hadn't changed all that much since those anything-goes days. True, things had gotten a tad tighter when the city was reintegrated into Morocco in 1956, but when we arrived, in 1967, selling currency on the black market was even more pervasive than dealing drugs.

The protagonist in one of Paul Bowles' novels gets involved in both the currency racket and cannabis consumption in Tangier, which ultimately leads him to hammering a nail into a sleeping cohort's brain. I was ignorant of Bowles at the time, which is a pity because back then I could probably have sought out the American expatriate writer and composer and maybe shared a pipe with him. Many did.

But my only knowledge of Morocco, outside of the old Crosby and Hope "Road" movie, had come from Terry. I remember him telling me the Rolling Stones had been there. If he'd mentioned that they had an audience with Bowles, it didn't register. But in the late 1960s, you didn't, have to be a character in a Bowles novel to maximize your currency in Tangier. Even the most dimwitted tourist could get more dirhams for their dollars in the Kasbah than at the bank.

During the taxi ride from the airport to Tangier, we drove past green hills dotted with small, one-story white houses, many of which had a couple of goats or a donkey grazing nearby. Watching it all roll by through the open taxi window seemed a bit like being trapped in a travelogue; you glide past but aren't really part of what you see, the car and the motion keeping everything impersonal and safe.

I'm not sure what Terry told the driver because he spoke to him in Spanish. That was one small edge we had over a lot of Nazarenes in Tangier, because many Moroccans spoke Spanish, which probably takes a bit of explaining.

Tangier was originally an ancient Phoenician city, but in the 5th century, it was conquered and occupied by the Vandals. This marked the beginning of a series of similar incursions by various European powers that continued until Morocco finally gained independence in 1956. At various times the Romans, Portuguese, Spanish, British, and French all annexed chunks of territory of varying size, usually by force.

The Brits married into the mix, so to speak, when Charles II was given Tangier as part of a dowry from Portugal's Catherine of Braganza, who, it is claimed, introduced the drinking of tea to the English. But it was no tea party, not even Boston style, when Sultan Moulay Ismail of Morocco blockaded Tangier in 1697.

The English eventually gave up and fled, but not before destroying the city and the port. And so it went. Western countries, unable to resist the geographically strategic nature of the ancient port, continued to impose themselves on what came to be known as "the gateway to Africa."

It was a gateway that swung both ways, for Tangier was the lower lip of the Mediterranean's mouth and, at the same time, a perfect staging ground for those seeking to exploit the rest of Morocco and the very continent itself. By 1912, Morocco was effectively partitioned between France and Spain, and the far north of the country was still called Spanish Morocco when

Terry and I embarked on our little adventure.

The taxi driver, who undoubtedly received a small kickback for every customer he delivered, took us directly to the Hotel Plaza on the Rue de Velasquez. It was drab and down-at-the-heels by U.S. standards, but far from a fleabag. As Terry haggled with the desk clerk, I was approached by a tall, middle-aged Moroccan wearing a djellaba and an oily smile.

He introduced himself in respectable if slightly accented English and showed me a passport-style document that had his photograph and a metal badge inside, which he claimed was proof he was an "official government guide." I wasn't quite sure what to make of him, but as he was conducting business right out in the open in the lobby and seemed as much a fixture as the ancient armchairs, I had no reason to doubt him.

He wasted no time in informing me that it was his honor to be at my service and could provide anything I needed, "kif, hashish, opium, cocaine, LSD, girls, boys," basically whatever my degenerate little heart desired. A bit taken aback by the blatant and sudden nature of his sales pitch, I demurred and told him I was weary from my trip and didn't need anything right now.

The room was large and airy with windows that opened out onto a narrow balcony overlooking the street in front of the hotel. The shower and the toilet worked and we even had a bidet, overall a splendid array of plumbing at a time when the average Moroccan toilet consisted of two footprints set in concrete, where you squatted over a sewer pipe.

The taxi driver had correctly calculated that we had enough money to stay at an establishment where you didn't have to shit in a hole and wipe your ass with your left hand. Even before we left London, Terry had schooled me on the importance in Moroccan of eating and greeting only with your right hand, so I knew the drill.

The hotel was in the European section of the city, so we were still on the fringe, a couple of hundred yards away from the Kasbah, where the arched portals once painted by Delacroix and Matisse, still led to a completely different world.

THE OLDEST WHORE IN TOWN

Terry and I hadn't traveled 20 feet beyond the hotel door, when a gang of street urchins, each carrying a wooden box and wearing a large brass badge, surrounded us.

"Shoeshine, mister?"

They jockeyed for position, the cheeky smiles on their faces contradicting the hunger in their eyes. None of them seemed to notice or care that I was wearing black suede boots, and I'm sure any one of them would have happily ruined them with globs of polish if I'd acquiesced.

"Not today."

"Tomorrow?"

The shoeshine boys eventually gave up as we continued down the hill toward Boulevard Pasteur, past the Café de Paris, and on to the Grand Socco—each step taking me closer and closer to a total departure from the familiar.

Tangier's Grand Socco (big marketplace) is where the old and new worlds dovetail at the northeastern gate to the Kasbah. Flanked by Western style buildings, this ancient whore still offered her gaping orifice and beckoned all to enter. Despite an undeniable stench of urine that grew stronger the closer we got, we were drawn inexorably through the ancient archway and into the medina, a generic term for the oldest part of many North African cities.

Extreme culture shock battled toe-to-toe with fatigue and wonderment for control of my thought processes. My carefully cultivated demeanor (art school bohemian from unflappable British stock) instantly began to crumble, my self-confidence suddenly as inconsequential as the fuzz on my chin.

The scene still comes back to me as isolated images, a series of snapshots illuminating the past in the same dim light that filtered into the Kasbah that day. Like most boys, I'd dreamed of adventure in exotic locales, a pleasant diversion that had never really faded. But now the real deal was right there in my face, a storybook movie set come to life, complete with villainous-looking characters lurking in maze-like alleyways.

A short walk into the Kasbah is the Socco Chico, a small square dominated by the Café Central. It is a gathering place for lowlifes of every stripe—dealers, pimps, smugglers, conmen, spies (the Cold War was at its peak in '67 and Tangier has always been an espionage center), thugs, hustlers, expatriates, artists, writers (William Burroughs wrote *Naked Lunch* in Tangier), moneychangers, merchants, and gay tourists. It was this last group that would provide our unofficial cover.

We didn't want to look like hippies because it would make us targets for police attention and not only because of drugs: Hippies had a reputation for being dirty and poor. What good was a Nazarene without money, especially a scruffy one?

Our plan was to stay in a respectable hotel (yes, the Plaza, complete with accommodating "officials guides," was considered respectable), dress well, wash behind our ears, and hopefully pass for two of the thousands of European homosexuals who vacation in Tangier every year, long a destination for gay travelers.

The medina, which is built on the cliffs overlooking the beach, is a labyrinth of narrow streets and even narrower alleyways, some so tight that you have to flatten your back to the wall to let somebody pass. The buildings are mostly two- and three-story hodgepodges of old and ancient architecture with whitewashed walls and shuttered windows.

There are dozens of flights of steps leading goodness knows where, and despite the modest and often shabby exteriors, there are some luxurious homes hidden behind anonymous doorways. Except for the TV antennae sprouting from the flat roofs, the Kasbah hadn't changed all that much in centuries.

I was too busy struggling to maintain my external cool to realize what a massive dose of the foreign I was absorbing and I failed to understand how powerful an effect this human rabbit warren was having on my psyche. But the Tangier Kasbah haunted my sleep for years. The dreams were basically all the same: I'm walking toward the Kasbah, excited to be back, but just before I reach the gate I always wake up.

Before Tangier, the only glimpse of anything remotely similar to Third World poverty I'd seen were the shacks of poor black folks in the Deep South, fleetingly witnessed through the windows of my father's Plymouth as we cruised past on our way to Miami Beach. I don't know what I expected, but certainly not the intense poverty or the stabbing stink, a kind of olfactory smell-track that followed us everywhere. I was simultaneously repulsed and attracted in equal measure.

Although it was late morning, the Café Central seemed to be just waking up for the day when Terry and I joined the only other customer sitting at an outside table. After the waiter brought our drinks, I felt calm enough to take in the surrounding as we drank our six-ounce bottles of Coca-Cola.

Even in the Kasbah, there were almost as many Moroccans dressed in Western clothing as there were wearing traditional apparel. More often than not, it was a combination of both. There were young men in T-shirts and jeans, their feet stuffed into impossibly long, bright yellow slippers that made the wearers look vaguely like Donald Duck. Old-fashioned Western-style suits, often just the jackets, were visible beneath djellabas.

There were also occasional furtive figures wearing the coarsest and grubbiest of djellabas, hoods up to hide dirty faces and haunted eyes as they scurried past. Westerners "gone native," guys who'd come to Tangier for whatever reason and had never gone home. Once upon a time, they were disgraced or deranged aristocrats, like Sebastian in *Brideshead Revisited*, but by 1967 most of them were just junkies or crazy.

"Let's look around some more," Terry said, draining the last of his soda.

We paid our bill and continued to explore the medina, where new sensory assaults lay around every bend. One of the most spectacular sights was a flight of broad steps that served as a market. Different types of fruit, vegetables, and spices were displayed every third or fourth step, a rainbow of raw colors that seemed to rise to the heavens.

New smells—incense burning in charcoal braziers, butcher blood, fresh bread—sometimes threatened to overcome the ubiquitous reek of urine.

Trying to regain our bearings, we turned into a narrow, residential street, where we saw a young Moroccan coming in the opposite direction. As he drew near, he muttered the magic word.

"Hashish?"

The three of us came together at the intersection of two alleys, a sliver of sun illuminated the spot where we came to a halt and faced one another. I felt like I had a feature role in a B-movie and was grateful that I was only the sidekick.

Terry spoke to the guy in Spanish, and the Moroccan dug into the pocket of his djellaba and came out with a matchbox from which he took a hunk of sandy-colored hash about the size of a bullion cube—the first I'd ever seen. He proffered it in his open palm, and Terry picked it up, smelled it, and showed it to me as if I knew what I was looking at.

"This is what we want," said Terry, first in English for my benefit and then in Spanish.

After a brief, animated conversation, during which the Moroccan glanced around several times, the guy nodded farewell and moved on. Just before he went around a bend and disappeared from sight, I noticed that he was wearing a pair of those Donald Duck slippers.

"That was all the hash he had with him," said Terry, "but he can get more and wants us to meet him in an hour at the Café Central."

Things were moving a hell of a lot faster than I'd anticipated, and I had to push down a paranoia that seemed to originate in my balls.

"Are we going to meet him?"

"Sure, why not?"

"How do we know he's not a nark?"

"I can tell; everything is cool," Terry cooed. "Let's keep walking and then double back after a while."

We wound our way through the Kasbah and found ourselves overlooking the harbor, which was dominated by a large and somewhat lonely looking cargo crane. In 1832, Delacroix painted a small band of seafaring men beaching a sailboat at the bottom of the cliffs on which Tangier is perched. The crane wasn't there then but the city is still recognizable, the white walls of the Kasbah peeking over the top of the menacing precipice.

The Brits built huge fortifications there in the 17th century, the same ones they later destroyed before beating a scorched-earth retreat back to Mother England. But remnants and a few old cannons remain—half-forgotten proof that the conceit of great and powerful nations is nothing compared to the enduring nature of this timeless city.

We walked along a sidewalk that skirted the beach, past brightly painted but peeling bathhouses with preposterous names such as "Miami Beach" and "Copacabana," a pathetic attempt to fob off this filthy stretch of sand as some sort of vacation destination. Still, it was easier to relax outside the claustrophobic Kasbah. There were several pick-up games of soccer taking place on the beach and a trickle of veiled women emerging from the dunes with bundles of produce on their heads.

We encountered two young Moroccan guys who tried to sell us their pipes and a bag of marijuana they were smoking. Their impromptu entrepreneurialism was impressive, but we politely declined. Terry had been right: Cannabis was as readily available as vegetables in Tangier. What I had yet to learn was that buying it was a lot more complicated than purchasing a kilo of onions.

THE DANCING BOY CAFÉ

"Do you think Yellow Shoes will show up?" I asked Terry as we neared the Café Central.

"Yellow Shoes? I think he said his name was Mohammad."

"Maybe. I don't know. Seems like everybody's called Mohammad."

"Well, it looks like he brought Red Hat with him!" said Terry, drawing my attention to our new friend, who was standing outside the Café Central with another guy, a few years older, wearing a red fez.

Yellow Shoes introduced us to Red Hat (it's been a long time, but I'm pretty sure his name was Mohammad) and we agreed to join them for tea at a nearby café. There was another exchange in Spanish between Terry and Yellow Shoes, during which Red Hat glanced at me a couple times, only to avert his eyes when I looked back. He was smaller but harder looking than Yellow Shoes, with none of his partner's boyish charm.

"They want to be careful," said Terry, looking over at me, "so we have to split up. I'll go with one of them and you with the other. Then we'll meet at the café."

"Do you think it's safe?"

"Yeah, it'll be fine. See you in a little while."

Terry turned to Yellow Shoes and they headed off to the right, talking and laughing. Red Hat and I went to the left in silence, into the heart of the Kasbah.

Red Hat set a vigorous pace, and it was all I could do to

keep up without breaking into a humiliating trot. Within the first minute, I was completely lost, unable to keep track of the frequent changes in direction as we shifted from reasonably wide streets to cave-like passages and winding staircases to nowhere.

Extreme apprehension, bordering on piss-your-pants fear, temporarily overrode fatigue. I found myself experiencing a mild case of the sort of heightened awareness you hear combat veterans and survivors of horrific accidents talk about. Every pore seemed on alert, sucking up incoming data and instantly forwarding it to my brain for interpretation. I simply couldn't process the information quickly enough and it heaped up inside my head like cars in a chain-reaction pile-up.

I'm not sure exactly how long Red Hat and I wound our way through the Kasbah, ten, fifteen minutes at the most, but long enough for my emotions to go from dread to semi-confidence and back to dread again half a dozen times. Red Hat just kept walking, changing direction, saying nothing but keeping an eye on me, whether a protective or predatory eye I hadn't quite figured out. In retrospect, it was probably a case of him not wanting to lose his meal ticket to another hustler.

It's weird, but I still feel a dim reverberation of shame for the fear I felt that day. It's silly really because I held myself together by calling on a lifetime's practice of pretending my shit was more together than it actually was, which, of course, is what everybody does. But that was another thing I hadn't figured out by the time I was 20.

The ironic part is that I really didn't have anything to worry about. It was all a mind game, which began to dawn on me when Red Hat and I scampered down a flight on steps and ended up right back where we'd all split up. Terry and Yellow Shoes were already waiting for us.

The four of us walked around the corner and up a few steps into a dark and smoky café that overlooked the harbor. It was a fairly large place with half of the 20 or so wooden tables occupied, exclusively by men, most of who were wearing djellabas. There was a soccer game on TV, a modern indulgence in an otherwise ageless establishment that received only casual attention from the patrons.

Everything looked brownish in the dim light. The brown floors, brown tables and chairs, and the various shades of brown djellabas the patrons were wearing, not to mention the brown color of the tea so many were drinking, emphasized an earth-tone aura.

Tea, super-sweet, piping-hot mint tea, is such an integral part of Moroccan life, it borders on religion. Nearly every visit, whether to a home or a store, begins with the tea ceremony. According to Moroccan poet Abdallah Zrika, "The entire universe is contained in the teapot. Or, to be more precise, the sinia (round tray) represents the earth, the teapot represents the sky and the glasses represent the rain; the sky is united to earth by rain."

Ignorant of this rudimentary custom and worried about catching something unhealthy, I ordered a bottle of coke.

The air was thick with smoke. Besides hookahs and cigarettes, men puffed on long-stemmed pipes (sebsis) with clay bowls (skuffs) like the one Terry had shown me in London. The pipes appeared with magician-like dexterity from the baggy sleeves of their djellabas and were smoked openly but discreetly before disappearing back up a sleeve or into a pocket.

Although technically illegal, cannabis has always been part of the culture, and the authorities pretty much ignored public smoking as long as it wasn't flaunted. On the other hand, there's a super-potent black Moroccan tobacco that is heavily taxed, and the police were much more likely to bust somebody for having illegal black tobacco than kif or hash. (Kif is two parts marijuana to one part tobacco, and the black tobacco is especially favored.)

After the waiter brought our drinks, Yellow Shoes produced his own pipe, filled it and passed it around. Red Hat and Terry took a few puffs, but I declined. I told myself I wanted to keep a clear head for business, but the truth was that I was already suffering from a sensory overload and didn't need any more cerebral stimulation. Shit, I was already tripping on the situation.

In one corner of the café, there was a low platform that I hadn't noticed until a small group of men sitting there began to play a squawking, thumping, rhythmic kind of music. There was a drummer, a guy playing the lute, and a third blowing flute, but I didn't pay too much attention to the musicians or their instruments. I couldn't take my eyes off the fourth member of the group, who was busy wrapping a strange-looking belt around his hips. This nimble young man began to undulate gently to the music, the belt, which was decorated with tassels, accenting the movement of his gyrating hips.

The dancing boy seemed to get even less attention than the soccer game on TV, but it was hard for me to look away. His movement was sensual in an efficiently professional way, and I found him mesmerizing, almost as if his dance was casting a spell.

I wasn't totally naïve about such things. I'd heard the old, allegedly Arab saying: "Women are for babies; young boys are for fun," which could have been made up by some supercilious Anglo asshole for all I know. But until that moment I hadn't even begun to understand how deeply ingrained the pretty-boy fetish was in the culture.

A female exotic dancer would have scandalized the local men who frequented the Kasbah teahouses. They wanted a dancing boy with their tea and kif, even if it seemed like they weren't paying him much attention.

Among tribal people in remote areas, the village dancing boy is considered the flower of the community, a prized possession. Great rivalries develop, and if one tribe kidnaps the local cutie from another, it could lead to considerable bloodshed.

Some believe the dancing-boy phenomena can be traced back to the Dionysian Mysteries. The Phoenicians, Greeks, and Romans have all occupied portions of Morocco, and it has been suggested that perhaps the old religions found refuge in this distant outpost, especially in the out-of-the-way regions of the Rif Mountains.

If that's true, the dancer I saw that afternoon was a living remnant of a primal practice still celebrated in this den of iniquity. With his androgynous costume and stylized movements, the dancing boy's performance had a ritualistic quality to it, and a link between him and the temple prostitutes of antiquity seemed even more appropriate when he drew closer to where we were sitting.

He wasn't a boy at all, but in his late 30s or early 40s, still slim, agile, with one of those Dick Clark faces, the sort that never seems to age until you see it up close without makeup.

After many cups of tea and several more bowls of kif, Terry struck a deal for a kilo of hashish while I sat there and tried not to look too stupid. There was one hitch: According to Red Hat, they didn't have that much hash readily available, so we would have to meet again the following afternoon.

On our weary way back to the hotel, we happened upon an eatery called "The American Restaurant," which reminded me that I hadn't had a proper meal since we had left London almost two days ago. My stomach, temporarily assuaged by coca-cola and some stale biscuits we'd bought from a shop on our way to the medina, remembered too.

"I'm starving. Want to give it a try?"

Instead of answering, Terry stepped forward and held the door open for me with one hand and bade me enter with a theatrical flourish of the other.

"*Tengo muy hambre tambien*," said Terry, as he followed me inside.

There was nothing particularly American about the food: nondescript soup, couscous with chicken and a salad of inappropriate and stunted-looking vegetables. But the place was brightly lit and reasonably clean, and soon after we were seated, The Beatles' *Rubber Soul* replaced the Moroccan pop music emanating from the record player. They also had some Stones and Hendrix, with Jimi the only "American" of the bunch. But it was rock-n-roll, and rock-n-roll was American, which was close enough as far as they were concerned, and close enough for us too.

The staff was friendly and we ate there every day until our funds began to dwindle, at which point we strayed to less salubrious establishments for our daily sustenance, an error that was to cost me far more than it did Terry. I'm sure growing up in Mexico had a lot to do with that, his plumbing blissfully immune to all but the most exotic strains of Moulay Ismail's Revenge.

I, on the other hand, was virgin meat waiting to be ravaged by the first parasite to slither out of a 600-year-old sewer pipe and into my Anglo digestive tract.

THE ZIPPO AND THE SWITCHBLADE

As Terry and I made our way toward the medina to meet Yellow Shoes and Red Hat, I was overly conscious of the bulge in the pocket of my corduroy jeans. Terry said I should hold the money but under no circumstances was I to produce it or even pat my pocket to reassure myself it was still there until he gave me the word.

For someone who had craved adventure, this caper didn't feel particularly adventurous, certainly not in a storybook or Hollywood way. Instead, I was feeling acutely apprehensive. Just a thin layer below the surface, I knew I wasn't really a drug smuggler, just a failed art student fucking around in territory where I had no business fucking around.

But there was no thought of turning back, and not just because I didn't want to lose face with Terry. I wanted to do this, the first step toward a glamorous career that fit the image and lifestyle I coveted.

Our new friends were already outside the Café Central, wearing the same clothes they had on the day before. Yellow Shoes smiled as we approached and exchanged a few words in Spanish with Terry.

"They're taking us to their boss's house," said Terry, as we fell in behind the two Moroccans and walked down the road that led to the harbor gate. Just before leaving the medina, we turned left and went up a short flight of steps and knocked on a light-blue wooden door.

The door swung open to reveal a barefoot boy of eight or nine who squinted at us from behind his forearm, crooked across his forehead to keep the glinting sun from shining in his eyes. He didn't look at all surprised to see us.

The boy took us down a dark hall and into a room lit by sunlight coming through windows located high on the wall, almost at ceiling level. Like many houses in the Kasbah, there was no furniture as such, just a collection of colorful cushions on the floor. On one of them sat a thin, deeply wrinkled man in his 50s who glanced at us, smiled faintly, and indicated that we should be seated with a sweep of his hand. He was wearing a blue skullcap.

Red Hat and Yellow Shoes sat to their boss's right at a respectful distance, while we arranged ourselves facing them—three against two. As we peered at each other across a space of two or three yards and a cultural gap wider than the Atlantic Ocean, I wasn't sure if they saw us as walking, talking wallets or invaders from another planet.

A brief uneasiness was broken when Blue Hat clapped his hands and spoke sharply to the boy, who'd been lingering in the doorway. He raced away and soon reappeared with a brass tray, laden with a teapot, sugar bowl and five small glasses stuffed with fresh mint leaves. I couldn't help wondering if the Moroccans shared tea with their victims before skinning them alive and staking them out in the desert for the ants to finish.

These weren't full-blown fears, just thoughts floating through my paranoia as we drank tea and I looked around the room, the walls of which were covered in small Moorish tiles, arranged in pleasing geometric and floral designs. The same three photographs hung on the wall that I had seen inside the café where the deal had been made and would later see in virtually every home or business establishment we entered—King Hassan II, the local soccer team, and John F. Kennedy.

Seeing JFK was a revelation and a compelling indication of the impact the martyred U.S. President had on people throughout the world, regardless of their personal political views. That this young American politician had struck a resonant cord with people so far away and so radically dissimilar still amazes me. Apparently, the same sense of hope and optimism that Kennedy imparted on much of America reverberated far from the Yankee Camelot.

Later, I learned that many Moroccans were also impressed that a head of state had such a sexy wife.

After several cups of tea, it was time for the deal to go down, and Blue Hat rose to his feet and walked to a small fireplace, where he fished a parcel from behind an unlit pile of kindling. He returned to his seat and placed the parcel in front of him. It was wrapped in newspaper and tied with string.

Blue Hat then reached into the pocket of his djellabas, and in one well-practiced movement, produced a switchblade and flicked it open!

For an instant I flashed on the blood-crazed Thug chieftain in *Gunga Din*. How pathetic is that? I don't know why I didn't jump up and bolt for the door, but a second later I was thankful I didn't. Clearly enjoying his little joke, our host bent forward and used the knife to cut the twine around the package.

Relief turned into disappointment when we saw that the package contained not hashish but a bundle of marijuana. For a change, Terry was not smiling, but he recovered quickly and began engaging the Moroccans in a level tone of voice. According to the dealer and his underlings, it was all just a misunderstanding and could be easily rectified.

As if to prove his case, Blue Hat stood up again and walked over to the wall where the three ubiquitous photographs hung and took something from behind each of them. There was a walnut-size piece of white crystal, allegedly cocaine, a small bottle of tiny pills Blue Hat claimed was LSD, and a hunk of hash that had to weigh at least an ounce and a half, which he handed to Terry along with a Zippo lighter.

"This is more like it," said Terry, glancing at me, the customary grin back in place.

Terry held one corner of the hash over the Zippo flame until it caught fire and then blew it out and inhaled the smoke. A nutty aroma filled the room and everybody, even Red Hat, began to smile.

We were assured that there would be no problem supplying us with what we wanted the next day, but part of the "misunderstanding" was the price; the hash would cost twice the original price. It was still ridiculously cheap by European standards, so we agreed and took our leave.

"They knew what we wanted all long, right?" I asked as soon as we were a safe distance from the house.

"It's just part of their negotiation technique," said Terry. "These guys are born hustlers and try to fuck with your head, like when he pulled the knife. It's just mind games; don't worry about it."

NO TEQUILA IN TANGIER

We weren't scheduled to pick up the hashish until the evening, so there was plenty of time to do whatever we pleased for most of our fourth day in Tangier. Terry wanted to smoke some dope, so he headed to the Kasbah, while I opted for the beach. This was the first time I'd really been alone since we had arrived, an opportunity to think things over away from Terry's intoxicating influence.

I took off my boots and socks and walked along the edge of the surf, sandpipers scurrying out of the way as I splashed along. There was a breeze coming off the water, so I kept my shirt on until I found a couple of deserted sand dunes where I was sheltered from the wind and had some privacy. There were several soccer games taking place a couple of hundred yards away, but other than that, there was nobody around, so I peeled off my shirt, rolled up my pant legs, and lay on my back, squinting up at the sky.

I felt obligated to return to damp and chilly London with at least a hint of a suntan. After all, we were in Africa, and even though many parts of Morocco can be quite cold in the winter months, the sun was shining and I was determined to trade my pasty complexion for something less funereal.

The problem with sunbathing is that it forces you to be physically still, which in turn quiets the mind and clears away many of the distracting thoughts that protect us from the torture of self-awareness. It is during these moments of accidental meditation, while I exposed my body to the rays of our nearest star, that my mind invariably drifted toward some disagreeable truth. It was no different on the beach in Tangier. I knew I was caught up in a game of my own creation, quite possibly a very dangerous game, and the only thing I really knew for sure was that I wanted a suntan.

After about twenty minutes, I rose to my feet, brushed the sand off my back and headed up the beach toward the hotel, anywhere was preferable than being alone with my fears. Fuck the suntan.

■■■

Terry was already at the Plaza when I returned. He was sitting on his bed, carefully opening one end of a plastic bag filled with something that looked like brown powder. He glanced up and flashed a distracted smile.

"What's that?"

"It's pollen, the stuff they make the hash out of. "You press it into slabs in a kind of vice."

"How are we going to do that?"

"We're not. I'm going to exchange it tomorrow. I ran into Yellow Shoes in the medina, and he said that the guys who made the hash were busy filling a big order, so he thought that perhaps we'd rather have the pollen right now, instead of waiting. I told him no, but he said to try it tonight and if I didn't like it, we could exchange it tomorrow. Besides, I wanted to smoke some and see what it was like."

"Did you try it yet?"

"No, I'm going to try it right now. It's too fine to roll a joint, so I'm going to put some in the end of a cigarette. Want to try some?"

I watched Terry as he removed the first inch of tobacco from a Woodbine, replaced it with a mixture of pollen and tobacco, and lit it. He laid back on his bed, feet up, a haze of smoke drifting around his happy head.

My efforts were considerably less successful. I'd failed to mix the pollen and tobacco correctly, which meant it wouldn't burn properly, and I had to keep relighting it. When I'd finally finished the pollen-laced cigarette, I didn't feel much different than before I started, just mildly annoyed at my failure. Exactly what I'd failed wasn't clear until Terry asked:

"Did you get off?"

"No, I don't feel anything."

He laughed gently.

"Don't worry about it. This stuff is okay but nothing special. I'm going to trade it for the hash tomorrow."

"Are they going to want more money?"

"Most likely, but that's okay. Once they realize we are regular customers, it will be easier to deal with them. We're just paying our dues."

"What do you mean?"

"Sometimes, especially if you act like an asshole, these guys will dime you out to customs. Then the customs agents bust you and give the hash back to the dealer, who sells it again and splits the profits with them. But by overpaying this time and going along with the program, they won't double-cross us because they want us to come back and do business with them again."

"I hope you're right."

Terry smiled, swung his long legs over the edge of the bed, stood up, and walked to the window.

"Let's get something to eat," he said, looking out the window as he spoke. Then he turned and walked toward the door. "Come on, let's go. I've got the munchies."

■■■

The sun was already fading on our fifth day in Tangier when Terry returned from a meeting at Blue Hat's house and tossed a brown parcel on his bed. The pungent smell of freshly pressed hashish instantly permeated the room.

"It will dry out a bit before we leave and won't smell so

much," said Terry, anticipating my apprehension.

The final price of the hash was more than twice the original quote, but still cheap enough to cover our expenses and make a nice profit, providing everything went well. We weren't scheduled to fly back to London for three more days and, in the meantime, we had a nice little pile of dope to baby sit.

Even after we wrapped up the hash in a cloth, put it in a bedside cabinet and closed the door, you could smell it. Nonetheless, we left the hash in the hotel room on several occasions, and it was always undisturbed when we returned, even though the maids must have smelled it when they came in to change the linen and clean.

Terry said it was because we were respectable-looking Europeans who overpaid for the drugs and acted like gentlemen. We were good for the overall local economy, and as such were considered worthy of a certain amount of respect and protection. It was in everybody's best interest not too rip us off too badly.

Maybe Terry was right or maybe we were just lucky. I don't know. It sounded good at the time and that's what counted. I was about to do something that could put me in prison, so it was essential that my head be in the right place. Thankfully, Terry was very good at putting it there. It never even crossed my mind to wonder if he believed the things he told me and, under the circumstances, that too was a good thing.

Even though we were sitting on thousands of dollar's worth of hashish, our ready cash was dwindling. We needed to economize for a couple of days if we were going to have a few pounds in our pockets when we got back to London. We'd already spent considerably more than we'd planned and it was going to take a while to sell the hash. Our daily visits to the American Restaurant would have to cease. Instead we'd buy food at the market and eat in our room.

On the way to the vegetable market, I saw Blue Hat's son, the one who had answered the door and served us tea. He was rushing somewhere and only spotted me out of the corner of his eye as he trotted past. He glanced back and grinned. I smiled, but he was already gone, around a corner and out of my life.

It's unlikely he ever gave me another thought, but I remember him, a small but reassuring figure in unsettling circumstances, a barefoot angel who helped blunt the fear aroused by his father's switchblade.

We bought bread, tomatoes, feta cheese and a sweet onion, took it back to our room and made sandwiches.

"Not bad, huh?" Terry said, brushing a few breadcrumbs from his mustache.

"I guess, but it sure could use some mayonnaise and mustard."

■■■

I woke up sweating and nauseous about four hours after consuming my makeshift meal. It was dark in the room and Terry was asleep, but the light was on in the bathroom and the door partway open. I made a spastic dash toward the glow and made it just in time to hurl my supper into the bidet.

"Bummer," said Terry. "Guess it must have been something we bought at the market."

He was standing behind me in the doorway, his voice groggy with sleep.

"How do *you* feel?" I asked as I stood up and wobbled toward the sink.

"I'm fine, but you need a bottle of tequila?"

"Tequila!"

"A lot of gringos get dysentery when they first come to Mexico, and down there you can just go into any drugstore and buy paregoric. You don't need a prescription or anything. You just go in and ask for it. It works great, takes the pain away and stops the shits. But when you stop taking it, the dysentery usually comes back.

The best way to cure it is drinking tequila. You just stay drunk until all the symptoms are gone. It takes a while and you'll probably have a couple of rough days, but once it's gone, it's gone for good."

"There's no way I could keep any alcohol down right now. I feel like I've got to throw up again."

"There's probably no tequila in Tangier anyway."

Before I went back to bed, I vomited two or three more times, and the bidet, which had only received the first baptism, was so clogged I couldn't flush away the evidence. So after washing and drying my face, I carefully spread a towel over the befouled plumbing fixture, turned out the light and closed the door on the scene of my private disaster.

I didn't know it at the time, but the worst was over, and although my stools were black for the next few days, I didn't suffer too badly after that initial hour of misery.

Soon a different kind of torment replaced the gastric uproar. Each minute brought us closer to back-to-back moments of truth. First we had to get the hash past Moroccan customs and then, a short flight later, the Brits would have their crack at us.

Maybe Terry had brainwashed me with his if-you-don't-think-about-getting-busted-you-won't riff. Maybe he hadn't. I'm still not sure, but it made total sense to me at the time. Even so, having the courage of your convictions is something altogether different, and it was a struggle to fend off the stray doubts that ambushed me with increasing regularity as our departure drew closer.

All along, the plan had been to body-pack the hash out. There was never any question about that. Nonetheless, it didn't prevent harebrained schemes for concealing it in my luggage from spontaneously combusting in my brain. Again and again.

They reminded me of a nightmare I once had, where I was in a jail cell waiting to be executed the next morning. I imagined that I could dig my way free by widening the drain in my washbasin with my fingernails or maybe crawl down the toilet bowl and escape that way.

As preposterous as those ideas were, in my dream they seemed more plausible than dying a few hours later.

Instead of avoiding death, this time my subconscious was searching for a way to distance itself from the deed before it happened, a layer of insulation between myself and the incriminating pound of hashish I would soon be trying to sneak past the authorities and myself.

It was all foolishness; there was no way I could hide that much dope in my can of shaving cream or stick of deodorant. There was no false bottom in my suitcase and no secret compartment in my boot heels. Those and countless variations on the theme were readily available in Tangier. They'd make you a pair of sandals with solid hash soles if you wanted or sell you a hollow donkey stick crammed with goodies.

But the local customs agents were wise to all that sort of stuff and would spot it right away. We didn't need that crap. All we had to do was use the power of our minds, a force over which my partner seemed to have considerably more control than I.

LET IT COME DOWN

I awoke early our last day in Tangier and just lay in my bed waiting for Terry to stir, trying to pretend nothing out of the ordinary was happening. Noise drifted up from the street below and through the open window, and after a while I got up, lit a cigarette, and stood looking out onto the street as I smoked, comforted by the nicotine and everydayness of the ritual.

I was back to eating the same thing I'd eaten the first day: stale shortbread cookies imported from Scotland and bottled Coca-Cola—the breakfast of champions and diarrhea sufferers throughout the Third World. How come James Bond never got a dose of dysentery?

Ironically, although Agent 007 was still my puerile point of reference for international intrigue of any sort, I had already left Fleming's cozy confines and strayed into Bowles' enigmatic milieu. Fortunately for me, I didn't even realize it.

"What time is it?" Terry said, finally awake.

"It's almost 10:30. What time do you want to leave for the airport?"

His answer was drowned by the sound of pissing, and when I heard the shower running, I walked over to the closet, pulled out my suitcase and began to pack. Most of my clothes were filthy, but I'd saved the shirt and slacks I'd worn the evening we left London, which were still relatively clean, despite sleeping in them the night we spent in Gibraltar. After a shower and a shave, we would still have a reasonable chance of passing for a respectable gay couple returning home after a week's frolic with Arab street boys.

"I'm going to strap on my hash in a few minutes," said Terry as he came out of the bathroom toweling his hair.

"Why so soon? Our flight isn't until 3:45."

"I want to get used to moving around with it on me. That way it will feel natural by the time we leave."

It wasn't as pungent as before, but even after wrapping it tightly in cellophane, you could still smell the hash. It was also still soft enough that we could mold it to the contours of our bodies. Next we taped it to our sides, just above the beltline with white medical tape we'd purchased at the chemists in London. We'd also bought some wide, elastic bandages that we wrapped around us, cinched tight, and secured with those little claw-like metal clasps. This was topped off with a sprinkling of talcum powder and a generous dosing of Old Spice, which masked, I hoped, any olfactory trace of hashish.

Thanks to the weight I'd shitted off the last few days, there was no discernable bulge beneath my shirt.

"Let's go buy a few souvenirs," said Terry. "We'll seem more like tourists that way."

We walked one last time down to the medina, where I purchased an embroidered pillowcase and Terry found a carved wooden comb for Susan. As we passed out through the same venerable gate that had beckoned so seductively the day we arrived, there was no pang of regret, no attempt to indelibly imprint the unique tableau in my memory bank.

We were on a mission and I fully expected to be back as soon as we had sold the contents of the package I bore, albatross-like, around my sweaty waist.

Just before we left our room and checked out of the hotel, Terry stared at me for a moment, his head cocked slightly to the side. He looked at me like a trainer sizing up a boxer before escorting him to the ring. Finally, he smiled and said, "Just forget you've got the hash and everything will be okay."

■ ■ ■

"See anything you like?"

I looked up and saw the stewardess standing in the aisle, next to my seat. She smiled and handed me the gin and tonic I'd ordered shortly after our plane had taken off from Gibraltar.

"You know," she said, smiling again and nodding her head in the direction of the *Playboy* magazine I was reading. She was leaning over slightly, and I was suddenly aware of her body heat and how she smelled.

She was flirting, but my mind couldn't catch up with my libido and I felt like a 10-year-old who'd been caught reading his father's porno collection. I blushed and said something politely curt; her smile turned professional and she moved on down the aisle to the next row.

What was I thinking of anyway, reading *Playboy*? I was supposed to be one half of a gay couple. I stuffed the magazine into the seat pocket and took a slug of gin. It wouldn't be long now, just a quick dash over Portugal and the Channel—then Heathrow.

Moroccan customs had been reassuringly easy. All they cared about was the exit tax and getting back that little card, the one supposedly listing all of our purchases. They didn't even look at it, just threw it in a pile with the rest and waved us on.

I'd settled my mind during the taxi ride from the hotel to the Tangier airport, and while I didn't exactly forget that I had more than a pound of hashish strapped to my waist, I didn't focus on it either. I was no James Bond when it came to the opposite sex, but I had pretty much mastered the unflappable Englishman part. That, along with Terry's gentle persuasion, served me well. I was nowhere near as nervous as I should have been.

Terry had fallen asleep almost as soon as we were airborne, so I was left alone with my thoughts for most of the flight. On the few occasions I felt something uncomfortable creeping up on me, I silently recited a bit of Zen doggerel I'd picked up somewhere.

"Just as a solid rock is immovable in a hurricane, the truly wise are shaken not."

It sounds corny, but it helped.

There was no internal debate as to whether or not the "truly wise" smuggle drugs across international borders. It wasn't the time to ponder that riddle and I didn't. I'd even grown so accustomed to the feel of the hash around my middle, it was almost as if it wasn't really there, just as long as I didn't think about it.

Terry woke up when the pilot announced that we were approaching Heathrow. As the plane began to lose altitude, he buckled himself into the seat and leaned close so nobody but me could hear what he was saying.

"See? I told you it would be cool. It's going to be just as easy on this end."

Then he sat back straight in his seat, brushed his bangs out of his eye, and produced a familiar-looking cigar from the inside pocket of his double-breasted blazer. He held it up for me to see, ran it under his nose with the flourish of a silent movie actor, arched his eyebrows, and returned it to his breast pocket.

It was like being in a movie again, just like the first time we met Yellow Shoes in the medina, only this time I felt more like a co-star than a sidekick. I was carrying an equal share of the goods and was facing the same jail cell if we were caught. But as we touched down and taxied up to our gate, there were no thoughts of turning back or stuffing the hash down the toilet. I was totally committed to the moment. The only way out was to go forward.

Compared to Billy Hayes' meltdown, my demeanor was impeccable, the epitome of a young English gentleman returning home after a spot of fun abroad. I had pushed all thoughts of the hashish so far into the back of my mind and hidden them behind so many layers of deception that I felt almost nothing, which was perfect.

In the end, it was all mercifully brief. Terry and I had to get in different lines at immigration and customs because he was traveling on a U.S passport, while mine was British. We didn't even look at each other when we parted.

I approached the custom officer's table, handed him my passport and placed my suitcase in front of him. He was a large, capable-looking man, in his 50s, slightly overweight. The skin on his face was pink and closely shaved.

"Good evening, sir. Have you brought anything back with you from Morocco?"

"Yes, let me show you," I said, reaching for clasps on my suitcase.

"No, just tell me."

"Well, I bought this embroidered pillow case ... "

"Welcome home, Sir," he said in a brisk but friendly fashion, stamping my passport with an authoritative thud and handing it back to me. I felt like saluting but restrained myself. Instead, I thanked him, picked up my suitcase, and walked through the doors into the brightly lit and noisy terminal.

It had been so easy, that when I patted my sides and discovered that the hashish was still there, it was almost a surprise. Terry, however, was nowhere to be seen, and for the first time, I could feel a cold, sticky fear rising up from my balls again.

Five minutes went by and then ten. Still no Terry. What if they'd caught him? Would they be coming after me next? Should I get the hell out of there while I still could? Would I be able to find my way back to the flat without him? Even if I did, then what?

Stay cool. Don't panic. Breathe deeply.

"Just as a solid rock is immobile in a hurricane ..."

"Do you have a light?"

I whirled around. It was Terry, standing behind me smiling and fingering his victory cigar. I don't think I'd ever been so happy to see anyone in my life and it must have shown. Terry laughed, wrapped a long arm around my shoulders and hugged me.

"No problems?" I asked.

"No problems, just a long line. Let's get out of here."

I removed the wrapper from my cigar and lit Terry's with my

Zippo and then lit my own. We strolled together into the English twilight with smoke issuing from our grinning cake holes.

"Let's get a bus to the city and then the tube home," said Terry, gesturing with his cigar toward the queue we needed to join. A bus was coming, so we hurried over and managed to find a couple of empty seats, the hard plastic kind that last forever if they don't catch on fire.

I felt relieved but detached at the same time. The quick transition from old Tangier to modern London made it seem like we'd been passengers in a time machine, not a jet plane. Compared to Tangier, London seemed like the set of a sci-fi flick, eerily lit in fluorescent shades of artificiality. As I looked out the bus window at the alien landscape, I wondered why I didn't feel happier.

Maybe I'd been so busy shutting down my emotions throughout the smuggling trip that I couldn't turn them back on when I had something to celebrate. It was like holding a piss for so long that, when you finally have an opportunity to relieve yourself, the piss won't come.

As we got off the bus at Acton Town and took the Victoria line tube to West Kensington, I felt like a robot whose battery was running low, still dutifully going about my appointed task but without my former vigor. At that point, all I wanted to do was to reach safe harbor and unburden myself of the hash.

But when we arrived at the flat, we discovered that the girls had moved!

At first, it seemed like a cruel twist. Susan had been talking about finding a new flat for a while now, but it never occurred to us that it might actually happen while we were out of the country. It was only a little more than a week ago that we'd scribbled them a note and headed to the airport.

We managed to roust the landlady, a cockney crone with hair in rollers and a fag hanging from the corner of her mouth. She didn't seem very pleased to see us, but Terry turned on the charm, and she told us to wait "aff a mo" while she went back inside. She reemerged with the girls' forwarding address, and soon we were off again, lugging our suitcases along the street, looking for our new digs, carrying enough hashish to get half of Kensington high.

You couldn't help wondering what the hell was going to happen next. The end of the journey was starting to look like a mirage, always shimmering just out of reach whenever we thought we were almost there. But there was no stumble at the finish line. The new flat wasn't far away, and we found it without too much trouble. The girls were out (again), but, thankfully, they'd left a key with a neighbor, and we were soon standing in a strange flat, pulling off our clothes.

It had been more than 12 hours since I strapped the hash to my flanks, and I could hardly wait to unwrap the elastic bandage. It was sweat-stained, and the talcum powder I'd sprinkled on to help hide the smell of hashish had turned to paste. My torso looked paler than the medical tape affixing the hash to my sides— so much for the African tan. It was then that I realized what a painful mistake I'd made, one I was going to pay for right then and there.

I'd forgotten the body-hair factor.

Instead of shaving my belly hair and the peach fuzz on my sides, I'd just applied the tape right over top of every fucking follicle. There was no good solution. It was either prolonged agony or instant death. I ended up with a bit of both.

You had to go slowly at first, just to get a corner lifted, and even that stung. Once I had a good hold of a portion of the tape, I gritted my teeth and tried to get it over with as fast as possible. It took three or four excruciating rips on both sides and a good bit of shouting before the ordeal was over. It took almost two weeks for the welts to heal.

There was a point, right after we'd peeled off the booty, when Terry and I looked at each other, smiled, and shook hands. It was officially over, officially a success. We had smuggled drugs out of Morocco and into the United Kingdom. It had been easy.

Now came the hard part: selling the stuff.

IT'S NOTHING LIKE BEING DRUNK

Terry and I slept late the day after we'd returned from Morocco and awoke in surroundings that made the Hotel Plaza seem comparatively luxurious. The only time sunlight found its way through the flat's grubby windows was early in the morning on a clear day. But despite the dreary environment, my memories of that gloomy room are enchanted, a handful of magical weeks that shaped my future even more than the Moroccan adventure.

It was actually two flats, two rooms across the third-floor hallway from each other—the girls on one side, Terry and I on the other. Both rooms had a sink and running water, but we shared a bathroom with the rest of the tenants on the same floor. It wasn't as cozy a setup as the old place, but there was more space.

The room was thinly furnished, two cot-like beds and a small table on which sat a single-burner electric hot plate where I learned to cook Mexican-style eggs. The two rear windows looked out on the rooftops and backyards of neighboring houses; a mirror sat on the mantelpiece of a bricked-up fireplace. We used Terry's sea trunk for a coffee table and set his record player on an upside-down milk crate.

Shortly after sundown the first day in our new abode, Terry cut a chunk of hash off one of the slabs with a large pocketknife and invited me to join him in a smoke. He lit several candles that were stuffed into the necks of empty wine bottles and turned out the lights. Then he held a tiny piece of hash over one of the candles until it caught fire and then quickly blew it out. I instantly thought of Blue Hat.

Terry crumpled the warm hash onto the cover of a record album (*Evening & Morning Ragas* by Ali Akbar Khan) and then stuffed a small portion of it into the bowl of the homemade pipe he'd shown me the day he first told me about Morocco.

"Want to go first?" he asked, smiling and holding out the pipe.

I struck a match, held it to the clay bowl and inhaled. At first, it seemed easier on the lungs than cigarettes and tasted a bit like a mixture of dirt and spices. I held it briefly and then exhaled, a spectacular column of smoke rising in the candlelight. I tried to stifle the cough welling up in my chest but finally had to give in to it.

Terry laughed, seemingly delighted by my sputtering, much the same way a father might when a toddler takes a clumsy spill.

"Don't take quite so much next time," he advised. "It will be easier to handle that way."

Terry finished the bowl I'd started, filled the pipe again, and handed it back. I took a smaller puff this time, and Terry took a bigger one. He leaned back on a pillow, his face partly swallowed up by the darkness beyond the candlelight. Out of the shadows, a plume of smoke appeared, floated through the golden light, past my head and into the darkness again.

"How do you feel?" Terry asked, his questions dissolving into a smile.

"I don't feel anything. What about you?"

"I feel high."

"How come I don't feel anything?"

"I'm not sure. Just relax and let it happen."

"Let what happen?"

Terry didn't answer right away. He groomed the sides of his wispy mustache with his forefinger, seemingly pondering my questions. There was something dreamily theatrical about him, so maybe he was just pausing for effect. You never really knew for sure with Terry.

"Sometimes it takes people a while," he said finally. "They might even be high and not know it."

"How come?"

"You might be looking for the wrong thing. It's nothing like being drunk."

"Okay, so what's it like?"

"Don't worry about it. You'll know it when it happens. We'll try again tomorrow."

And we did—and the next day and the one after that. Every evening for well over a week, we sat together and smoked hashish—and still I felt nothing. After two or three bowls, Terry would laugh uproariously when I reported that I felt no effect whatsoever. At one point, he said that "some people are so up-tight they never get off," which didn't exactly fill me with confidence.

I persevered, nevertheless, hopefully participating in the nightly ritual of fire and smoke, just happy to be young and in London with a new and fascinating friend. Eventually I was rewarded for my perseverance with a mind-bending encounter with a different way of thinking and feeling, my first peek behind the curtain of what I'd assumed, up until that moment, was reality.

It happened on the eleventh consecutive night Terry and I had sat on the floor in the candlelight and smoked the hashish we'd smuggled back from Morocco. By then, I'd stopped expecting much and had begun to think of it pretty much the same way you would think about sharing a cigarette with a friend. No big deal, just a minor social event. But on that particular night, fate provided a catalyst that dissolved the mental barrier between a larger view of existence and myself.

After a couple of tokes, I laid back with my head on a pillow, my feet sticking out in front of me. I rested the pipe on my chest, the bowl nestling in the hollow of my sternum, clasped my hands beneath my head and closed my eyes.

The clay bowl was still warm, and I felt the heat penetrating through my shirt; it radiated outward from the bowl and seemed to flow into my circulatory system. Behind closed eyelids, I could see the heat spreading through every pour of my body like an expanding river of golden light that filled me with a newfound joy.

It was as if I finally understood the punch line of the funniest joke in the world, an orgasm of insight after a lifetime of mental constipation. It all happened so fast, it took me a moment or two to grasp the obvious—I was high.

Then I started to giggle.

Like the first time you have sex, the first time you get high is a landmark occasion, a rite of passage that remains an integral part of you, the particulars of which, though perhaps glazed by memory and the passing of time, linger forever in your psyche. Is there a stoner among us that would deny this truth?

My maiden cannabis-induced epiphany washed over me like a series of waves, one after another for several hours. Each wave caused a new synapse to click, and the relationship and connection between all things blossomed in my consciousness as never before. It was simultaneously revelatory and great fun, a rush of comprehension that had me laughing at the same time it showed me a new prism through which I could view the world.

It's never like those first days again. You can get close by quitting for a few months or by scoring some connoisseur cannabis after a long diet of dirt weed. But nothing is ever again quite like when you first start smoking.

It's not so much the heightening of the senses that make those original highs so special. That aspect remains a major part of the experience no matter how long you've been indulging. Rather, it is the sudden recognition that this alternative outlook is authentic, a way of relating to the universe that changes the way you think about life in all of its confounding intricacies.

At one point that first time, I realized I'd been sitting with my back to the wall for hours, hardly moving a muscle as I observed the thoughts passing through my mind. I felt like a statue and wondered if that was why it's called "getting stoned." My reverie was interrupted by a voice that seemed to emanate from a far distance but was actually coming from just a few feet away.

"I'm going to bed," purred Terry. "Why don't you do the same? If you stay there all night, you'll be stiff in the morning."

Standing up and moving across the room was an adventure in itself, time and space taking on a whole new meaning. I felt like an unwieldy robot as I lowered myself onto the cot, where I lay for a long while, absorbed in the shadows on the ceiling. Sleep finally overtook me, and when I awoke around nine the next morning, I felt unexpectedly invigorated.

I recalled that Terry had told me a couple of times that there is no hangover from cannabis, but I didn't really believe him until then. It seemed implausible that so much pleasure could be had without paying a price, no vomiting your guts out, no skull-splitting headache, no overpowering desire to curl up in the fetal position and die—just a good night's sleep and a new perspective upon waking.

Even before I peeled off the bedcovers, I was thinking about getting high again.

LIFE IN LONDON

There was a knock on the door around 7:45 in the morning. I was still half asleep, my bladder doing battle with a deep desire to slumber on.

Another knock ... quicker, louder!

Terry and I sat up in our cots and glanced at each other. He wasn't smiling.

Then there was a third knock ... followed, mercifully, by a familiar voice.

"Terry, Oliver is here to see you," said Susan in a stage whisper.

Oliver was a friend of theirs, the lay-about son of an upper-class family, living off a modest stipend. I'd met him at a party before we left for Morocco, and he'd waxed poetically about the "marvels of majoun," and said he couldn't wait until we got back from "dear old Tangier," to see what "yummy delights" we'd brought with us.

"Hold on," said Terry, getting up from his cot and crossing the room in leisurely strides, pulling his bathrobe around him as he went. He paused before opening the door and looked back at me.

"He probably wants to score," said Terry, and then he opened the door.

Oliver swept in, bushy-tailed and beaming, his Spanish cape swirling in his wake. He fancied himself as a bit of a dandy and looked like a young Peter Ustinov. Susan tiptoed in behind him, giggling quietly behind her hands, her eyes darting from Terry to

Oliver to me, and back again.

"Terry, my dear boy. I'm so happy you're back," declared Oliver as he peeled off his leather driving gloves. "Susan has been telling me all about it. I hear it was a successful trip and that you brought home some splendid souvenirs."

Terry laughed but didn't say anything. He walked over to the closet and took the stash off the top shelf, where it was hidden beneath a stack of sweaters, and handed Oliver a piece of hash about the size of a poker chip.

"Ooh, this looks interesting," said Oliver, inhaling deeply, his bloodshot nose too close to the hash for my taste. "I've got to visit my Aunt Margaret today and I simply can't handle it straight. Can I take this piece with me and give Susan the money in school tomorrow?"

Terry glanced over Oliver's shoulder at Susan, who nodded almost imperceptibly.

"Sure, that's cool. Here's something to wrap it in," said Terry, handing him a piece of silver-coated paper from the inside of a box of cigarettes.

Terry knew his sister would give him the money the moment Oliver left and then try to collect on her own behalf. Sometimes it was difficult to know whether Susan was a sap or an angel. Maybe there's no difference.

Word that we had hash to sell spread quickly through expat and art school circles, and it wasn't long before a steady trickle of people started stopping by the flat and scoring a few grams. It might seem like it was easy money, but we had mixed emotions whenever somebody wanted to cop.

As much as we counted on the money, every gram we sold in London cut into our potential profit, as it was worth significantly more in the U.S. But we needed the money. I had spent more than anticipated buying the hash in Tangier, making up for Terry's shortfall when the price kept going up. Consequently, I was running critically low on funds.

Initially, Terry borrowed a few pounds from Susan, but that

didn't last long and most of his next stipend check went toward the rent. We ate in cheap Indian restaurants when we had money and cooked up various frying-pan monstrosities on our hot plate when we were down to our last few shillings. As I was newly acquainted with the munchies, everything tasted scrumptious.

We'd decided to mail some of the hashish back to the United States before it was all gone. Terry had a friend in New York City, who said he would sell it and mail us our share of the profit. Even though it seemed risky to me, Terry apparently trusted the guy, and besides, we didn't have a good alternative.

"We'll put it in a candle," said Terry. "They'll never find it unless they chop it in half. And even if that happens, they can never trace it back to us."

"What about your friend in New York?"

"If worse comes to worse, he'll play it dumb. But nothing's going to happen."

It took almost all afternoon and half the evening to make the candle. First, Terry wrapped almost three ounces of hash in a layer of plastic and two layers of aluminum foil, sealing the seams with candle wax. Next he took an empty soup can and dripped an inch-and-a-half of wax into the bottom.

After the wax had hardened, I placed the package of hash on the middle of the wax base and held it in place with the blade of an old pocketknife while Terry dripped melted wax into the soup can.

Slowly the area between the hash and the sides of the can began to fill. The hash stopped a couple of inches below the top of the can, and when the wax reached that point, an unburned wick was inserted before we added the final few inches of wax. The sucker would have actually burnt for a while if somebody lit it.

After the creation had cooled and we'd eased it out of the can, it looked like exactly what it was, a crude candle molded in a soup can. But there was no sign of its hidden secret, and after we dripped additional wax all over the outside, it looked like one of those candles you might see at an arts and crafts bazaar.

We wrapped the candle in tissue paper left over from Christmas and put it in a shoebox, which was then bundled up in plain brown paper and secured with a combination of tape, string, and sealing wax. Terry was a big believer in sealing wax.

Using my left hand to disguise my handwriting (does that work?) I painstakingly addressed the parcel to Terry's friend and filled out the custom's declaration form, euphemistically describing the contents as a "gift." Then I signed a phony name: "George Hayes," after Gabby.

The next morning, sweet, angelic Susan, knowing full well what was inside, took the package to the post office, where she batted her eyelashes at the clerk and watched him blush as he affixed the correct number of airmail stamps and sent it on its merry way across the Atlantic. All Terry and I had to do was relax and wait for the money.

By then, I had abandoned all pretense of writing a movie script, a chore that seemed exceedingly dull compared to experiencing life in London high on cannabis. Everything appeared so full of previously unnoticed allure—even the streaks on a grimy window or the pattern of condensation on a beer glass were fascinating in a way I'd never noticed before.

The relationship of all things to all other things started to come into focus, and soon I began to have a fuzzy understanding of how those relationships molded the whole. The best part was that I wasn't learning any of this from teacher, preacher, parents, or book. It was a spontaneous reaction to experiencing life from a slightly different angle and seeing the world with much more clarity and appreciation than ever before.

I do believe that children see and know so much more than adults, but I'm among the latter group now (legally, anyway) and can only recall snatches from my age of innocence. A bowl of marijuana, on the other hand, has seldom been beyond my reach for very long since those first months in London.

Although the divine Miss Jane has never stopped giving,

those early lightning bolts of insight gave me a foundation upon which I'm still building, higher and higher—so to speak—with each puff. I have no illusions about ever touching the sky. And no regret either—our earthly roots contain more than enough magic to fill a thousand lifetimes.

THE YELLOW CANARY

To be young and high in London during the late 1960s was to be in the epicenter of a cultural shift unlike any other in the 20th century, and drugs were both a primary part of that movement and its currency. By the time Terry and I had been back in London for five or six weeks, we'd sold most of the hash, except for what we'd mailed back to the States in the candle.

We used most of the hash money to pay for our day-to-day expenses, and it wasn't long before we'd consumed the few grams we'd saved for personal use. The night we smoked the final few bowls, I was too buzzed to worry about it. I blew out my candle, lay on my back, and watched the green and orange lightshow on the inside of my eyelids fade to black.

We'd acquired new contacts through selling off the hash and became a trusted part of our little corner of the scene. Oliver, who was just as much at home picking up a bit of rough trade in the East End as he was drinking champagne and snorting coke with the sons and daughters of the landed gentry, was a major part of that scene. The morning after the last of our stash went up in smoke, he showed up at the flat about 8:30, looking to score.

"Sorry, man," said Terry. "It's all gone."

"Oh, well, I guess I'll have to go back to buying from Tex at the Yellow Canary," said Oliver, sighing dramatically and looking around for somewhere to park his ample backside.

"Who's Tex," I asked, "and what's the Yellow Canary?"

"It's a pub at the bottom of Portobello Road, where the

antique shops end and the outdoor market begins," said Oliver, settling gingerly on the edge of Terry's empty cot. "You can't miss it. Tex will be the one wearing cowboy boots and a fringed jacket. The poor man thinks he's Buffalo Bill or somebody. His hash costs more than yours, but it's usually pretty good."

"I guess we'll go check him out," said Terry. "Want to come with us?"

I knew the second the invitation came out of his mouth that Terry hoped he could charm Oliver into buying him a few grams. And under other circumstances (perhaps if I wasn't there) maybe he would have allowed Terry to take advantage of him just so he could enjoy his company for a couple of hours. I guessed it wouldn't have been the first time.

"Not today, I'm afraid," said Oliver. "I'm frightfully busy. You boys run along and say hello to Tex for me."

"Okay," said Terry as he opened the door just enough for Oliver to squeeze past into the hallway. Terry glanced at me and followed Oliver into the hall.

I could hear his muffled voice through the door but couldn't understand what he was saying. Oliver laughed and, a few seconds later, Terry came back into the flat. He smiled and held up two ten-pound notes.

"I promised to have a drink with him later," he said, shrugging. "But first, we're going to Portobello Road."

"What sort of place is it?"

"It's cool; you'll like it. It's a sort of combination antique row and street market. It's been there forever and goes on for miles. I wanted to go back there anyway to see if I can find any genuine Hester Bateman silver. My mother wants to buy some."

"Who's Ester Bateman?"

"Hester, with an 'H.' She was a famous 18th-century silversmith. My mother says we're related."

"No shit."

Hester Bateman silverware was just one of the terribly expensive things on Terry's list of things to buy. The previous week, we'd taken a train to one of London's suburbs to look at a Vincent Black Lightning, the legendary vintage motorcycle that Hunter S. Thompson wrote about in *Fear and Loathing in Las Vegas*. But it turned out to be a Vincent Black Shadow, the stock model of the custom-built Lightning, so Terry wasn't interested.

And he never tired of talking about the Aston Martin he wanted. The fact that Terry didn't have much more than Oliver's twenty pounds didn't faze him in the slightest. Being practically broke wasn't even a consideration, and when we got to Portobello Road, we stopped at six or seven shops and inquired about Hester Bateman. We got mainly are-you-daft looks and one "Does this look like a bloody museum?" for our trouble.

But Terry was undaunted by even the rudest rebuff. "I knew none of these places would openly sell Hester Bateman," he confided as we continued our stroll. "But they fence a lot of stolen shit, so you never know. I was hoping somebody might have steered us into a back room for a private chat."

"Want to keep trying?" I asked.

"No, let's keep going. The Yellow Canary is still a ways down the road yet."

It was a cold and sunny day, but I was comfy in my pea jacket, a long knitted scarf wound around my neck. I admired my reflection in a store window. With Terry's black Spanish hat pulled down low on my brow, I looked like an extra in a Spaghetti Western.

It was Saturday, the day of the week Portobello Road, the largest antique market in Europe, comes alive. The scene crackled with the buzz of humanity punctuated with shouts, laughter, and an occasional car horn in the distance. In some ways, it reminded me of the Kasbah in Tangier, but nowhere near as claustrophobic or pissy smelling.

Still, both were public gathering places where diverse elements of the community mingle in the name of commerce. Besides antique shops, there were a number of stores selling turn-of-the-century clothing, which was becoming fashionable among rock stars and the decadent children of decadent members of the aristocracy. There were also military and band uniforms from the same era, some of the latter similar to the type the Beatles wore on the cover of *Sgt. Pepper's Lonely Hearts Club Band*, which would be released that June.

There were open-air stalls selling used books, furniture, old phonograph records, cooking utensils, and toys. A guy with a cockney accent had set up a folding card table in the middle of the road and was selling the "eleventh wonder of the world," which turned out to be a combination potato peeler and can opener. His singsong spiel was mesmerizing, and we stopped to listen for a few minutes before moving on, our boot heels clicking on the pavement.

The Yellow Canary was right where Oliver said it would be, and we could hear the jukebox through the open front door a hundred yards away, as the din of the patrons competed with The Rolling Stones pounding out "Under My Thumb." Inside, the sunlight coming through the windows crisscrossed the pub like a series of searchlights, highlighting the smoke rising from a smoldering forest of cigarettes. Everybody seemed to be talking at once, as three bartenders and two waitresses struggled to keep up with the voracious thirst of the Saturday afternoon stampede.

It was an eclectic mix of customers: A mini-skirted girl lounged against the bar talking to a pensioner, while a huckster, anxious to return to his stall, chugged down the last few swallows of his pint. A toff, complete with a rolled umbrella and yellow gloves, sipped a gin and tonic as he chatted up an expensive-looking tart in knee-high boots and a fur coat. A tall black man with rings on every finger watched the pair from a discreet distance, his face impassive as he nodded his head in time to the music.

Tex, wearing his fringed jacket and cowboy boots as advertised, was situated about halfway down the bar, talking to a small cluster of people, one of whom patted him on the back, picked up his change from the bar, and headed for the door. This gave us an opening to get within speaking range, and Terry sidled up to him.

"Tex?" he said, smiling widely.

Tex turned his head in Terry's direction and shook the proffered hand.

"Oliver told us to say hello."

The look of mild apprehension disappeared from Tex's face and was replaced by a nicotine-stained smile. He was shorter than both of us, even in his cowboy boots, and had a bit of a belly protruding over his rodeo-style belt buckle. His shoulder-length brown hair looked like it hadn't been washed in months and his industrial-strength body odor cut clean through the beer and tobacco when you got within a few feet.

"Good old Oliver," said Tex. "I haven't seen him in a month or so. How's he doing?"

"He's cool," said Terry. "He said he'd be coming to see you soon."

"Good. I miss old Oliver. Have you known him long?"

"He goes to art school with my sister."

"Oh!" said Tex, realization dawning in his bloodshot eyes, "you must be the blokes who went to Morocco."

"Yeah, that's us. But we sold everything already, and Oliver said you might be able help us with something to tied us over."

"Sure. How much do you want?"

"Ten quid's worth."

"Okay, but why don't you buy a round to make it look good."

As Terry attracted the bartender's attention, Tex rummaged through the inside pocket of his buckskin jacket and came up with a matchbox, which he slipped into my hand as smoothly as Blue Hat had whipped out his switchblade in Tangier.

Tex handed me a beer with one hand and grabbed his own with the other. I noticed his fingernails were overgrown and dirty.

"Cheers! Welcome to the Yellow Canary."

"Cheers!" said Terry as the three of us clinked our glasses together.

I handed the matchbox to Terry, who slid it partway open and lifted it to his nose.

"Smells good. Are you here every Saturday?"

"Pretty much, and most evenings. Gotta take care of my regulars."

'What else do you have?"

"Just hash and a few pills every now and then. There's a guy down the road who has some excellent acid."

"LSD?"

"Blotter. Two pounds a hit."

"How do we get to his place?" asked Terry, glancing at me and grinning.

"I'll take you around to see him now if you like. I get a free hit for every ten customers I take him."

"Let's go," said Terry, downing the rest of his beer.

A KODAK MOMENT

The afternoon sun was starting to sink below the rooftops as Terry, Tex and I left the Yellow Canary and continued down Portobello Road, where some of the fruit and veg vendors were starting to pack up for the day. Evening was nigh, and Tex turned the collar up on his buckskin jacket.

There were a few forlorn shops in back of the stalls, but most of the buildings had been converted into cheap flats, a far cry from the upscale antique stores and trendy boutiques a mile or so back up the road. There was an empty gin bottle on one of the doorsteps and a pigeon pecked at a soggy, half-eaten sandwich in the gutter.

About a quarter mile from the pub, Tex knocked on the door of one of the neglected old row houses, and after a brief wait, none other than Flash, the Portobello Road Pied Piper (and purveyor) of lysergic acid diethylamide, opened the door.

"Oh, hello Tex," said a tall, gaunt man in his early 20s wearing wire rim glasses. "What's all this then?"

"Friends of Oliver wanna score some acid."

"You'd better close the door and come on up then," said Flash, turning and taking the stairs three at a time. I noticed as his left hand grabbed the banister that he was wearing gloves with the fingers cut out.

We followed Flash up a dusty flight of stairs and into the living room of his second-floor flat, where a pretty young woman was curled up on a tattered armchair in front of the fireplace. She was wearing several sweaters over her dress and an old, leather aviator's helmet, the sort with earflaps, pulled down tight over her head. She was motionless, almost as if in a catatonic trance, with her hair sticking out of the helmet at odd angles.

"This is Lucy," said Flash, gesturing offhandedly in her direction.

The girl never looked up or acknowledged us in any way. She just stared into the fire, as the broken crates, scavenged from the fruit and veg market, crackled in the hearth and sent sparks flying up the chimney. In the firelight, I could see that her face was dirty.

Flash threw a few more scraps of wood in the fire and then led us to a small darkroom. He took a brown bottle off the shelf and carried it into the kitchen. It had a yellow Kodak label that identified the contents as developing fluid.

Flash set the bottle on the counter next to the sink where the evening sunlight was the brightest. Then he went back into the darkroom and reemerged with a pair of scissors and a large piece of paper. It was a sheet of blotting paper, the sort people used to keep on their desks when fountain pens were still in common use, and somebody, presumably Flash, had drawn a rudimentary grid on it with a ruler and pencil. A few of the postage stamp-size rectangles were missing, carefully snipped free of the sheet, though you could see that the scissor blades had strayed slightly outside the lines on a couple of instances.

Flash placed the blotting paper on the counter and fished an eyedropper out of his baggy corduroys. I felt like I was back in junior high school chemistry lab watching a brainier student perform an experiment. He dipped the dropper into the bottle, drew out a tiny amount of clear fluid, and then painstakingly deposited a single drop on each of two squares. The drops hit the paper and spread out to form a damp discoloration about the size of a dime.

After cutting out the two squares, Flash wrapped them in a scrap of tin foil and handed them to Terry.

"That will be four pounds, please."

Terry gave him the money.

"Wanna cuppa tea before you go?" asked Flash, stuffing the money into his trouser pocket.

"No thanks," said Tex. "I've got to get back to the Canary."

"We're going to split too," said Terry. "Next time, maybe."

"I'll let you out," said Flash and headed for the stairway.

Tex turned to Lucy before he left and said goodbye. His words hung in the air—the only reply came from a teacup that rattled on the draining board when Flash opened the front door.

It was getting dark, and nobody spoke until we were once again outside the Yellow Canary, where we bid Tex farewell and headed for the tube station at the top of the road. A lot of the antique shops were still open, but with a pocketful of hashish and acid, Terry seemed to have temporarily forgotten Hester Bateman.

Scoring the acid wasn't exactly a spur of the moment thing. Terry and I had talked about it on and off for weeks, but there had been no definite plan. Terry had always said he wanted to see how I handled cannabis before we tripped together, but until he jumped at Tex's offer, I had no idea he deemed me ready.

Once, two or three weeks after I started smoking hash, I asked Terry what he thought was the biggest difference between me now and the way I used to be. He didn't say anything for a while, but then allowed that I was " less argumentative now."

It seemed faint praise at the time, especially as I was so eager for his approval, but it was true: Certain aspects of my personality were beginning to mellow under the influence of the benign weed, which made me open to all sorts of possibilities that I'd never even considered before.

The truth was that I would have willingly taken the acid without an apprenticeship with the pipe. Now that I had peeked behind the curtain and glimpsed a larger vision of the world, I was even more enthusiastic about the impending journey into the deeper recesses of the mind. I understood that the straight world was just one layer of the onion, and the desire to peel back and explore the other layers was one I could not resist.

Back at the flat, we sampled a few bowls of Tex's hash, agreed to take the acid first thing in the morning, and settled in for the night. Rain pelted the windows and somewhere outside I heard a car door slam and high heels clacking on the pavement. A Thelonious Monk record was playing softly and I felt very cozy, snuggled beneath my blanket with a head full of hashish.

When the album ended, Terry propped himself up on one elbow and leaned forward to blow the candle out. But before he did, he looked over at me and said, "You'll never be the same after tomorrow, you know."

Then he blew out the candle, leaving me suddenly wide awake and staring at a wisp of candle smoke evaporating in the faint glow of an electric alarm clock.

YOU WILL NEVER BE THE SAME AGAIN

I'd already pulled on my jeans and a sweater, groped my way down the hall to the communal bathroom, and was sitting on the commode when I remembered what day it was—the day that Terry said would change me forever.

He was right, of course, but is there anybody who isn't changed by their first experience with psychedelics? It's a matter of how and to what degree you change. Dosage also plays a major role in what kind of trip it is, and all I can say about Flash's acid was that it was the best I ever had—so far.

Was it because it was my first trip or because the acid was good? A bit of both, I suspect. But as I flushed the toilet and headed back to the room, I had no idea what was going to happen to me. All I knew for sure is that I wanted it to happen.

Terry had the kettle on when I got back.

"Let's take it with a cup of tea."

"Okay. Then what?"

Terry stopped fiddling with the teacups and looked at me.

"We just wait until it comes on. Once it does, you probably won't feel like going anywhere for a while."

An involuntary shiver passed through me. I wouldn't have admitted it at the time, but to a minor degree, I had been influenced by all the sensational horror stories that had been in the papers, some of which have become archetypical tales, a mixture of urban legend and doper lore: Trippers, thinking they could fly, plummeting to their deaths after jumping out of windows. Trippers staring into the sun until their eyeballs were fried. Instant insanity. Ritual suicides. You name it.

The establishment media was so full of bullshit in its eagerness to demonize LSD, after a while you could not believe a word. Still, as the decisive moment neared, a sliver of doubt slipped past my defenses.

"Don't worry, you're going to like it," said Terry. "And I'm going to be here with you. Everything is going to be cool."

I put the piece of blotting paper in my mouth, took a swig of tea, and turned the acid-soaked sacrament into a spitball. Then I took another swig of tea and swallowed it like a pill.

I was worried it wasn't going to work and then I worried it would. After a while, I didn't care.

I was staring out the window when the acid began to take hold. Our third-story flat looked down on an alleyway where two trees pushed up past our window in their quest to touch the London sky. At first, I looked at the trees without really seeing them.

I was absorbed in playing the role of the young bohemian, striking a pensive pose as I looked out over a winter cityscape. I imagined myself a modern-day De Quincey substituting acid for opium, but that was just a façade. Inside, I was a jumbled mess of insecurity and foolish courage.

I believe the trees triggered the trip because they were the only living things visible outside the window. Most of the leaves had fallen off and blown away, but there were seedpods still hanging from the branches, thousands of them, potential trees destined to fall on barren concrete.

Of course, I had known since childhood that seeds housed potential life, but suddenly I felt the miracle of it like never before, felt it in my body as much as in my mind. The sudden comprehension made me laugh, and I felt the same golden light spreading throughout my body that I had felt the first time I got high on hash. It felt like an old flannel shirt, warm and comforting, but then something shifted and the experience accelerated.

I had the first of a series of what some might call mini-hallucinations, visions that came and went in an instant, as if someone had struck a match and illuminated a primeval cave for a split second and then quickly blown it out. They were multi-sensory insights, based very much in the corporeal world, half-forgotten knowledge surfacing from antiquity.

The nearest tree outside the window turned into an archetypal tree of life, and then instantly turned back to the tree in the alleyway. But some kind of time warp allowed me to absorb much in that ephemeral moment. The same golden light that flowed through my blood vessels also flowed through the tree, shimmering with life and spreading up from the roots until it reached into the veins of the leaves and seedpods. I saw the tree's seasonal cycle go from full bloom to barren and back to bloom again. The simple yet wondrous beauty of it filled me with a peaceful joy I had never known before.

"I can't understand why anybody would think this is bad," I said to Terry, who was sitting on the floor with an even bigger grin than usual on his face.

"Me neither," said Terry, nodding benignly and stroking his mustache.

I lay down next to him, too high to do anything more than just be there as an ever-expanding understanding swept away old assumptions and countless layers of assorted bullshit. There were no journeys to other worlds, just a highly intensified version of the world I had always occupied—a version where you sensed the interconnectedness of all things.

If that sounds trite, so be it. That is what we need the most, a refresher course on the true nature of our existence, one that reminds us that we too are part of the whole. There is nothing revolutionary about the concept, but for me that day in London, it was no longer an abstract theory, it was simply a fact, the way things were.

At times, the revelations rushed to the surface like carbonated bubbles in a soda, popping helter-skelter as they broke the surface. But just before they disappeared forever, another link in a chain of understanding flashed through me. It was such a blissful feeling that euphoric laughter erupted from time to time and then faded as the rush subsided, only to spew anew when the next one rolled over me.

I experienced no fear or apprehension whatsoever, not a trace of a bummer. Why anybody would think this was bad was becoming my silent mantra. There were, however, a couple of startling instances, both of which involved an encounter with somebody other than Terry, one of whom was I.

An hour or so into the trip, I tried to get up and walk around a bit, a task that felt like operating a large, cumbersome piece of construction equipment. I slowly stood up ... and then quickly sat down again, my skewed equilibrium not quite up to a task I had taken for granted since I was three years old.

I waited a while, gathered my wits—such as they were—and tried again. That's when my muscle memory took over and I managed to get up and walk four or five feet to the mantelpiece.

This brought me face to face with the mirror, and instead of a reflection of myself, a satyr grinned back at me. I involuntarily glanced down to see if my feet had turned into cloven hoofs— they had not—and when I looked back up at the mirror, the satyr was gone. And I was back. Just like that.

Okay, I'll admit that with my rumpled curly hair, unkempt goatee, and stoned-out sparkle in my eyes, I did look a bit like a youngish satyr, at least from the waist up. But there were no budding horns on my forehead, and what I saw in the mirror was not I looking like a satyr. It was a satyr. I only saw him for a second, at most, and that was a long time ago. But his memory lingers, a flashing neon sign on a psychedelic road trip that has never really ended.

I like to flatter myself by thinking that the satyr was a window into my true nature, and there's no denying I would have been right at home at the Dionysian Mysteries. Who knows? Maybe that's too obvious an interpretation. But with Occam's razor in my hip pocket, I seldom fear to follow in his hoof prints.

When I told Terry what I'd seen in the mirror, he laughed, "You're just high. That's all."

Yeah, I know, but what do you think it means?"

"It means you're high."

We were several hours into our trip and still peaking when there was a scratching noise at our door. Terry and I looked at each other and then at the door. He had told Susan when we came home from Portobello Road the night before that we were going to drop acid the next day and didn't want to be disturbed. But the scratching noise persisted. It sounded like some sort of burrowing rodent clawing at the door.

Terry lurched to his feet, looking a bit like a praying mantis in blue jeans and a turtleneck, and walked to the door in what seemed slow motion. He put his ear up to the door, listened for a few seconds—or was it a few minutes—and then turned toward me with a loopy grin on his face.

"It's Miranda. She needs the can opener."

When my art school friend scurried into the room, I had another experience similar to when I looked in the mirror. For a heartbeat, when I first saw her, Miranda looked like a giant groundhog walking upright and wearing clothes. Although there isn't a groundhog in Kenneth Grahame's classic, she would have looked right at home with Ratty, Mole, and the rest of *The Wind in the Willows* crew.

Then, just like the satyr, the groundhog was gone and Miranda was back.

There is a tenuous but intriguing connection between the mythical creature in the mirror and metamorphosing Miranda: The cover of the first edition of *Wind in the Willows* is embossed with an image of perhaps the most famous satyr of all—Pan, who is pictured sitting on hairy haunches playing his pipes. The primordial rascal also makes an appearance in Chapter 7, "The Piper at the Gates of Dawn," just as he did at the dawn of my psychedelic gateway.

My encounters with the satyr and Miranda's fleeting anthropomorphic transformation were gifts, two portals into a world beyond any I had known. They were as real as the trees in the alley and the empty teacups on the table. Everything was as it had always been.

The difference was in me—just like Terry had said it would be.

BEGINNER'S LUCK

Terry kept refilling the pipe with Lebanese Red until the taxi arrived. By the time we floated down the stairs and tumbled into the cab, I was enveloped in an invisible cannabis cocoon through which I perceived the world with an appreciative heart. I had twenty quid in my pocket, and, as the taxi headed for a casino in Soho, I stared dreamily out the window, absorbed in the lights shimmering in the puddles left by an afternoon shower.

As a would-be painter, I was cognizant of the quality of light and the interplay between illumination and darkness as an essential element in visual medium. True, my severely limited capacity with brush and pencil prevented me from expressing this yin-yang of artistic vision with anything resembling success, but the concept was still part of the way I viewed the world. With cannabis enhancing my sensory palette, however, that comprehension bypassed intellectual insight and blossomed into a corporeal pleasure as elemental as food or sex.

As the taxi weaved its way through the wet streets, the liquid light show on the other side of the window glass temporarily diverted my thoughts from a letter that had arrived a few days earlier. It had been forwarded from my parents' home, but the original return address was still in the upper left-hand side of the envelope: The United States Selective Service!

I'd been fucking drafted—and my mother had passed on what could very well turn out to be my death warrant as casually as a month-old magazine. It was, as Terry casually observed when

I told him, a "bummer."

Quite possibly the casino trip was a collective effort to cheer me up, and if so, probably engineered by Susan and Miranda, with Terry's compliance. Not that I had any such suspicion at the time, too absorbed in my own problems to see beyond myself. Why it didn't dawn on me when Miranda had slipped me two ten-pounds notes, I'll never know.

Maybe it was the hash, bowl after bowl of it, the best I'd ever smoked. It was a gift from Oliver, who had finally come into his inheritance, his aunt dead and buried the previous month. The day his estate check cleared the bank, he'd purchased a kilo of primo Lebanese Red from an old school chum in Oxford.

The high was sweet and dreamy. It slowed down the world just enough to give you time to soak it all in and spin it around your head before it passed. London that night looked a neon-painted dream, a world where everything dissolved into a funhouse reflection where the rainwater gathers in the gutters.

As we approached Piccadilly Circus, Terry leaned over and tapped me on the knee, interrupting my private reverie. When I swung my head around to face him, he was smiling at me the way one might smile at a favored child.

I grinned back, happy to be the beneficiary of his benevolence. Our relationship had been strained the last few weeks, which filled me with a sadness that threatened to slide into self-loathing.

While I won't deny that I was the architect of my fate, circumstances had also been instrumental in my plight. Back in Tangier, when I put up more than twice as much money for the hash as Terry had, we made an agreement: We would both live off his monthly check from his parents until we had sold the hash.

Now both the hash and the money were gone, and to make things worse, we'd received just a fraction of what we'd expected from the candles caper. I had become a burden, a burden with very few prospects.

But that night in the taxi it was suddenly like old times again. Maybe the hash had carried us past our pettiness. Maybe I'd been paranoid all along. Who knows? Who cares? At that moment, Terry and I connected again, and that's all that mattered.

"You should try roulette," he said, looking at me the way he had before we had left the hotel in Tangier, hashish already strapped to our bodies, headed for the airport. I knew that look well, and as always, it was accompanied by a gentle, persuasive tone of voice.

"Just play either black or red until you start to feel a connection with the wheel. Be conservative and wait until a number pops into your head. It will seem out of nowhere, like a hunch, but trust it and bet on that number. The trick is not to force it; be patient and just let it come on its own."

"Is that what you're going to do?"

"That's what I always do. Sometimes it works and sometimes it doesn't, but I think you're going to have beginner's luck."

"You think so?"

"Sure, just don't get greedy"

Terry leaned back in the seat and laughed, and even though I wasn't sure what the joke was, I laughed too.

"I wish I had one of those magic beans," I ventured.

"I don't think you're going to need one."

∎∎∎

Terry was right. Less than an hour later, I was sitting at the casino bar, drinking a gin and tonic, more than 200 pounds in my pocket. James Bond would have continued playing, maybe even tried to break the bank. But all I needed was airfare back to New York.

Everything happened exactly the way Terry said it would. A number popped into my head after about 10 minutes at the wheel, and I didn't hesitate to put all my money down or walk away after I hit. I surrendered to my instincts, stopped rationalizing, and went with my gut. Somehow, I knew I was going to win, and when I did, it wasn't a surprise. I somehow felt in sync with fate and was able to act accordingly.

It took me decades to realize what had happened, but I've come to understand that it was Terry's parting gift to me, the last spell cast on my behalf—a final taste of Mexican magic.

I never saw Terry again after leaving London, but he's still with me. Our time together was brief, his influence deep and enduring. Even now, his face, framed by a halo of hashish smoke, smiles at me down through the decades.

Sometimes it seems like I imagined the whole thing, including Terry. But there are a couple of faded stamps in my old passport that tell me otherwise.

PART

Two

Maneuvers

NIGHT TRAIN TO DIXIE

When I finally managed to force the window open, the sound of the train click clacking along the rails intensified and the smell of honeysuckle and diesel fuel wafted into my compartment. It would be mid-morning before we reached our destination, and I knew this would probably be my last chance to cop a buzz, maybe for months.

I still had about half a gram of the hashish I had stuffed in my Zippo before leaving London. After locking the door, I rolled the last of my stash into three small balls, found a safety pin in my toilet bag, and stuck one of the balls on the end of the pin. Then I unscrewed a ballpoint pen, clamped the bottom half between my teeth, and set the hash ball on fire with my Bic.

I only allowed the hash to burn for a couple of seconds before blowing it out and inhaled the resulting column of smoke through the barrel of the pen. I held the smoke in my lungs as long as I could and then slowly exhaled what was left out the window and watched it disappear into the darkness.

I repeated the process twice more and then lit a cigarette to overpower any smell of hash that may have lingered. The day was coming to an end pretty much the same way the previous one had, wrapped in a comfy cloak of cannabis. My body relaxed as one world closed and the doors of another swung open, my inner journey illuminated by a familiar golden glow.

But it was impossible to forget that this was not just another night. It was, in fact, unique, my first night as a member of the

U.S. Army. As the train made its inevitable way south, I knew I had embarked on an expedition from which I might never return. The war in Vietnam was as real as the train carrying me to Fort Bragg, North Carolina, a factory that turned boys into killers and victims. For many, basic training was the first stop on the road to Southeast Asia and, quite possibly, a trip home in a body bag.

You think that sounds overly dramatic? Well, that's exactly how it works. You think it can't happen to you, but you get caught up in a time-tested system, and before you know it, you're in a combat zone, a shit-smeared punji stick embedded in your foot, wondering how the fuck you got there.

Somehow, I managed to herd that thought into a box, nail it shut, and push it to one of the deeper recesses of my mind, where it stayed, more or less, long enough to find a refuge of sorts in the fitful sleep that eventually followed. But before I drifted off, I thought about a discussion Terry and I had had after I told him I'd been drafted.

"You should drop acid right before you go," said Terry, pausing to light the pipe he'd just stuffed with hash. "You'll be on a totally different level than them; they'll be so freaked out that they won't take you."

He exhaled a plume of smoke, grinned, and passed the pipe.

"Sounds like a plan."

I took a toke and passed the pipe back. Whether it was the hash or Terry's suggestion, I'm not sure, but I felt better right away. But two months later, as I rolled toward the dawn, the only mind-altering substances in my system were cannabis and alcohol.

The plan to score some acid before leaving London was spoiled when a last-minute trip to Portobello Road yielded nothing. Terry and I knocked on Flash's door for five minutes, but nobody answered. Then, just as we gave up and started to walk away, I thought I spotted Lucy's pale face in the upstairs window.

"Look," I said, pointing, "there's Lucy."

Terry spun around and looked up, but she was gone.

"Where?"

"Up there in the middle window. Maybe she's coming down."

We went back and waited by the door, but Lucy didn't come, not even after I knocked again and yelled her name through the mail slot.

"Let's go," said Terry.

"But my flight is tomorrow."

"Don't worry. I'll score a couple of hits and mail them to you."

Just like Lucy on that final trip down Portobello Road, the acid never came, so I spent the night before I was to be inducted smoking hash-laced Gauloises and drinking wine with Harvey, a painter and old art school friend. He had an apartment in the city, a brief walk from the induction center, and we talked into the early morning.

I nodded off a few times, but woke at the first light of dawn, a bad taste in my mouth, apprehension gnawing at my nut sack. Harvey was still asleep, curled up in a thin Indian bedspread, snoring softly, when I let myself out. As I headed down the street, fortified by the bowl of hash I'd smoked before leaving, I figured that with a little luck, I'd be back in a few hours.

I passed a storefront with a hand-written sign taped to the window, along with an assortment of flyers and posters. The sign read "Draft Counseling" and was decorated with several peace signs in different color felt-tip pens. The flyers advertised various anti-war activities and the poster was for a benefit rock concert featuring a local band. I peered inside: The lights were out; the only sign of life a calico cat asleep atop a radiator.

I walked on, wishing I were headed anywhere but where I was going, but lacking the courage to outright defy Uncle Sam and head for the border. Instead, I was going to outsmart the system, beat the Draft without going to jail or skipping the country.

I felt it would have been easier with the acid, and maybe it would have been, but it worked anyway. Not the way I thought it would and not as quickly as I would have liked. Not even close. But I did bullshit my way out of the Army. It just took longer than expected.

That very morning, after leaving Harvey's apartment, I started the chain of events that eventually led to my early discharge. It began at the induction center, where I filled out the first batch of forms that the Selective Service used to screen out undesirables. They were setting the bar pretty low back then, but they still made you take a battery of tests, just to make it look good and perhaps weed out a few basket cases and one-legged guys.

It was easy to know what answers they wanted in the questionnaires intended to probe your psyche for deviant characteristics, so most of the time I gave them exactly what they didn't want. The trick was to tell them just enough but not too much, tease them without getting yourself thrown in jail or the nuthouse. I did this instinctively, sensing when to be truthful, when to lie, when to exaggerate (and how much), and when to hold back.

Much to my glee, there was a series of questions about drug use, part of which was a laundry list of mind-bending substances. You were supposed to check off the ones you'd taken. I told the truth, admitting to using marijuana, hashish, LSD, amphetamines, cocaine, and morphine. The last was a bit of a stretch, as my one experience with morphine had been totally legal, taken in hospital after breaking my leg one summer as a laborer on a construction job.

One of the questions asked if you were addicted to any of the drugs you'd taken, and although I knew full well it was totally preposterous, I claimed cannabis addiction. I figured, what the hell, it was worth a try. Besides, if they tested me, I would certainly have been positive.

There was also one crucial part of the physical exam that I faked, something so simple it's surprising a lot more guys didn't do the same: While taking the eye exam, I pretended my vision was much worse than it really was at the time.

I'm nearsighted and had worn glasses since tenth grade, so it was believable when I kept saying I couldn't read the eye chart, even when they tested lenses three or four times the strength of the glasses I'd worn to the induction station. When I admitted I could read the chart, I was roughly in the same league as Mr. Magoo.

I credit the self-survival instinct with which all living creatures are hardwired for much of what I did that day. Even so, the enhanced awareness that accompanies cannabis intoxication helped give me a single-minded focus.

It was as if an internal ally helped guide me through a bureaucratic maze, pointing out potential opportunities, but also restraining me when I was tempted to do something foolish. It was like fishing for a whale in a rowboat—I had to set the hook and then hang on for a rough ride without being pulled overboard and drowned.

Who knows? Maybe if I had dropped acid as originally planned, I would have been back at Harvey's apartment in time for a late lunch. But although I had unknowingly tipped over the first domino in a chain reaction that would eventually set me free from Uncle Sam's grasp, as the sun set, I found myself on a train, rolling slowly south toward an uncertain future.

MISERY LOVES COMPANY

A line of olive drab buses was waiting for our train when it finally chugged into Fayetteville, and as I joined a couple hundred other miscreants spilling onto the platform, I fervently wished I'd saved one of the previous night's hash balls for the morning.

As the bus rolled out of the station and toward Ft. Bragg, I peered through the grimy window and couldn't help noticing how pretty North Carolina looked in the springtime. On both sides of the road, forests of fragrant evergreen trees pushed out of red soil and reached for the sun, shining in the cloudless blue sky.

I felt the calming effect of being close to nature and took comfort in the way it reminded me that there really was something bigger in the world than the U.S. Army. Of all the things I did during my time at Fort Bragg, the one I treasure the most was being outside for both the sunrise and sunset almost every day for approximately three months. Each was different, a collection of excruciatingly beautiful canvases that provided a counterpoint to the nasty business at hand.

I suppose that if you're young, in relatively good physical shape—and there's no war going on—basic training might even be fun for some guys, sort of an extended Boy Scout outing, complete with barbed wire, tear gas, and live ammunition with which to play. But knowing that the killing fields of Southeast Asia were probably waiting for you at the other end of the production line cast an ominous shadow over the experience.

Then there was the nagging knowledge that for the first time in your life your freedom was restricted. You weren't a prisoner, but you weren't a free man either. You were trapped in a parallel universe, one that interacted with the rest of the world but was, at the same time, a world apart.

The one thing that helped you get through the day-to-day grind and never-ending bullshit was that you make friends easier and quicker than at any other time in your life. I was lucky in that respect because I found a lifetime friend, all because he was the only other guy on the train to Fort Bragg with long hair.

It seems quaint and naive in retrospect, but there was a bond between longhairs in the '60s, and for a brief moment in time, it did really mean something. It generally meant that the person smoked pot, was against the war, and was, to one degree or another, a peace-loving freak that disavowed violence. There were exceptions to the rule, of course, but the cliché was rooted in enough truth to work as a reliable tribal marker.

Charlie Manson changed all that forever a few years later, but when I first spotted Jimmie the day we were inducted into the Army, it was his shoulder-length hair that caught my attention.

I liked Jimmie right away. He was bright, funny, easy to talk to, and, just like me, a would-be hippie caught up in the war machine because he was too chicken shit to refuse to step forward or run away to Canada. You would be surprised how many guys like us there were back then.

One evening soon after we arrived at Fort Bragg, as we sat on the barracks steps smoking cigarettes and killing time until "lights out," I told Jimmie about my recent Moroccan adventure.

"You can buy hash on the streets as easily as you can buy vegetables over there," I found myself saying.

"Where do I sign up?" said Jimmie, laughing and stubbing out his cigarette, as a recorded bugle call sounded over the public address system.

"Yeah, Tangier is a hell of a long way from North Carolina. I wonder if there's any weed for sale in Fayetteville?"

"Sounds like a suicide mission to me, but I'm definitely going to check out Tangier first chance I get."

As we ambled back into the barracks and climbed into our bunks, my spirits were lifted by the knowledge that I had a kindred soul up shit's creek with me.

The next day, Jimmie and I watched as our hair fell to the barbershop floor and the symbol of our identity was swept up in a pile along with the hair of dozens of other guys. To my surprise, I felt relieved. The last thing you want in the Army is to stand out among the herd, and although thoughts of getting out filled my waking hours, I realized keeping a low profile would make my life easier until that day came.

In the meantime, I was just another fresh recruit being fed into a human sausage machine designed to strip us of our individuality and reduce us to the lowest common denominator. My mind was still in London, but my ass belonged to Uncle Sam. Everything depended on how I balanced the two.

THE MERCIFUL SERGEANT

Sgt. Jones was standing between the two-story wooden barracks that would be our home throughout basic training and the recruits. His back was to the sun, and you had to squint to see him clearly, a slender, athletic-looking black man, probably in his late 20s, with a handsome face and flawless teeth. His fatigues were freshly laundered and starched, and he wore his Smokey the Bear hat pushed slightly forward so that the underside of the brim almost touched the frames of his aviator sunglasses. He had his hands on his hips and seemed to be sizing us up.

"Is there anybody who doesn't want to be here?" said Sgt. Jones, sounding as casual as if he were asking if anybody wanted a cup of coffee. "Is there anybody who wants to get out of the Army?"

There was a ripple of nervous laughter, but almost half of us either raised our hands or verbally acknowledged we wished we were elsewhere.

Was he serious or what?

"Okay," said Sgt. Jones, "here's what you do: In a week or so, you will have a class on the Uniformed Code of Military Justice. You have to do what I'm about to tell you before you have that class because, afterward, they can throw the book at you and you'll probably get court-martialed. But before you have the class, they can only do so much to you."

You could not see his eyes behind the shades, but you could tell he was scanning us because his head swiveled, almost imperceptibly—left, right, and then back to center—before he continued.

"All you have to do is walk away when nobody is looking, lay low for a couple of days, and then turn yourself in. Tell them you were afraid and panicked. But whatever you do, do not, I repeat, do not throw away your dog tags or military ID. If you do, you will be charged with desertion, but if you keep your dog tags and ID, the most they can charge you with is being AWOL, confine you to the barracks and maybe dock your pay.

"Then, a day or so after turning yourself in, do the same thing again. Do it three or four times, and you'll be sent to a psychiatric hospital, where they will keep you for a month or so and then give you a medical discharge. But remember, you must do it before your class in the Uniform Code of Military Justice, and whatever you do, don't throw away your ID and dog tags."

We all stood dumbfounded, blinking in the morning sunlight, and when Sgt. Jones had said all he had to say on the matter, he segued into explaining that he would soon march us over to the PX, where we could purchase any personal grooming and toilet item we had neglected to bring with us.

Just like that, he switched gears from giving us an unauthorized blueprint for beating the system to discussing toothpaste and boot polish. There was no pause, no change in his tone of voice or facial expression. It made the escape plan seem a routine part of the indoctrination process. Were the other drill sergeants telling their platoons the same thing?

It was a surreal moment, and I didn't really know what to think, and I don't believe anybody else did either. Maybe it was a trick. One of the first things you learn in the military is not to believe anything until it happens. There's a million times more bullshit in the army than bullets. Even reality is relative.

Like the civilian version of reality, military reality is an agreed-upon set of perceptions to which virtually everybody subscribes, regardless of whether they want to or not. Military reality, however, is based on a different set of rules, and although the dissimilarities can seem subtle at times, this is just a ruse to make it appear more acceptable to the world in which so-called civilized society likes to believe it lives.

I'll never know for sure, but I like to believe that Sgt. Jones was sincerely trying to show us a way out. He had recently returned from a tour of duty in Vietnam, where he had seen and done god knows what, but whatever it was, I think it's plausible that he was giving us one last chance to get off the lethal merry-go-round before it was too late.

I wasn't bold enough to do anything so audaciously overt and, as far as I know, nobody else was either. Sgt. Jones never mentioned it again.

DEAD-EYE DICK RIDES AGAIN

Thirty-five guys wearing combat boots kick up a lot of dust running around a dirt and cinder track. On that June afternoon in North Carolina, it swirled around close to the ground, forming little clouds and making it difficult for the runners to see.

That's why I didn't notice the guy lying on the track until I was almost on top of him. Instinctively, I jumped, the way you would over a log, and kept going, the wind in my ears drowning out the pounding of my heart.

Stopping to help the guy was never a consideration. The Army had honed my sense of self-preservation whether I wanted it to or not. Each recruit had to complete the course within a certain time or repeat basic training, and that would mean an additional 11 weeks before I got leave, another 11 weeks before my next taste of freedom.

Later, we heard that the guy had died of heat stroke. Who knows if it was true or not? He wasn't in my platoon and I didn't know him. A couple of days later, everybody stopped talking about him and it was as if he had never existed. But I can still see him, stretched perpendicular across the track, face down—an obstacle to be cleared so that I didn't trip and end up lying next to him.

Maybe these training mishaps help prepare you for worse to come, chip away a bit more innocence before the real shit hits the fan. Not that the Army sabotages selected recruits to make a point—there's more than enough idiots to fuck up without any help.

There was the geeky-looking guy from Detroit in my company who stabbed himself in the face with his bayonet. You don't forget seeing something like that. He was having trouble pulling the bayonet off of his M14 and yanked too hard.

Surprisingly, considering the sophomoric nature of barracks humor, nobody laughed. We laughed plenty later, but not then.

Luckily, the business end of the bayonet hit a few inches below his eye and it only took four stitches to sew him up. The clumsy blunder made this clown an instant celebrity, partly, I think, because his last name was Bodner and the alliteration was irresistible.

"Bayonet Bodner" was the most popular guy at the beer hall that night and didn't pay for a round. We had a perverse pride in having the company's most spectacular screw-up in our platoon, and he retained a mascot-like popularity until basic training was over and we went our separate ways.

The Army has a very simple and effective method of getting recruits to do what it wants them to do. They control access to the two things every living creature needs—food and sleep.

If you're ravenous and are told you have to crawl through a mud pit before being allowed into the chow hall, you are going to start crawling. If you are ordered to clean the shower tiles with a toothbrush and bottle of vinegar before you can go to sleep, you're going to start scrubbing.

I did enough to get by but no more, which turned out to be trickier than I had anticipated when it came to qualifying with my weapon, the M14. Like the timed run, you had to qualify with your weapon to get out of basic.

There were three qualifying categories, starting with Marksman, the lowest passing classification. Then came Sharpshooter, the middle grade, and finally, Expert, the top grouping. As I was pretending that my vision was far worse than it actually was, I figured that I'd shoot for Marksman, just good enough to get out of basic but manifestly ordinary by army standards.

But there was a problem: For some reason that I've never

really understood, I'm a naturally good shot with a rifle. Maybe it was all the cowboy movies I watched as a kid. I discovered I had the knack when I was around 12, taking target practice with my buddy's .22-caliber, bolt-action Marlin. I even bought a few issues of *Gun Digest* when I was 13 or 14.

By the time I was drafted, however, I was no longer enamored with firearms—quite the opposite, in fact—and was mildly surprised when I shot so well our first day on the firing range.

There followed week after week of painstakingly detailed and repetitive instruction, and only the few dweebs who could never get past being afraid of the noise and recoil seemed likely to fail. My dilemma was different: I needed to do well but not too well.

In order to qualify, you had to knock over a series of targets, shaped like the top half of a human torso that popped up at various distances downrange. Your score was determined by the percentage of targets you hit. An NCO sat next to you, holding a clipboard, keeping tally of your hits and misses.

I lay on my belly, propped my M14 on a sandbag, and adjusted my sight. I'm not sure what came over me. Maybe it was the desire to hurry up and get it over with or some ego-driven need to show off. It was like I couldn't miss—bang, bang, bang, plop, plop, plop—the torsos toppled over as if by magic.

"Yer doing good, soldier," said the NCO, "real good."

Shit, he was right. Halfway through, and I'd already knocked down enough to make Marksman. So I started to miss a few deliberately, but it got embarrassing after a while.

"What's the matter, soldier?" barked the NCO. "You were doing so good. Take your time. Don't jerk the trigger. Squeeze it."

So I knocked over a few more, and before you know it, I was a Sharpshooter. Things weren't going down the way I had figured. What a fool I was for acting like some dumb-ass Annie Oakley. I had to be careful, or the NCO might guess that I was faking it.

Down the stretch, I'd knock one down and then miss the next. It came down to the last shot. If I hit it, I'd be a fucking Expert.

"One more, just one more, soldier," said the NCO, encouragingly. "You can do it."

Just to make sure I did not, I aimed a good three feet over the top of the torso.

Bang! A clean miss.

"Shit!" said the NCO. "You missed, but you were so close, I'm giving it to you anyway. Congratulations."

"Thanks, sergeant."

I stood up, feeling slightly nauseous, brushed the sand off my fatigues, and went over and joined the rest of my platoon, most of whom thought I was bullshitting when I told them I'd shot Expert.

JAY-D AND THE POACHER

The coolest part of the day that San Antonio summer was just before first light, down by the creek under the willow trees. We lay on the grass and rested our heads on our helmets, gathering ourselves for the daily dose of army chicken shit. In the half-light, we looked like a group of peaceful corpses, floating in the morning mist that gathered near the water.

Upon completion of basic training, Jimmie and I had gone directly from Fort Bragg to Fort Sam Houston. That's the base where the U.S. Army turns recruits into medical corpsmen. They're the guys who, along with bedpan and clerical duties, patched up the casualties on the battlefields.

That's a heavy enough trip itself, but there was also the commonly held belief that the enemy always tried to pick off the medic first because of its demoralizing effect on the surviving troops. They supposedly went after the officers too, but the medics were target Number One, or so our instructors were fond of telling us.

The thing is, nobody else worried about that shit, and if they did, they kept it to themselves. Why drive yourself crazy fretting about things you can't control? We all knew that most of us were headed to Nam, but of more immediate concern was the remorseless Texas sun.

Those precious few minutes down by the creek, between reveille and morning chow, were probably the only time that day we would not be soaked in sweat. A couple of classrooms were air conditioned, but our barracks sure as hell weren't. Sundown brought far less relief than you might think. It never dropped below the mid-90s in those spit-shined ovens.

Nobody told us that the creek bank was the best spot to be as dawn approached. We just naturally gravitated to a place of respite, drawn by some rudimentary instinct toward whatever relief we could find. That's the thing about the military; it brings out the animal in everybody.

The chief task of such an elementary mindset is focusing on the immediate goal, which in our case was surviving the murderous heat. The sun is a far tougher taskmaster than any drill sergeant, and to make matters worse, the Army added it's own twisted, little complication: If you got sunburned, they could court-martial you for damaging government property—your own body.

Like I said, there was a lot of chicken shit. Daydreaming helped. Everybody daydreamed about one thing or another, but no matter what it was, it was something you couldn't get on base. My thoughts generally drifted to sex, drugs, and a weekend pass that held the promise of procuring both.

What we all really wanted was to be free—free to forget for a couple of days that we were in the Army. That was the real prize; the sex and drugs, or whatever you thought you desired, just enhanced the illusion.

Jimmie was in a different company and other than a few beer-hall sessions and a trip to the local drag strip to watch the funny cars, I didn't see much of him during our stay in San Antonio. But the bond was strong, the seeds of a lifetime friendship already planted.

Instead of Jimmie, I palled around with Curtis—an alligator poacher from the Florida everglades who had been given the choice of jail time or joining the army—and Jay-D, a beautiful, bisexual black guy from Washington, D.C.

Jay-D wasn't overtly bisexual and had no trouble passing as straight, probably because he loved pussy as much as he loved cock. There was genuine sincerity in his skirt chasing and macho bragging. But to me, the wrestling was a dead giveaway.

Jay-D participated in and often instigated the friendly wrestling matches that took place on the grass between the barracks during off-duty hours. He was built like a NFL cornerback and capable of crippling any one of us in a serious physical confrontation. But he grappled like he was everybody's big brother, allowing his opponents to be successful enough to have fun, while maintaining an effortless control of the situation.

As far as I could judge, none of the other guys thought anything of a homoerotic nature was taking place as they rolled around on the grass, slathered in each other's sweat. Jay-D even let some of them win on occasion, but most of the time, he allowed his partners to exhaust themselves and then gently pin their shoulder to the grass, smiling down on them good-naturedly as they writhed beneath him. Then there was the dancing.

Even on the hottest night, Jay-D would dance bare-chested on a footlocker placed in the middle the aisle between the two rows of bunks that ran the length of the barracks. He was good—*Soul Train* good—and the troops would gather around, laughing, cheering, and clapping as he shook his ass to anything from Motown to James Brown and the Rolling Stones.

The louder they cheered, the more he shook it.

I never said anything to anybody about my theory, not even to Jay-D. Actually, I didn't have to—one night Jay-D told me about a tryst he had with a gay lieutenant who worked at the base JAG office. They'd met in the stairwell after lights-out for a quickie.

I don't know what sort of response Jay-D was expecting, and I don't know why I said what I did, but I told him to ask for money the next time. He smiled and said okay, but the subject never came up again.

I'm not exactly sure what drew Jay-D, Curtis and I together, beyond the common plight of hating the military and fearing the war. Like everywhere else, there were plenty of assholes in the Army. But there was also a seemingly endless assortment

of human flotsam from which to choose your buddies. I chose
Curtis and Jay-D, or maybe they choose me. Most likely it was no
more complicated than enjoying one another's company. In the
military, that's more than enough.

You give up one type of freedom in the military, the corporeal
kind, but you gain another sort—the freedom to be almost
childlike again in the intensity of your emotions and relationships.
The Band of Brothers Syndrome doesn't start on the battlefield;
it begins the day you take that fatal step forward and they ship you
out with a bunch of other suckers.

The unspoken understanding that not all of us would
be coming back automatically jump-starts a series of coping
techniques, one of which is surrounding yourself with new
friends. It's those relationships, sort of an instant extended family,
that help keep you sane most of the time.

It was almost completely light, and the ghosts were coming
back to life, rising reluctantly from repose, each lost in his thoughts
as a new day dawned in Texas. Our moment of peace had passed,
one world had closed, another opened, and there wasn't a fucking
thing any of us could do about it.

"Let's go eat," said Curtis, sitting up and fumbling for the
pack of cigarettes in his shirt pocket.

"Where's Jay-D?" I muttered, watching the shadows turning
back into people.

"I dunno. Haven't seen him this morning. Guess we'll catch
up to him in the chow hall."

Curtis was right. Jay-D was already seated at a table, forking
a small mountain of scrambled eggs into his mouth when we got
there. He looked up, beckoned us with his free hand, and grinned
as Curtis flipped him the finger.

"Mornin', General," said Jay-D as I slid in next to him on the
bench. "Did you hear that everybody who passes the test today is
gonna get a weekend pass?"

"No shit?" said Curtis, his spoon poised midway between his
cereal bowl and his mouth.

To pass the test, you had to draw blood from the vein of another trainee into the barrel of a syringe. You had to show blood in the barrel. Just sticking the other guy and spilling some plasma wasn't good enough. There was no bullshitting. You either did it or you didn't.

Needles designed to extract blood have a beveled edge, without which, drawing blood, even from somebody with so-called "good veins," would be vastly more unpleasant than it already is, and much messier.

You don't just stab the needle into the vein. After the arm has been tied-off and the vein pumped up, you slide the needle under the skin at a low angle, and locate the vein the way you would the top of a beer can with an opener.

Then, in the all-essential second step, you pull up on the needle, and just like the pointed end of the beer can opener, the beveled edge of the needle punctures the vein with relative ease. Jabbing at a blood vessel is just like opening that beer can with a screwdriver. You can open it, but the beer does not necessarily go where you want it to go.

We'd been practicing on a rubber tube for a couple of weeks, but this was different. Way different. For me, doing the procedure correctly was the easy part. Having your partner get it right was the big worry, especially as mine was a nearsighted alligator poacher with a decidedly twisted view on life.

I succeeded in putting it out of my mind for most of the morning, but the moment we filed into the classroom where the test was to take place, I suddenly developed a severe case of the skeeves. By then, of course, it was too late, and five excruciating minutes later, I was just about ready to bolt for the door.

"Jesus fucking Christ! You're butchering me!"

Curtis looked up, a weak and worried grin on his lips. Sweat was pouring down his face, his glasses were sliding off his nose, and he held a blood-smeared needle in his left hand. He had just blown his third attempt to draw blood from my arm. I had three puncture wounds and assorted bruises blossoming beneath the flecks of blood, which mixed with sweat and ran down into the cradle of my elbow.

It was my own dumb-ass fault and I knew it. I was an idiot for agreeing to buddy up with Curtis in the first place. What was I thinking? Was I thinking? But it was too late for regrets and too soon for recriminations. I just wanted it over with before serious damage was done, so I gritted my teeth, closed my eyes, and awaited what I fervently hoped would be the final assault.

"Give me that fucking thing, Curtis!" barked the sergeant in charge of grading our section of the class.

The voice of an angel couldn't have sounded sweeter. The Sergeant took control of the needle, glanced at me, and then drilled me like the pro he was, drawing just enough blood into the barrel to pass muster. He did it quickly and effortlessly. My ordeal was over. I could have kissed him.

"Okay, Curtis," said the sergeant, holding up the hypo between the thumb and the forefinger of his right hand and shaking it just enough to make the blood jiggle in the barrel. "You pass."

The sergeant shook his head sadly, made a notation on his clipboard, and threw the dirty needle into the sanitary receptacle. Then he glanced quickly at both of us, as if to seal the conspiracy, and walked over to the next table without saying another word.

I'm still not sure to whom he was giving a break—Curtis, me, himself? All of us? Did this sort of thing go on all the time?

Actually, I didn't give a shit. It was over. The cosmic wheel had turned, lifted me out of the muck, and taken me high enough to taste the fruits of life. Curtis, Jay-D, and I were headed for the border, three soldiers on their way to Mexico with a weekend pass and gringo dollars in our pocket.

Does it get any better? Well, maybe if we could score a little weed.

WEEKEND PASS

We rented a new Mustang in San Antonio and headed south. I drove, Curtis rode shotgun, and Jay-D was sprawled across the back seat, his bare feet sticking partway out of the open window. Sonny and Cher were on the radio, and we all sang along.

"I Got You Babe" had never sounded better than on that bright Saturday morning in the Texas desert.

We didn't have to be back to Fort Sam until Sunday evening, and who knew what would happen in the time between? Life was about as sweet as it could get for three misfits in civilian clothes and army haircuts.

San Antonio is about 150 miles from Laredo, where we planned to cross the border into Nuevo Laredo—a town that had been servicing the military's recreational needs since General Pershing was chasing Pancho Villa during the so-called Punitive Expedition of 1916-'17. Pershing and his men never did catch up with Villa, but in hindsight, it wasn't a total waste of the taxpayers' money. Not only did the general allow a small group of vendors, launderers, bartenders, and prostitutes to set up businesses next to the Army camp at Ciudad Juarez, he established a flat rate for sexual intercourse.

Thank you, General Pershing. Generations of horny grunts owe you a debt of gratitude.

Within a few decades, the concept had spread along the U.S.-Mexican border to a number of cities, including Nuevo Laredo. Legal prostitution is controlled by the local governments and restricted to certain areas called *zonas de tolerancia*—or Boy's Towns.

One of the few good things about the Army is its sensible attitude toward sex, just so long as it was heterosexual sex, of course. They harped on us about wearing condoms, but hastened to add that if we messed up and caught a dose of the clap, they'd take care of us down at the infirmary. Just don't wait until you can't urinate and pus is running out of the end of your dick.

Whores and soldiers go together like nurses and cops. Everybody knows that. I think it's in the Bible somewhere. But it wasn't lust alone that drew us closer and closer to Mexico as the Mustang whizzed down the highway; it was a heady mix of adventure, hormones, and rediscovered freedom. The temporary nature of our situation gave it an edge somewhere between euphoria and desperation. And at some level, I think all of us harbored a secret wish that something miraculous would happen that would prevent us from ever going back. It almost felt like we'd broken out of jail.

A little past midday, somewhere in the desert along Interstate 35, we pulled off the road into a Mexican restaurant. There was a weather-beaten sign along the highway, but the restaurant was set back off the road about fifty yards and occupied the bottom floor of an old two-story wooden house.

It was dark and cool inside; a bar stretched away from the door, with tables and chairs set up in a large area to the left. The curtains looked homemade and the tablecloths were freshly laundered. Two old Mexican men were sitting at separate tables— one waiting for his grub, the other sipping coffee, an empty dessert plate and dirty fork pushed to the side.

The place looked like it hadn't changed since Harry S Truman was in the White House. But the smell wafting from the kitchen was yummy and the Mexican woman who greeted us was motherly and welcoming. She showed us to a table on a screened porch, where a slight breeze augmented a slowly revolving fan.

There was a strip of flypaper hanging from the ceiling in

the middle of the porch, which I tried to pretend wasn't there, especially after the food arrived. Good thing too, because it was the best Mexican food I've ever eaten. Nothing fancy, just tacos with beans and rice and a salad, prepared fresh for us by our hostess. Out of this world delicious.

We topped off the meal with apple pie and strong Chiapas coffee and sat there, savoring the moment and smoking cigarettes while our food settled.

"You know," said Curtis, looking round to make sure nobody could overhear him. "If we had some money, we could cross the border and just keeping going."

"Well, we don't. So forget it."

"Shit," said Jay-D. "We got enough money to have a weekend to remember. Let's pay the bill and split. There's a lot of Mexican pussy waiting on down the road."

Jay-D was right, of course, and finding pussy in Nuevo Laredo was even easier than finding hashish in Tangier, though there were some similarities in the procurement process. We crossed the Rio Grande into Mexico mid-afternoon, where the border guards glanced at our license plate and then waved us on. They knew a car full of randy GIs when they saw one.

Except for the short ride across the international bridge, there was no buffer zone. It was sensory overload time again, Mexican border-town style. One minute we were rolling down a major U.S. interstate, and the next we were in Nuevo Laredo, driving along a street lined with every manner of tourist trap imaginable. There was no way to slow down and absorb it gradually, this movie was already rolling and I was driving the stagecoach.

What a place: bars, nightclubs, strip joints, pool halls, pawnshops, liquor stores, pinball arcades, souvenir stands, eateries, street vendors of virtually every stripe. There were even a couple of those old-fashioned photo studios, where you could have your picture taken in front of a painted backdrop. One of them had an old burro tied to a hitching post out front so that tourists could sit on it to have their picture taken.

Every time we stopped for a red light, men ran up to the car, trying to sell us cheap watches and fake gold chains. They were more persistent than Manhattan squeegee guys, and the helter-skelter way they approached from so many different angles was disorienting, clearly the desired effect.

After the second light, it felt like an ambush you knew was coming but couldn't do anything to avoid. Well, I couldn't anyway. I was too consumed with trying to get away from these guys without running over any of them. Curtis, on the other hand, seemed to be thoroughly enjoying himself and knew exactly what to do. As we approached the fourth light, he leaned out the window and yelled: "Hey, which way to Boy's Town?"

"I will take you there, senor," said a wiry, middle-aged man who came sprinting up to the car a few steps ahead of the pack. "It's not far."

The man was wearing blue jeans and a western-style shirt and was about the same age as Blue Hat. He even looked a little like him, except for the eyes, which were softer than those of our stiletto-wielding friend in Tangier.

Curtis scooted over to make room, and the man climbed into the front seat. When the light changed and we pulled away, one of the remaining hustlers yelled something in Spanish and the others laughed.

"Don't worry about them," said our passenger. "They're just jealous. Turn left at the next light."

Following the man's direction, we were soon on the outskirts of town and just up ahead was a long adobe wall that was too high to see over. It looked like something out of a Zorro movie and there was an arched entrance about 100 feet ahead with a cop at the gate.

Terry had warned me that all Mexican lawmen were corrupt and utterly ruthless. Even so, their unkempt appearance, complete with mix-and-match uniforms and odd assortments of handguns, gave them a ragtag quality. It made them seem less threatening than the spit-and-polish breed north of the border. A naïve illusion no doubt, but probably the reason I obeyed when our guide shouted, "Don't stop! Keep going," as we approached the gateway.

I didn't ask questions, just zipped past the guard and into the dusty streets of Boy's Town. Father Flanagan wasn't there to welcome us, but there was no shortage of fallen angles ready to carry us to paradise or at least a commercial approximation.

Within the compound, there was a sizable collection of what looked like motels with bars attached, which was pretty much what they were, except that each had a string of girls working the premises. We cruised past several nightclubs featuring sex shows, including the infamous donkey act. Later, it occurred to me that the worn-out beast of burden outside the photo studio might have worked the Boy's Town circuit in his youth. If so, the photo-studio gig must have been quite a comedown.

Our guide directed us past these establishments, deeper into the compound, where he told me to park next to one of the motels. It was no fancier or grungier than the rest, just your generic Boy's Town fuck palace. It was, of course, also the establishment with which our particular man had an arrangement.

The tout whisked us past the pistol-packing guard perched on a bar stool near the entrance and into the interior, where a large, well-dressed man emerged from behind the bar, all teeth and gold jewelry. He smiled at us and engaged our guide in a brief conversation in Spanish, after which we were told that we could rent a girl each and a room for $20 per man.

That was a much better deal than what we would have gotten for the same amount of money back in San Antonio—we'd have the girls to ourselves all night and a place to sleep. I was just about to accept when something happened that didn't immediately compute.

"I have something special for you, amigo," our guide said to Jay-D, giving his shoulder a friendly squeeze. "Come with me. Just down the street."

Shit! I hadn't expected racial prejudice in a Mexican whorehouse. But what did I know? Apparently some establishments catered to blacks and others didn't. Now what?

"I don't know," I said, looking at Jay-D, who was still grinning. "Maybe we should stick together."

"It's cool," said Jay-D "Just let me have some money."

I glanced at Curtis, who shrugged and looked down at the floor. Although I've thought about this moment many times over the ensuing years with some misgivings, at the time it wasn't a crisis of conscience, just a testosterone-driven snap decision.

I handed Jay-D twenty dollars.

"Thanks, General. I'll meet you back here later."

Jay-D and the Mexican walked out the door and down the street, and as I dug in my pocket for another $20 to give the proprietor, I could hear them laughing in the distance. I never did figure out if Jay-D really didn't give a shit or was making it easier for us. Maybe he was just in a hurry to get laid. I know I was.

Just about the only choices for a lot of unmarried Mexican girls were the sweatshop, the convent, or the whorehouse. Because prostitution was legal and relatively profitable, among the poor there was no great stigma in selling your body, especially if you attended Mass on Sunday and put a little something in the collection basket. That was what Terry said, anyway.

All the girls had photo IDs with the date of their most recent medical checkup stamped on the back. But that was no guarantee your dick wouldn't fall off before you got back to base. What about all the tricks they turned between checkups? Such ruminations, however, instantly became irrelevant the moment two young women sauntered out of one of the bar's darker recesses and gently took us by the arm and steered us out the door and toward our room.

The whores apparently lived in the rooms where they conducted business, or at least did when they were on duty. Those who weren't busy with customers yelled at us good-naturedly from windows and doorways as we passed, inviting us to come see them next.

Their eagerness for our company was synthetic, but the weariness in their eyes was real, and so was the raw sexuality that infused everything inside the wall of Boy's Town. It felt more organic than evil, as if Dionysus had reappeared in the flesh, a cash register strapped to his back.

Our girls were dressed like a couple of poor teenagers, but some of the older women wore nylons and garter belts or some other sort of boner-inducing lingerie to compensate for the mileage. There was also a skinny French-speaking white woman with short red hair and an illegal sparkle in her eyes. Later, we learned she was the regular girl of an Air Force officer who drove down from Lackland AFB whenever he was off duty. He even kept some clothes and a stereo there, but that didn't stop her from trying to get some of our money on the side.

I got the prettier girl, but it wasn't because I was the moneyman. It was one of those rare instances when one's shortcomings prove an advantage. Mother Nature had compensated Curtis for his overall geeky appearance by blessing him with a cock worthy of a porn star, and as unlikely as it might seem under the circumstances, neither girl was eager to have it shoved up inside her. Of all things!

After a giggle-filled conference, the other girl reluctantly agreed to take Curtis, and the cute one told me that I smelled and should take a shower. By the time I came back, damp and with a raging hard-on, Curtis was already pumping away—his girl, apparently resigned to her fate, showed no sign of distress. Mine waited on the other bed, compliant but dry. I worked it in with spit and tried not to come too soon.

Communal fucking was new to me, and when another GI walked past the window, looked in, and said "hi," the absurdity of it all made me laugh. This elicited a tiny frown from the girl, and when I looked down at her and smiled, our eyes met for the first time. Two strokes later I came, but by then she'd looked away again.

As soon as I rolled off her, the girl got out of bed and went to the bathroom. Curtis was sitting on the edge of the other bed, smoking a cigarette; his girl sat on the other side, pulling on her clothes. He passed her his cigarette, she took a drag, handed it back and exhaled the smoke on her way to join her partner in the bathroom.

"Do you think we should ask them if they know where we can get some pot?" said Curtis.

"Maybe, but let's wait a while, see how things go."

The girls came out of the bathroom, fully dressed and wearing fresh makeup.

"We go get hair done. Come back soon."

Then they were gone, out the door in a cloud of cheap perfume before we could utter a word of protest. I sat there in my underwear, still struggling to get my bearings, listening to music from several sources competing outside the open windows.

PUSSY OR POT

We had to pass the red-haired woman's room to get to the bar, but by then the Air Force had landed and there was a party going on. The captain saw us looking through the open door and beckoned us inside. He was tall, skinny, in his late-twenties with the casual charisma of a high school quarterback.

There were about a dozen people in the room. Everybody was talking at once, trying to be heard over the sound of Rolling Stones pounding out of a set of expensive three-way speakers. Over in a corner, a guy was dry-humping a whore to "Time Is On My Side," while another played air guitar with his eyes closed, silently mouthing the words.

The captain passed a bottle of tequila. I took a swig and passed it to Curtis. The third time the bottle came around, I leaned in close when the captain handed it to me and whispered: "Do you know where we can get some pot?"

"Maybe later," he said, putting his mouth close to my ear. "If Red hasn't smoked it all while I was away."

The captain gave me a conspiratorial grin, turned away, and engaged another guest in conversation. Just the thought of getting high again after so many months was a high in itself, and I was buzzing with booze and anticipation when a voice, recognizable above the din snapped me out of my revelry.

"Hey, General. There you are. I've been looking all over for you."

A sweaty Jay-D maneuvered his way through the crowd and

gave me a hug. Curtis sidled over with three beers and we clinked bottles together, identical shit-eating grins slathered across our young faces. Then we chugged.

"I could use a few more dollars," said Jay-D, licking foam from his lips and batting his eyelashes.

"Sure, man. Here's twenty."

He gave me another sweaty hug and turned to leave.

"Where you going?"

"I've got somebody waiting. See you later."

As I watched Jay-D leave, I saw two familiar faces pass the room. Our whores were back from the hairdresser or wherever the hell they'd been. Curtis saw them too.

"Let's go back to the room," he said. "I'm ready for another round."

I hesitated, but only for a couple of heartbeats. The choice was guaranteed pussy versus the possibility of pot. Shit, the captain had said "maybe" later, so I wheeled and followed Curtis.

"We'll be back," I yelled over my shoulder, but nobody was listening.

The girls were not in a very friendly mood, and when we tried to initiate sex they shied away. The deal was that we got the girls and the room for the night. We knew it and they knew it. But they clearly had lost their appetite for the bargain. I was considering heading down to the bar to complain to their pimp, when the girl I'd been with said, "Fuckee and then let go?"

"What?"

"Fuckee and then let go. Okay?"

So that was it, they wanted to strike a deal. They'd be nice if we would let them out of the bargain after one more fuck. Curtis' lone contribution was one of his what-you-gonna-do shrugs, so I agreed for both of us. Fuckee and then let go.

And fuckee we did. It was no more passionate the second time than the first, but it lasted longer and toward the end I thought I felt her hump back a little. It was probably my imagination.

The fuckee part was over, and ten minutes after I ejaculated the let-go clause was consummated as the door closed behind them with a gentle click. Perhaps that was for the best. The tequila, the screwing, the beer, the drive from San Antonio had all slowed me down. And for the first time in months, I slept in a bed that didn't belong to Uncle Sam.

Some time in the early hours of the morning, I heard the girls return. To my bleary surprise, the one I'd fucked climbed in bed with me, snuggled close, spoon-style, and was soon snoring softly. I could feel her breath caressing the back of my neck as I drifted back to sleep, feeling happy and strangely wanted.

The girls had disappeared by the time Jay-D woke us up several hours after sunrise. Gone to Mass maybe. It was Sunday.

The three of us shared our last cigarette, climbed into the Mustang, and headed back over the Rio Grande. We had half a tank of gas and enough money for cigarettes and lunch. We couldn't have been happier.

At the border, they looked at our military IDs and asked if we were bringing back any switchblades or fireworks. Not guns and drugs, mind you, switchblades and fireworks! It was enough to give a recently retired-smuggler thoughts of making a comeback.

"Hey, Jay-D," I asked as soon as we were back on the road. "Did you ever run into any grass after we split up?"

"Yeah, at that Air Force guy's room. I went back looking for you late last night, but you were gone. I got a couple of hits off a joint that was going around."

"You fucker!" Curtis yelped. "Why didn't you tell us?"

"I tried to save the roach for you guys, but that red-headed whore stuffed it in the end of her cigarette and smoked it."

"How was it?"

"Tasted like dirt weed to me, barely got a buzz."

My first thought was to turn around and go right back, but there was nowhere to pull over, so I kept the Mustang headed north and stepped on the gas.

A WHITER SHADE OF PALE

Two goons from CID were waiting for me in a dimly lit office at company headquarters. They were wearing civilian clothes. One had on a cheap suit and the other, the younger, muscular one, wore a short-sleeved dress shirt, complete with clip-on tie—a couple of regular Joe Fridays.

The older one stubbed out a cigarette when I entered, and the other looked up from some papers he was stuffing into a briefcase.

"Have a seat, private," said the guy in the suit, pointing at the metal chair across the desk from him. He looked like a boozer and needed a shave.

"We want to ask you some questions."

"About what?"

"About your drug use."

A fly buzzed frantically, trapped somewhere between the olive drab curtain and the windowpane.

I knew these guys were trying to bust me, but I felt calm. This was the moment I'd been hoping for, the next move in the gambit instigated months ago at the induction center, operating on instinct, adrenalin and a lingering hashish high.

I'd given them just enough on those forms to raise a red flag but not enough for them to actually do something to me. I had to be careful though. My interrogators played this game for a living.

After confirming a lot of the things I'd claimed on my induction questionnaire, I was asked if I'd "used any controlled substances since being in the military." I told them no, which was pretty much the truth. I hadn't had a toke since the train-ride to Fort Bragg.

If they tested me, I'd be clean, thanks in part to the stiff dick that made me follow those whores back to the room in Boy's Town instead of waiting for the air force captain to break out the weed.

The goon with the five o'clock shadow asked a few more questions, but we were talking in circles, getting nowhere, so they played their final card.

"We want you to take a polygraph test."

"A lie detector test?"

"That's right."

"I'd like to get some legal advice about that."

They looked at each other. I thought I heard the older cop sigh, but I couldn't be sure over the whining of the air conditioning unit in the window.

"Okay, private, go see the officer of the day; he'll give you a pass to go to the JAG office."

■■■

"Those assholes must be kidding," said the JAG lieutenant after hearing my story. He was only about five years older than I, a fresh law-school graduate without a trace of gung-ho despite a well-tailored uniform. I could hear a radio playing faintly in another room. "A Whiter Shade Of Pale."

"Don't worry," said the lieutenant, picking up the phone. "I'm going to call right now and get those idiots off your back."

"Thank y ..."

He cut me off by raising the forefinger of his left hand to his lips and then began to bark into the mouthpiece. The way he yelled at whoever was on the other end of the phone took me by surprise. I wondered if it was at one of the cunt faces that had interviewed me. I'd never heard a commissioned officer chew out a noncom before, but my man immediately went on the offensive.

"You've got nothing on this soldier and you know it. Leave him the hell alone or you'll have me to deal with!"

Then he slammed down the phone, looked at me, and smiled. "They won't bother you again."

'Thank you, sir."

"My pleasure, private. Be careful."

He dismissed me with a parody of a salute and called out to the sergeant manning the reception desk.

"Please send in the next client, Sergeant Ackley."

As soon as I hit the sidewalk I was back on base, outside the JAG's friendly envelope of sanity and face-to-face again with the insanity of army life. Instant bummer. I felt a bit giddy. I don't know if it was the heat or hearing my persecutors being told to go fuck themselves. My mind raced, trying to sort through the implication of what had just taken place.

I sat on a bench, lit a cigarette, and waited for the bus to take me back to the part of the base where my company was housed. A lot had happened in a short period of time, and I didn't know exactly how to feel. It was cool that the CID was off my back, but if they couldn't bust me, what next? Would that be the end of it? Was this as far as my scheme would take me? Would I go back to being just another grunt riding Uncle Sam's lethal conveyor belt?

As the bus slowed to a stop and the door swung open, I wished for the millionth time since I finished my last hash ball that I could get high. Right about then, I would have given a month's pay for a single joint of the good stuff. I thought that maybe Sister Cannabis could shine a light on a path that no longer glowed with its original clarity. But I need not have worried; she had already worked her magic. All the pieces of my survival matrix would eventually mesh. I'd done a better job than I had thought. It just wasn't time yet. Things had to ripen a while longer.

When I stepped off the bus, I saw that every swinging dick from my barracks was swarming around the company bulletin board, jockeying for position like a bunch of college freshman trying to see their first-semester grades. But there was a lot more at stake in this crapshoot than a spot on the honor roll. The pieces of paper pinned to the corkboard told the fate of every man present, for next to each name was that soldier's next duty post. Life and death, literally, if not instantly, hung in the balance for some of us.

I lucked out big time, getting assigned to a stateside hospital. Jimmie and Curtis did okay too—they were going to Germany. But Jay-D was headed to Nam.

A KICK IN THE SHIN

My first permanent duty station also turned out to be my last, but for a few months it seemed I had found refuge rather than freedom.

Actually, I had a pretty cushy deal. I was assigned to a ward comprised mainly of guys back from Nam who were suffering from either hepatitis or malaria. There were also a couple of soldiers with jungle rot, which is some truly nasty shit. It looks like terminal acne, hideous ridges of scar tissue and fresh, puss-filled eruptions.

I was lucky in a lot of ways: Most of my regular patients were ambulatory and the only time I experienced the heavy stuff was when they were shorthanded in the ICU.

The guys in the ICU weren't patients; they were casualties, many of them shot in the back or ass, paralyzed from the neck down. The first thing the doctors would do when they visited the ward every day was to grab each patient's balls and squeeze as hard as they could, hoping for a reaction. They were virtually always disappointed.

Compensating for the occasional glimpses of horror were the black civilian nurses who worked on my ward. They shared cigarettes and flirted with the white soldier boys, who they seemed to find both humorous and endearing. I looked forward to seeing them, and not just because they were pretty. They brought a civilian vibe with them, the faint sound of freedom in the rustle of their rayon uniforms.

I had pretty much settled into a routine—show up for my shift on time, do my job, and try to remain as anonymous as possible. I was, therefore, surprised when I was told the commanding officer of the hospital wanted to see me in his office. I didn't know what to expect. I'd caused no problems since I reported for duty more than two months prior, so I was more curious than worried.

The major turned out to be an MD in his early 30s with a relaxed, informal manner that immediately put me at ease. He had one of those Peter Gunn hairdos that passed for hip in the early 1960's before longhair became a cultural war zone. He was wearing penny loafers and no socks.

"I want to show you something," he said, getting out of his chair and walking over to a small safe in the corner of the office. He dialed the combination, swung open the door, and lifted out a folder as fat as any big-city phonebook.

"This," said the major, dropping the bundle of papers on his desk so that it made a thud, "is your CID file."

"Jeez!"

"Yeah, that's what I thought too. Anybody would think you were related to Ho Chi Minh or something."

"What's in there?"

"Nothing, really, nothing they can hang you for, anyway."

He hesitated a second …

"Before we get into any of that, let me ask you something."

"Okay."

The CO leaned closer and lowered his voice slightly.

"How would you like to get out of the Army?"

It's rare, but I've had a couple of moments like this, times when you hear something you've been wanting hear for a long time. And then, when it finally happens, the joy is mixed with a vague feeling that this is the way it was supposed to be. Maybe the way you willed it to be.

"Yes, sir."

My heart began to beat very quickly as I began to comprehend what was happening.

"I'm going to level with you, but what I'm about to say is off the record. Okay?"

"Yes, sir."

"If you tell anybody about this conversation, I'll deny it ever took place. It will be your word against mine; I'm a major and you're a private. Who do you think they'll believe?"

He smiled and looked me in the eye.

"I understand, sir. This is just between you and me."

"Okay, here's the deal: The CID did a thorough investigation of you, interviewed everybody they knew that you know. But there was really nothing they could bust you for as long as you behaved yourself, and you have. But just the fact that you are under my command could prove an embarrassment to me."

"What do you mean?"

"Say, hypothetically, there are some drugs missing from one of the wards. My superiors would come down on me for having you around, even if you didn't have anything to do with it. Just the fact I didn't handle the situation before something happened could hurt my career. But I think there might be a way to help both of us."

I had been unconsciously holding my breath and found it difficult to get my words out when he paused to gauge my reaction.

"What's that?" I croaked, my mouth dry, my mind spinning.

"The military has a special classification for guys who somehow slip through the screening process. It's usually guys who can't tie their shoelaces; that sort of thing, but not always. Sometimes it can be used in situations like yours, but I'm going to need your cooperation."

"Okay."

"This kind of discharge, which will be an honorable discharge, requires the signature of three people: the base chaplain, the company shrink and myself. The only way this will work is if you go along with everything. You have the right to appeal, and if you do, you'll probably win the appeal and have to serve out the remainder of your two years."

"I'm more than willing to do whatever you say, sir."

"Good. It will take a month or so to get all the paperwork done, in the meantime I'll make appointments for you with the shrink and the chaplain. The shrink will do whatever I tell him to do, but the chaplain can be a pain in the butt, so be careful what you say to him."

"I will. Thank you."

"No problem, private, but do me a favor."

The CO picked up my file and stood in front of the safe looking back at me.

"Certainly. What is it?"

"After you're discharged, write a letter to your local senator and congressman. Tell them what a good guy I am. It just might help my career."

"Sure. I'll be happy to."

"Great. You're dismissed."

The CO was right about the chaplain, a squirrelly looking guy with a little beard. Our interview lasted for more than an hour, much of which involved him questioning me about my pacifist beliefs. I bullshitted right along with him, saying what I knew he wanted to hear.

We were seated opposite each other, with the chaplain on a couch and me in an armchair. The weird part came near the end of our talk, when he hauled off and kicked me in the shin. I was shocked but acted as if nothing had happened, and so did he, simply continuing to ask questions.

Originally, I thought it was an accident and that his leg had just shot out involuntarily in some sort of spasm. But the more I thought about it, the more I came to believe that it was a test to see how I would react to being physically violated.

Whatever the case, the chaplain signed off on my discharge, and about seven weeks later the paperwork was complete and I was honorably discharged. As I drove away from the hospital for the final time, I pumped my fist in the air and blew the horn. I'd served 10 months instead of 24 and never came close to a war zone. I'm still not sure whether I had outsmarted the system or had been extremely lucky, but I sure felt good as I headed toward Harvey's apartment.

I had been gone much longer than I expected the morning I left Harvey asleep and headed to the induction center, but I had made it back unscathed, toting a duffle bag full of memories and no regrets. Of all that happened during those months, the trip to Boy's Town remains the most vivid, a treasured rite of passage that grows in significance as the miles and years away from Nuevo Laredo grew longer.

I never saw Curtis or Jay-D after the morning in San Antonio when we headed out of town in different directions, but I did hear from Jay-D one final time. About two weeks after I was discharged, I got a letter from him. It was from Vietnam and stuffed with marijuana.

PART

Three

Amsterdam State Of Mind

ALL ALONG THE CLOCK TOWER

I looked over at JR and was surprised to see his eyes open. We had been in Amsterdam five hours and he had been asleep for three of them.

"It's getting late," I said. "Want to get something to eat?"

JR mumbled and lurched into the bathroom. Ten minutes later, we were outside on the sidewalk that ran between our hotel and the canal, headed back the way I'd traveled earlier in search of a coffee shop.

Actually, you don't really search for a coffee shop in Amsterdam, you just come across one the same way you come across a shoe store or fast food joint in other cities. Amsterdam has all the usual sorts of business establishments, of course; it just has coffee shops as well. In some neighborhoods, you can also find one by following your nose, literally, as the odor of smoldering cannabis filters out into the street.

Every guidebook mentions what a joy Amsterdam is to discover on foot and it's true. The Canal District, most of Amsterdam really, is compact and accessible. The city is an architectural marvel, a place where postcard perfect and coffee shop funk reside together in harmony. It makes for a cultured yet comfortable vibe, one that beckons you beyond the next corner with promises of new sensory delights.

Some cities are better for walking than others. New York is okay, London better, but Amsterdam is just about perfect. There's not even much dog shit anymore. But what the guidebooks fail to emphasize is how ridiculously easy it is to get lost.

We made the circuit of Rembrandtplein, checking out the more prominent eating establishments, most of them touristy looking and featuring large portions of what Beldar Conehead liked to call "charred mammal flesh." Finding little that satisfied our vegetarian sensibilities, we wandered along the side streets until we spotted an Indian restaurant. Thank Vishnu for the Hindus.

After stuffing ourselves with veggie curry, we stopped at a nondescript coffee shop and I bought a gram of weed. It wasn't quite a strong as the buds I'd bought earlier, but strong enough. It was easy to merge into the darkness of the room and become just another shadow, occasionally illuminated by the flick of a Bic.

About forty-five minutes and half a dozen pipes later, we were back on the street headed to the hotel. Or so we thought. Totally disoriented, we rambled around for another thirty minutes before admitting that we had absolutely no idea where we were or which way to try next.

"We can't just stand around here all night with our mouths open and our heads up our ass," I blurted in frustration.

JR's response was a cackling sound that seemed to both mock and celebrate our sorry situation.

When we left the coffee shop, we'd been about half a mile from the hotel at most, probably less. I wish I could tell you where we went wrong, but I can't. I certainly don't blame Amsterdam. The fault was all ours. I was starting to come down off the amphetamine (there's never a real crash from the pharmaceutical shit, just a gradual lessening of its affects) but still stoned on pot. What was JR's excuse?

Finally, with the help of one of those "You Are Here" street maps, we found our weary way back to our rented beds. It was, alas, not to be our last misadventure. An aging stoner and his eccentric friend traipsing through the streets of this magical city is perhaps my strongest memory of the trip.

I thought I had things figured out when we noticed an ornate,

17th-century clock tower within a few blocks of our hotel. There are few tall buildings in Amsterdam and practically none in the Canal District, so if we could spot the clock and head toward it, we should have always been able to find our way back to the hotel.

Smugness in my innate navigational skills soon soured and became the punch line of one of those jokes about not taking yourself too seriously. Much to our chagrin, we soon discovered that there are lots of clock towers in Amsterdam, and although they're similar in many respects, as is usually the case, the devil was indeed in the details. You can easily tell the differences once you get close, but by then you've already gone in the wrong direction.

The Clock Tower Theory was quickly abandoned and we began to study our maps with greater focus, a loathsome activity that always leaves me temporarily cross-eyed. In Amsterdam, you've got to be careful not to confuse Klovenierssteeg and Kloveniersburgwal, and Koekeokssstraat can morph into Koekoeksplein before you know it.

Whether written or spoken, Dutch doesn't come easily to English speakers, but in a happy twist of fate, the people of the Netherlands speak English better than the people of any other non-English speaking nation. And that, my fellow traveler, is far more valuable than a thousand trails of breadcrumbs and a stack of guidebooks as tall as any clock tower.

Jet lag finally caught up with me and I slept almost until noon the next day, which meant we were too late to participate in the free breakfast that came with the room. But that was a good thing. Hunger forced us into the street, and we were soon sitting on stools at the corner café, sipping coffee, wolfing down apple pie and sneaking peeks at the waitress' ass.

You're never served just coffee in Amsterdam; you always get a little something with it, usually a small biscuit or a piece of chocolate. After only a few days in town, it became my firm belief that you can judge the status of an establishment by the quality of the treat that accompanies the coffee.

While my "little something" always ended up in my gut along

with the coffee, JR got into the habit of saving his to feed a disreputable-looking duck that lived in the canal in front of our hotel. He would stand at the water's edge and let rip with a series of loud, semi-realistic duck noises, which would usually bring the freeloading waterfowl paddling in his direction.

JR's quacking attracted a few curious looks, but you learn to live with that sort of thing if you roll with him long enough. His milquetoast appearance and polite demeanor fool a lot of people at first, but beneath the reserved veneer lurks a world-class screwball.

The duck call was a mild example of one of JR's more endearing eccentricities—his mastery of the unexpected outburst. It can come at any time, the more inappropriate and startling the better. It's the lasting echo of a class clown who pretended to conform for pragmatic reasons but never really lost his love of the absurd.

Following our breakfast, we set off in search of a post office. Having no idea in which direction to go, we turned right as we exited the café and wandered down a picturesque side street lined with small shops. We passed a shop with a big mushroom painted on its sign; it was what the Dutch call a "smart shop," a store where you can legally buy psilocybin, peyote and other natural psychedelics.

How cool is that?

Your friendly, neighborhood purveyor of Mother Nature's mind expanders sitting there quietly among bakeries, cafes and antique shops. No big deal, just another business among the many, part of daily commerce, part of a culture of tolerance.

Things came together in an opportune way when the post office turned out to be in the Stopera, an architectural oddity built in 1986 as an oversized city hall and a music theater. It's also the home of the Netherlands Opera, and JR just happens to be an opera freak.

The next night was the final performance of Wagner's "Das Rheingold," an over-the-top melodrama based on a lot of the same Nordic myths that inspired Tolkien's *Lord of the Rings.* Considering that Amsterdam paid a bitter price at the hands of the Nazis during World War II and the Anne Frank House is still a major attraction, it seemed a strange fit for Amsterdam.

Wagner was supposed to be Hitler's favorite composer and an anti-Semite. The only other thing I remembered about Wagner was that it was his music Robert Duvall blasted over sound systems when his helicopters swooped to the slaughter in *Apocalypse Now.*

Tolerance stretches in a lot of different directions, and it would be nice if I could claim such noble purpose, but it was nothing more than morbid fascination that lured me on, that, and the wish to please my friend. Besides, where better to be culturally experimental than Amsterdam? Some smoke pot or eat mushrooms for the first time there. I was about to lose my opera cherry.

But man cannot live on highbrow culture alone, and, besides, our date with Wotan and his merry band of gods, monsters, and maidens (there's also a dwarf and a sorcerer in the mix) wasn't until the following evening. The rumbling in our tummies was a more urgent call.

After a quick trip back to the hotel to top off my cannabis level, we sallied forth again in hunt of the illusive veggie and ended up at a restaurant called Flying Saucer, which served the best potatoes au gratin I've ever eaten. And if there's a food of which I consider myself a connoisseur, it's the humble spud. Trust me, spaced out or straight the Flying Saucer's potatoes au gratin are out of this world.

As was our pathetic wont, we got lost on our way back to the hotel. The sun faded, the famous Amsterdam drizzle came on and we were soon reduced to anxiously scanning our surroundings for a familiar landmark. Then, as we approached the warm glow of a coffee shop, I suddenly realized that it was the Bluebird. *The Bluebird.* I'd never been here before but I knew all about it from Jimmie, who had raved about the place. I knew we'd found safe harbor.

"Hey, that's the Bluebird. Let's go inside."

JR, who had not yet taken a single puff of pot since we arrived, offered no resistance. As far as I know, the only time he partakes of cannabis these days is when he's with me. If I'm smoking and he's got time to kill, he'll take a couple of tokes. They're usually small ones and it kind of looks like he's just holding it in his mouth, rather than inhaling. I don't know. Maybe he's just being sociable, and if that's what's happening, that's okay too.

I'll never forget the time he came over to my apartment back in the 1970s and handed me a grocery bag filled with various odds and ends of grass. "Here, you can have all of this stuff," he announced. "I can't smoke any more; it's making me go nuts."

The funny thing is that the weed in his collection of partially used nickel and dime bags didn't even give me a buzz. If that low-grade shit was driving him crazy, he'd made the sensible decision. Still, there have been a number of recent occasions when I know he was stoned, so I'm not really sure what's going on with JR and the noble weed.

He used to remind me of Jack Nicholson in that campfire scene in *Easy Rider*, when Jack smokes his first joint with Peter Fonda and Dennis Hopper—high as hell but refusing to acknowledge it.

JR's relationship with cannabis seems to have warmed over the years and he willingly followed me through the door and into the dim light of the interior of the Bluebird, where we were greeted by a familiar sweet smell and the rhythmic sounds of Bob Marley pulsing softly in the background.

The Bluebird was fancier than most of the other coffee shops I'd visited, though no longer the state-of-the-art smoking emporium it was when it opened. Still, you could tell that considerable thought had been given to creating a stoner-friendly atmosphere. The whole front is a large two-story window that looked out onto the street, where the store lights shimmer in thousands of rainy reflections, creating an accidental light show with which homeboy Van Gogh could have done wonders.

Most of the seating was on the second floor, where one room had a hookah on a coffee table, surrounded by a large sofa and a couple of comfy armchairs. Many of the walls were covered in intricate murals of a vaguely psychedelic theme, most likely painted by a second-year art student intoxicated with equal doses of Dali, Bosch (another Dutchman), and psilocybin.

The Bluebird sold hashish as well as weed. There was a time when hash ruled in Europe, but that changed with the advent of the high-voltage, professionally cultivated cannabis that most everybody smokes today. Hash is out of style, and for good reason: The vast majority of it is nowhere near as potent as most of today's marijuana.

But the memory of the old days when hash was king is still strong in the minds of boomers who started smoking in the 1960s, and it's not just the high that's hard to forget. The unmistakable smell of smoldering hash and the distinct, spicy taste are also something that never completely leaves you. So I purchased two grams of zero-zero just for old time's sake.

Genuine zero-zero is the top grade of Moroccan hash and very difficult to obtain, even in Morocco. Most of the hash they sell is of varying commercial grades, while the dealers keep the zero-zero for their personal stash. The name derives from the size of screen used to sift the finest pollen and dust, while courser screens are used for the commercial-grade hash.

As the Bluebird's hookah was being used by a zonked-out group of locals who looked settled in for the duration, JR and I took a small table overlooking the balcony with a good view of the street. The Bluebird is a place where people hang out and get high, rather than a place where you pop in, buy a few grams and split.

I don't know if the zero-zero I bought was the genuine article or not. It smelled and tasted the way I remembered and the buzz was decent but still half a notch below even the weakest of the weeds I smoked in Amsterdam. That doesn't necessarily mean it wasn't zero-zero. The THC count in today's cannabis is so high, it might even make real zero-zero seem ordinary.

Be that as it may, I like to think that what I smoked at the Blue Bird was a pale imitation, something sold to tourists, and that the authentic item is still out there, the Holy Grail of old Morocco hands, just waiting to fill our lungs and brains with the ultimate blast from the past.

JR didn't want to try the hash, but shared a bowl of pot, which probably got him higher than he would have been if he'd smoked the hash. I mixed the two together for my third bowl and felt a cozy blanket of introspection wrap itself around me as I sank deeper into my thoughts. I'm not quite sure how long we stayed at the Bluebird—cannabis-induced time distortion is a very real phenomenon. But I do know that by the time we wandered back out into the street, I'd forgotten we were lost.

ZERO-ZERO FOR BREAKFAST

The breakfast buffet at the Nes didn't look much like the cholesterol bomb you find in your typical American establishment—no piles of bacon, ham, and sausage soaking in their own melted fat, no steaming pancakes, laced with butter and syrup, no avalanche of eggs, no cream cheese-covered bagels, no French toast sprinkled with confectioner's sugar. No home fries, hash browns, or grits, nary a donut to be found.

Instead, was a utilitarian spread of plain but wholesome food, all of it familiar, though in certain cases a bit incongruous to the Western stomach. Cold cuts, sliced cheese, and something I fear might have been pickled herring were standard fare, as were hard-boiled eggs, the only form of chicken embryos available. There was no warm food except beverages and toast. Bob Evans would have been horrified.

The hotel served exactly the same thing every day, which seemed weird at first, but when you think about it, most hotel and restaurants serve the same thing ever day. It was the austerity of the food and the way it was laid out with such precision that emphasized the almost military sameness.

I soon fell into the habit of eating the same thing every morning, pound cake and fruit cocktail (the kind that comes in a can), washed down with multiple cups of coffee. But on that particular morning I added the rest of the zero-zero, almost a gram and a half, to my meal. A couple of hours later, I was glad I did.

Undaunted by our previous navigational disasters and emboldened by the desk clerk's directions, we struck out early for the Museum Quarter, which, much to my relief, turned out to be a pleasant 15-minute tram ride away. Holland's public transportation system is efficient, clean, relatively inexpensive, and easy to use. Like most everything in this country, it is thoughtfully delineated, with different modes of transportation designated for specific tasks.

It starts with the canals, of course, but the locals seldom use them anymore to travel from one place to another. Today, most of the canal traffic is comprised of tourist and weekend merrymakers.

The sidewalks of Amsterdam can be tricky, and I'm not talking about their mesmerizing ability to lead the directionally challenged astray. Running parallel to many sidewalks is an outer lane for bicycles, where countless tourists have discovered how it feels to have a bike run over their heels or up their butt crack.

I had a few close shaves the first couple of days, as cyclists whizzed past me, yelling angrily at my stupidity. The bike paths are clearly marked, but unless you're paying attention, it's easy for a newcomer to assume the bike lane is just an extension of the pedestrian thoroughfare, especially if you're stoned and gawking at the scenery. I felt like such a jackass after the first few times, and it wasn't long before I was warning JR to watch his step.

The ubiquitous bicycles of Amsterdam are as much a symbol of the city as the canals. There's something like 500,000 of them, and you see them everywhere, not just being ridden but parked and padlocked to any bit of available railing. There are bike racks, of course, but nowhere near enough. At busy intersections, you see layers of bicycles, sometimes two or three deep, all leaning against the same stretch of railing or fence.

A favorite tethering spot are the railings across canal bridges, and if you look closely, you can see that some of the bikes have been abandoned, tires flat, spokes rusted. But most of them are in good working order, awaiting their riders and another pedal-powered zip through the streets of this bicycle-friendly city.

There's supposed to a problem with junkies stealing bikes and selling them cheap to tourists, and it's probably true, but the upside to the bicycles of Amsterdam is monumental, especially when it comes to pollution control (I didn't take a single sinus pill during my entire stay), traffic congestion and the health of the riders.

But for me, the happiest consequence of all this pedaling to and fro is the slender legs and firm bottoms of the female riders.

While Amsterdam is a truly multicultural city, the indigenous Dutch, mostly tall, fair, and thin, are easy to spot. I still have visions of row upon row of slender Dutch girls riding past me, sitting up straight on their old-fashioned bicycles, breasts thrust forward into the future, their lithe legs and shapely buttock propelling them by me with a gentle whoosh.

If you don't want to walk or ride a bike, the electrical trams are the easiest way to get around the city. JR and I had no trouble finding the tram stop the desk clerk told us about; it was exactly where he said it would be, at the top of the road, about 100 yards away from the hotel.

I'm always surprised when directions of any kind work. Maybe it's because I'm just as terrible at giving directions as I am at following them. I've learned to compensate by trusting my internal map, but with no previous data to process, the intuition that has instinctively guided me on more familiar turf was of little use the first few days in Amsterdam. At such times, even the smallest victory is heartening.

We found seats and the tram lurched forward, gaining speed, its wheels squealing faintly on the tracks whenever it rounded a curve. As we made our stop-and-go way toward the Museum Quarter, the sun broke through the gray and I had one of those "pinch me" moments. It's not quite the same as being "in the moment," because if it were, I wouldn't be thinking about anything but the moment.

The "pinch me" moment is a close cousin, a pleasant reminder of how wonderful life can be. I think the hashish in my digestive track was already starting to stir the cerebral stew.

VAN GOGH vs. WAGNER
(NO HOLDS BARRED)

I may as well come clean right here and now and admit that I've had a crush on Van Gogh (pronounced "Khokh") for years. The first art book I ever purchased had a Van Gogh reproduction on the cover. I saw *Lust for Life* at the movie house when it first came out in 1956 and loved it—Kirk Douglas' face still sometimes flashes in my mind's eye when I think of the painter.

It was Van Gogh who first seduced my aesthetic sensibilities and if I ever had reason to doubt my taste, it vanished a few years ago when a Van Gogh exhibit came to my hometown's art museum. The whole show was magnificent, but it was the final picture, the last one you saw before exiting the gallery that really flipped me out. It was a self-portrait, one with the artist wearing a felt hat. I'd seen reproductions of varying quality many times, but not even the finest print could come remotely close to capturing the painting's magic quality.

The canvas seemed alive, and not just in the sense that the person it portrayed appeared bursting with life or that it seemed that the subject would come to life and walk out of the frame. No, it was the painting itself that was alive, the paint a moving, squirming, shimmering organism held together by the sheer willpower of the painter's genius.

I had to back away and approach the painting several times before I could come to grips with the miracle before my eyes. It is one thing for an artist to live on through his art, but an entirely different proposition when a painting has a life of its own more than a century after the artist's death. It was as if Van Gogh had infused the paint with his emotions and that they live on, poltergeists sealed in pigment, still pulsating with the same passion that created them.

I didn't have a similar epiphany at the Van Gogh Museum or at the Rijksmuseum, which was the second stop on our first Amsterdam arts ramble. A major part of the problem was overkill. There was simply too much to see at one time, and the temptation is to rush from one gallery to the next, afraid you might miss something, and you end up missing everything.

When the breakfast hash kicked in full force, so did my playful side. It wasn't long before I was teaching JR how to play Spot the Dog, a game I invented on one of my countless trips to various art museums and very easy to play.

All you do is count the number of canines you find in the various works on display and to try to discover as many dogs as possible. The medium doesn't matter, painting, drawing, prints, sculpture, and photographs are all fair game. But there is one rule: Works of art where a dog or dogs are the main subjects don't count. The dog has to be tangential, part of the scene but not the focal point. I don't remember when I first noticed how many dogs make their way into artwork, but you'd be surprised how frequently it happens.

I'm not sure why Spot the Dog is so irresistible, but once it gets into your mind, it takes over and supersedes a wider appreciation of the works. Something about the irreverence of the game appeals to me, like poking fun at the saints in church. There's also a faint resonance of that warm feeling dogs have long provided mankind, which, somewhat ironically, never fails to help humanize the work of art in question.

But if truth were known, dogs would probably prefer leaving the scent of their pee on the gallery walls to being immortalized in oil or bronze.

There is a large, grassy park between the Van Gogh and the

Rijksmuseum called the Museumplein, which was the site of the 1883 World Exhibition, and about halfway across we stopped at a coffee stand. The hash was starting to take my legs, but the caffeine and few milligrams of amphetamine sent me on my merry way again, and when we reached the home of Holland's premiere art collection, Spot the Dog continued unabated.

With some 5,000 paintings on display in 200 rooms, the Rijksmuseum is another visual overload. What percentage of it we actually laid eyes upon is hard to say, but I came away feeling like one of those tourists on a whirlwind package tour that visits 10 European countries in five days. If there weren't so many other things to do, we could have spent most of the week there, soaking in more than must-see masterpieces such as Rembrandt's "Night Watch" and Vermeer's "Milkmaid." But our next scheduled brush with culture was not at a museum. We had an appointment with Wotan and the rest of the "Das Rheingold" gang.

Due no doubt to my severe limitations, opera is one of the few musical categories that I've never enjoyed. And, alas, this imaginative production of "Das Rheingold" did not change things.

I've always felt much the same way about opera as I felt the first time I heard Bob Dylan sing: Jeez, that sounds like shit! But my feeling about Dylan quickly changed. As soon as I began to listen to his lyrics, I instinctively sensed the poetry and knew it was worthy of respect, even if the way it sounded was grating to my ear. Once I began consorting with a certain Miss Cannabis, however, Dylan's music also came alive for me. I was still romancing the same mistress when JR and I took our seats at the opera house.

I was half-hoping for a similarly transforming experience at "Das Rheingold," but even though that didn't happen, there was a moment that met my highest standard for any musical event—that moment when you leave your body and become one with the music. Or maybe the music becomes one with you; it amounts to the same thing, a joyous connection that lifts you out of your day-to-day existence by means beyond your control.

My "Das Rheingold" moment came before the first note was sung, when the orchestra began to play. The music soared majestically out of the dimly lit pit and filled the theater with warmth you could feel as much as hear. It swirled around the hall and seemed to enter through my pores, and for a handful of seconds, I was no longer a guy listening to music but part of something larger. What a rush.

Musically, for me, it was mostly downhill after such a satisfying start. It didn't sound "like shit," but I didn't enjoy it either. Maybe I lack the opera gene or some element of my hardwiring is faulty. But ultimately, it didn't really matter whether or not I enjoyed the singing; just being there was a hell of a kick.

The staging was wildly unorthodox and much of the action took place on a series of inclined planes as opposed to a flat stage, which gave everything a disconcerting feeling and added an unavoidable tension to the proceedings. Much of the time the performers appeared to be teetering on the brink of falling into the orchestra pit.

More than anything else, I had trouble ripping my eyes away from the plastic wigs many of the characters wore. They were not plastic in a cheesy way, as in "bad rug." I presume they were designed to look the way they did, which was like Jimmy Neutron's hair, a cartoon hairdo styled in colorful plastic. As befits the top god (dog), Wotan's wig was the snazziest, a bright orange with black highlights to match his black eye patch, the perfect accessory for his deep red robe.

It would be an insult to even the most casual opera buff for me to attempt to explain "Das Rheingold." But even an opera oaf could sense that all was not well on the Road to Valhalla, and in the vocal bickering that went on and on and on, none of the characters seemed particularly laudatory. Even the Rhinemaidens were cruel to the dwarf. Still, I wouldn't mind scoring a few of Freia's golden apples, the ones that keep you young forever.

I'm sure I missed a lot. I know I nodded off a few times, but

I'm pretty sure I didn't snore. And when the curtain came down to great applause, including mine, I hoped like hell it wasn't just intermission.

It wasn't, thank Wotan, and when we strolled out into the Amsterdam evening, I felt strangely elated. It reminded me of the time I went to see Buddhist monks from Tibet perform sacred music at a university.

They blew these impossibly long horns, rang bells, and chanted in a guttural way that sounded like it was dredged up from the Himalayan taproot. Like "Das Rheingold," the monks were not particularly pleasing to my auditory system. Nonetheless, both experiences are treasured for the tiny spurt of growth they afforded, even though the groove felt alien.

There are certain things that fall into this category, things you're very glad you did, but having done them is better than the actual experience itself. Of course, there are plenty of other things that are never better than at the very moment they're happening. The trick is to realize it at the time.

BLUES FOR MISS KEEVER

Thanks to five mgs of amphetamine on my part and grim determination on JR's, we were up and about reasonably early the morning after our night at the opera and off on our first road trip. Our destination was Edam, an old fishing and shipbuilding village better known today for its cheese, the kind that comes coated in red or yellow paraffin. In its heyday some of the finest sailing vessels in the world were built in Edam, including the "Half Moon," the ship in which Englishman Henry Hudson set out in search of a northern route to the East Indies in 1609. He ended up in Manhattan, of course, but we can't blame the good citizens of Edam for that.

Where we were going was secondary; mainly we wanted to explore beyond the city limits, and this was our first tentative probe. We wasted half an hour figuring out that we needed to take a bus to Edam, not a train. In Holland's eminently sensible and efficient public transportation system, trains are reserved for longer journeys.

Edam is less than 20 miles outside of Amsterdam, but before we were halfway there we were passing rich green fields complete with cows, sheep, and the sickly sweet bouquet of manure. You don't have to go very far outside of Amsterdam to find a different side of Holland.

Upon our arrival in Edam, we strolled along the picturesque streets and canals, which were almost deserted. Besides manufacturing cheese and being a minor tourist destination,

Edam has become something of a bedroom community for the affluent who work in Amsterdam but prefer a more idyllic place to lay their heads.

We had a leisurely lunch in a pleasant pub, and I'm proud to say I had an Edam cheese salad with my beer. The food was okay, but I couldn't see a coffee shop anywhere. So we got on the bus and headed back to where the Amstel River empties into the Zuiderzee. Had we known about Trijntje Keever, however, we would have undoubtedly lingered in Edam a while longer.

I subsequently learned that there is a life-size portrait of Keever hanging in the Edam Museum. She was reputed to stand more than 8'4", a mind-boggling height, which, if accurate, would quite possibly make her the tallest woman, ever. Trijntje was a minor celebrity who had visited royalty at The Hague, where she reportedly went every year to be measured. She also toured with a circus—or, as an email from Edam's info Web site so quaintly put it, "exposed herself on markets."

The "Big Maid," died of cancer in 1633 at the age of 17. What a heavy price to pay for such a small and morbid slice of immortality. But then again, it could very well have been worse for her in the first decade of the 21st century. Today, the unfortunate Miss Keever, once her 15 minutes of fame had elapsed, might have found herself sitting in a custom-made window in Amsterdam's Red Light District, peddling her gargantuan ass at 100 euros a pop.

I suppose such a base thought doesn't speak too highly of your humble correspondent, but there's no denying that as a boy I was as eager as the next lad to pay my shilling to see the carnival freak show. And I'm still kicking myself for not paying my gawking respects when we were in Trijntje's old neighborhood.

It was getting dark by the time we got back to Amsterdam, and after a cheese fondue at a sidewalk café and a few pipes back at the hotel, we set out in search of Maloe Melo, the city's only blues club. The venue was a family affair, owned by music-loving patriarch Jur Scherpenzeel, who is assisted by sons Patrick, bartender and a rabid music collector, and Marcel, billed as "Holland's best blues guitar player."

A light but persistent rain fell as we scurried along unknown and deserted streets, two damp but determined blues lovers following a course we'd charted with the aid of a guidebook map. On and on we trudged until we finally found it, a small, dark, and atmospheric joint covered in old posters and a heavy layer of grime.

At the end of the bar was a door that led to another narrow room with a tiny stage at the far end. The only music was coming out of the jukebox, but the bartender told us it was "jam night" and that the live music would be starting in about half an hour.

The long, wet march had killed much of my buzz, so while JR nursed a bottle of beer, I sucked down several rum and cokes in an attempt to dry myself from the inside out. Although the posters and photographs that decorated the walls bespoke of past glories featuring such stalwart blues performers as Gatemouth Brown, Sun Seals and Eddy Clearwater, we had to settle for a collection of game but mediocre wannbes.

Jam night was built around three members of the house band—guitar (the only black guy in the club), bass, and drums—that accompanied any musician who wanted to play. Those who did on that particular night were all markedly inferior to the members of the house band, who did their best to accommodate and cover up for the amateurs.

The jammer who stood out for me was a guy around 30 who played a soaring, feedback-loaded guitar solo with a certain amount of panache and skills. The problem was that he had absolutely no idea how to get in or out of the solo, which finally came to a disjointed, car wreck of a conclusion, much to the chagrin of the house band that was struggling mightily to compensate.

The rain had stopped by the time we left and the journey back to the hotel didn't seem nearly as long as the outward voyage. JR and I grabbed a quick meal at a falafel franchise, a brightly lit wedge of white tiles and stainless steel incongruously located half a block away from our friendly neighborhood 17th-century clock tower. After gulping down our food, we stopped at a Rasta coffee shop just off Rembrandtplein for a few bedtime tokes before finally wending our way back to the hotel.

Earlier in the day, on our way from the bus stop back to our hotel, I purchased some "philosopher's stones," a truffle-like form of psilocybin. I intended to eat them the next morning, so some shut-eye was mandatory.

AN OBVIOUS SOLUTION

One thing experienced stoners should keep in mind on their first visit to Amsterdam is that the recommended doses on the various natural psychedelics are strictly for the novices. The Dutch government doesn't want a bunch of tripped-out tourists cluttering up emergency wards or wandering the streets in a daze, easy prey for pickpockets and petty thieves.

The sales person in the smart shop where I'd bought the philosopher's stones suggested JR and I split a package. JR said he wanted to see how they affected me before sampling them, so the morning after the sodden trip to Maloe Melo I sat on my hotel bed and ate half the stones. They tasted a bit like walnuts and went down easier than mushrooms.

It took about 45 minutes for the effect to take hold—a modest buzz and a vague feeling of uneasiness, as if the dose had taken me to the edge of something but wouldn't allowed me to cross. Maybe for a psychedelic virgin or very occasional tripper, it would have been a transformational experience, but I was mildly disappointed. I should have eaten the whole package and I knew it.

So why didn't I eat the rest?

I'm not quite sure myself, but it had a lot to do with the taste and the queasy feeling they gave me in my gut. But at the same time, the buzz did provide a slightly amended worldview for the next few hours, a kind of weary acceptance of fate that seemed philosophical, in the darkest of ways of course, but philosophical nonetheless.

We decided to take a canal tour. A small fleet of tour boats docked close to our hotel, which suited me just fine. I was suffering from an acute combination of sleep deprivation and toxic shock, which resulted in a low energy level with spacey undertones, perfect for a laid-back cruise through time.

For the next hour, we glided along canals, under low, picturesque bridges, and past hundreds of genteel canal houses, sentinels from the past that derive a distinctive look from their gabled roofs. The style of gable, or even the lack thereof, indicates the era in which the house was built, starting with the "spout" gable in the 1580s, progressing through the years with the "step," "neck," and "bell" gables, until the 18th century, when they switched to straight, horizontal tops, frequently with richly decorated cornices.

What would the original owners think about the refrigerator magnets resembling the houses, along with all the knickknacks bearing similar images that are available to the tourists? You can't know for sure, but considering that a lot of these houses were built by merchants, they probably wouldn't mind too much as long as they got their cut.

Today, the government subsidizes some of the residents to help them maintain these living museum pieces. It's all part of the magic of Amsterdam and helps create the feeling that you have one foot in the past, one foot in the present—and they're keeping perfect time.

We were both pretty burnt out by the time we got back to the hotel, so we spent a lazy afternoon laying on our beds, smoking pot, and shooting the shit. Somehow the conversation turned to writing, or more specifically my inability to get involved in any sort of writing project that wasn't directly connected to my day job as a journalist.

It was something that had been nagging at me for a long time. I knew that I should be writing outside my employment context but had never done very much about it other than talk. There were a few halfhearted attempts, but nothing clicked.

It would be easy to say that I was simply too tired to get motivated to write in my free time after writing and editing all day at the office. But it wasn't that, and I knew it wasn't. I felt a persistent need, which I knew could only be satisfied by writing. The hack work that paid my bills had long ago ceased to gratify this nebulous urging, but the discomfort this realization caused was more irksome than painful. It just percolated somewhere in the part of my brain where the muse tossed and turned in fitful slumber.

The more I thought about it, however, the more I realized that the major problem was that I didn't know what I wanted to write about, and after a while I began to seriously consider the possibility that I had nothing to say, which was even more disheartening.

My relationship to writing has always been a bit unconventional. I wasn't the kind of kid who grew up dreaming of being a writer, but it was always something with which I had a certain facility. When I first went to school, around the age of five, I wrote a story about a cowboy who lived in a cave. I hadn't learned to read or write yet, but I dictated the story to my father, who faithfully wrote it down in longhand in my notebook. I also provided a series of illustrations, which was the part of the project that seemed to interest adults the most.

Over the next few years, my ability to draw recognizable objects with a fair amount of proficiency (and, of course, the attention and praise I received for my scribbling) distorted everybody's perception of where my talent, such as it was, resided. It was assumed by my elders that I would eventually do something with what they called my "artistic ability," and I gladly went along with the notion because of all the positive reinforcement.

After a while, I started to believe it myself, but it was never something I felt compelled to do in order to satisfy an inner desire. Drawing and painting started as a pleasing childhood activity, a pleasant way to fill an only child's lonely hours, and they undoubtedly should have stayed that way.

As my experience with the world outside the protection of my family grew and I saw what marvels other people could accomplish with a pencil or paintbrush, I began to understand that my talent was decidedly modest. Still, it was convenient to pretend it was more than it was, especially as my academic career was hopelessly mired in mediocrity.

I recall a high school guidance counselor, who probably should have been drawn and quartered for gross incompetence, telling me I should either get a job in a factory or join the Army—just the tonic for the artistic soul allegedly dwelling somewhere beneath my teenage angst.

As much as others overestimated my ability to draw and paint, I undervalued my ability to write. I breezed through book reports and term papers with relative ease throughout school but took it for granted, something I could do without working too hard. Instead of thinking of it as a gift, it became a way to earn gas money for my 1956 Nash Rambler. There were plenty of guys my age that figured they had better things to do than homework, so I started writing their book reports, essays, and term papers for a modest fee.

My biggest success as a high-school ghostwriter involved my buddy, Motts, who was not going to graduate with the rest of the class if he flunked biology. He did poorly the final semester, but our teacher, Miss Berger, said she would give him a passing grade if he would write an extra-credit term paper. I offered my services, but Motts balked at the five-dollar price tag and said he was going to have his private-school-attending girlfriend write it for him.

She did a good job, better than I could have done, but there was a problem: No way Miss Berger would believe that Motts wrote the fucking thing. It was profusely peppered with words that neither of us understood—in a panic, he paid me the five dollars to dumb it down to an acceptable level. I did, and he graduated.

After that glorious triumph of mediocrity over excellence, I didn't write another thing for money until I finally backed into a journalism career almost two decades later. Don't ask me why I was so blind because it sure seems like nothing short of sheer stupidity.

If there is an explanation to my finally seeing the light, maybe it has something to do with that blind pig that every now and then finds a truffle. Only in this swine's case, however, a philosopher's stone might be a more appropriate symbol.

About 25 years ago, following a five-year run as full-time, reasonably well-paid journalist, I suddenly found myself unemployed and broke, so I wrote a nonfiction book, which was published and even made a few dollars for all concerned, including me. JR was my poorly paid proofreader and also supplied considerable encouragement throughout the ordeal, so it was only natural that I used him as a sounding board that smoke-filled afternoon.

JR has always been a most amiable conversationalist, the sort who listens carefully and asks probing questions. He has a sharp, inquisitive mind and seems interested in what you have to say, but if your thought process is faulty, he'll call your bluff and challenge your point of view, which makes for stimulating and often demanding banter.

Shortly after my book was published and (perhaps more significantly) the advance spent, I came up with an idea for a private detective novel featuring a protagonist I hoped would be likable enough to spawn a series of sequels. It fed well into my hazy dream of quitting the rat race, retreating to an exotic and cheap locale, where I would support myself by churning out a couple of semi-popular novels a year. Not the most original fantasy to be sure, but a pleasant one nonetheless.

So I banged out a couple of chapters and showed them to JR. He quickly provided some constructive criticism and a list of suggestions concerning the direction the story should take. It looked briefly like we would collaborate on the book, but I took another full-time editorial position soon afterward, and the project was shelved indefinitely.

As JR and I talked and smoked our way through the afternoon, we came around to the obvious conclusion that what I needed was a jump-start to get me going, a warm-up exercise I could get into or maybe something that would lead to something else, anything to get me writing. This was hardly revolutionary thinking, but a sensible enough solution that just might have a chance of working. But the old bugaboo was still there: What should I write about?

"You like travel narratives," said JR. "Why not write something about this trip?"

SHITTY PIZZA AND BAD DRUGS

As the light through the hotel window began to fade and the afternoon rain blew away, JR and I roused ourselves from the lengthy pot and bullshit session. I didn't realize it at the time, but a seed of an idea had been planted and was already germinating somewhere inside me. At the time, however, hunger took immediate precedent over any vague literary ambitions, so we hit the streets again.

After a relatively short stroll, we found ourselves in Leidseplein, Amsterdam's leading nightclub district. I wanted to eat at one of the many sidewalk joints in order to people watch, but due to the recent rain and still threatening sky, a lot of restaurants were only serving inside.

After a couple of laps of the quarter, we settled on a generic pizza place, where the semi-obsequious proprietor did a half-assed job of wiping rainwater off the chairs and table with a ridiculously small towel. I knew then and there that this was going to be a gastronomic debacle, but pushed aside my intuition, sat down and ordered.

The pizza was probably the worst I've ever eaten, a horrifying fusion of a ketchup-like substance and some sort of white goo masquerading as cheese, served on a flaccid, pasty-looking circle of what tasted like damp cardboard. True, I've never eaten damp cardboard, but I've masticated enough of it making spitballs to know what I'm talking about.

When the waiter served this monstrosity, he seemed

astonished that I accepted it and quickly scurried away.

JR's pizza looked suspiciously like mine, except his had a topping of banana slices, which I thought was asking for trouble. But when I complained about mine, he actually said with a straight face that his "tasted great." You never know when JR is putting you on or not, and along with the unexpected outburst, he derives great pleasure from getting a rise out of people.

You probably knew somebody like him in school, the sort of kid who provoked unruly behavior among his classmates and then had a good laugh when they were hauled away to the principal's office.

Although in his defense, I should mention that I'm given to understand that JR was hauled away on a fairly regular basis himself, much to the delight of his cohorts I'm sure.

There are countless variations on this theme, and JR has mastered most of them, including publicly calling attention to others' faux pas, usually in a loud stage voice designed to wring as much embarrassment as possible out of the situation. For years, whenever he visited me, he pounded on the door as loud as he could and yelled, "DEA! Open up! We know you're in there!" And that's just for starters.

We lived in the same small, suburban town and every time JR drove past my place, and I mean every time, he'd scream my first name at ear-piercing volume, elongating the annunciation in order to prolong the agony. It could come at any time of the day or night and was utterly random—while I'm watching TV or at my computer, eating a sandwich, taking a piss, lacing up my sneakers.

I even heard him when I was in bed half-asleep, and my bedroom was in back of the house as far away from the road as you can get. I'm sure a lot of the other drivers thought he was deranged, suffering from a rare and esoteric form of road rage -- Tourette's Syndrome maybe.

For me, the sound of this madman shrieking my name as he passed became strangely reassuring, one lone wolf howling to another across the impersonal void of civilization.

JR and I lingered over our pizza and beer, watching the growing crowds wander past, a mixture of tourists and locals out for a bit of fun. Next to the pizza place was a nightclub with a couple of shaven-headed musclemen manning the door, from which salsa music leaked every time somebody went in or out. At one point, a trio of pretty Latinas switched their way inside, all tight jeans and laughter, identical orange cowboy hats perched on their heads.

A bicycle cop pulled up outside the club and hung around with the doormen for a while, shooting the shit in Dutch. The cop was also muscled up; perhaps they all worked out in the same gym or bought steroids from the same dealer. Maybe both.

On the way back to our hotel we crossed a dark canal bridge where street dealers lurked, dispensing small bags of powder. The ones I encountered were all shabbily dressed black men, maybe junkies themselves, but never threatening or pushy. In hush tones they would offer coke, meth, heroin – stuff you couldn't score in a coffee shop or smart shop. What was actually in those bags, however, was anybody's guess.

Everything I'd read and heard indicated that the vast majority of the shit these guys sold was a rip-off, so I never even considered doing any consumer research. But I did overhear a British couple sitting near me in a coffee shop talking about the "bleeding rubbish" some street dealer had sold them instead of the promised chemical of their choice.

That was confirmation enough for me, and with so many delicious mind-altering goodies legally available, it seems piggish anyway. Greed is never a good reason to tempt fate. According to Terry, even a gambler who had faithfully followed the ritual and possessed the magic bean would lose if he had gotten too greedy.

VAN GOGH'S BICYCLE

How many able-bodied Baby Boomers do you know who never learned to ride a bicycle? It's got to be relatively rare. Not as rare as conjoined twins, but rare just the same. Even if your family couldn't afford a bicycle, there was always some kid in the neighborhood who had one and would let the other kids bum a ride. Even I can ride a bike for cripes sake.

JR, however, has yet to master this everyday skill and readily admitted it when we planned our trip to Hoge Veluwe National Park. Even so, I'd harbored the foolhardy notion that I would be able to teach him. My fantasy was ignited by the fact that visitors are encouraged to use the park's 1,500 bikes to explore its 13,750 acres of forest, shifting sands, and heathery moors. I somehow convinced myself that after a brief demonstration and a few false starts, we would be off, pedaling side-by-side through the beautiful old-growth forest.

JR would probably take a few spills, but nothing serious, just a few scrapes and bruises. Maybe, if we were really lucky, we'd catch a glimpse of a wild pig rummaging through the undergrowth.

My harebrained scheme to transform JR into an instant cyclist wasn't the first hiccup of the trip—although things certainly got off to a splendid start: Fortified with breakfast (and for me several pipes of cannabis and five mgs of amphetamine), we took a tram to Centraal Station, a majestic structure that looks more like a gingerbread palace than a transportation hub. It is the work of architect Pierre Cuypers, who also designed the Rijksmuseum, and merges Gothic and Dutch-Renaissance brickwork to create a wonderfully over-the-top edifice worthy of Walt Disney.

Following our guidebook's directions, we purchased round-trip tickets to Ede-Wageningen, a small town just west of Arnhem, the site of fierce fighting between the Germans and Allied airborne troops in 1944. The train was clean and swift and deposited us at Ede-Wageningen in about 45 minutes, where we were supposed to catch a bus to the park. But after about a half-hour of waiting, it began to dawn on us that something had gone awry.

Numerous buses came and went, none of which were headed for the park. Finally, a friendly local told us that the bus we were waiting for was no longer in service—so much for what our trusty guidebook described as the "easiest option" to get from Amsterdam to Hoge Veluwe.

It was at this point that we became the beneficiaries of a generous sampling of Dutch goodwill. A bus pulled up and discharged a couple of passengers, so we approached the driver and explained our dilemma. If this had been in the United States, the most cordial reply would probably have been a shrug of the shoulders; a more likely response would have been the door closing in our face as the vehicle roared away in a cloud of carbon monoxide.

The bus driver in Ede-Wageningen, however, spent a good five minutes graciously flipping through various schedules and maps, looking for a route that would be best for us. He rejected several before settling on a short ride to Otterlo, which would take us within a mile's walk of one of the park's three entrances.

The park is the best-preserved part of the Veluwe, which was formed during the Ice Age and was once a vast forest. Patches were cleared for cultivation and livestock grazing during the Middle Ages, which eventually led to erosion and sand drifts so large they buried entire villages. Reforestation in the 19th century prevented additional erosion and drifting, but if it hadn't been for wealthy businessman Anton Kroller and his wife, Helene (nee

Muller), the entire Veluwe would probably have been gobbled up for industrial or agricultural development.

The wealthy couple, both art and nature lovers, purchased the land that eventually became the park in 1935. Today, native animals such as red deer, roe deer, wild pigs, and moufflon (wild sheep from Sardinia and Corsica) populate the park in which the Kroller-Muller Museum is located.

Mr. Kroller made his fortune in shipping and mining, while his wife spent a significant chunk of it building one of the finest private art collections in the world. It was too early in the year for the red deer rutting season (always a big hit with the tourists), but we'd still have an opportunity to see some of the fauna and flora in an unspoiled setting and play a round of Spot the Dog, all thanks to Anton and Helene's twin passions.

The walk from where the bus deposited us was pleasant and we soon found ourselves at the park. No sooner had I paid the eleven-euro entrance fee and passed through the gate, I spotted the little beauties—sturdy mid-size bicycles, painted white, waiting for us in tidy rows, well-maintained and ready to roll. Not, however, with JR at the controls.

In a hopeless attempt to teach him, I tried all the same things that worked with my daughter when she was nine, but my optimism proved absurdly delusional. I might as well have been trying to teach JR to fly by flapping his arms. There were no hilarious pratfalls. Shit, he was never on the damned thing long enough to fall off. Instead it was a series of staggering starts and stumbling failures. The closest he came to a real spill was a rapid one-foot hop in a desperate attempt to stop the crossbar from smacking into his balls.

Even when I tried balancing him by holding the seat and running behind the bike, it didn't work. I shouted encouragement and fed him the old line about how the faster you go the easier it is, which is true, of course, but virtually impossible for a novice's body to believe when all survival instincts are screaming "GO SLOW!"

In the end, everything failed. The most essential thing cannot be taught: You've got to take a leap of faith to ride a bicycle. That's why kids are good at it.

Half a mile down the paved trail that led through the forest, we gave up and decided JR would walk his bike to the museum and leave it there. I, meanwhile, would bike on ahead and wait for him. It was the best plan under the circumstances and I raced off, happy to be free at last, surging forward, rediscovering the familiar bond between man and machine, rejoicing that my legs and lungs would still allow me to participate in this essentially youthful activity.

I doubled back two or three times to see how JR was doing and always found him dutifully trudging forward, a wry smirk on his lips, his now-docile charger gliding gently at his side. Then I'd rush forward again, whizzing down the almost deserted trail under a canopy of old-growth forest, the musky smell enveloping me like an invisible fog.

I stopped where two trails intersected and smoked a pipe of primo cannabis. No sooner had I put my pipe away than a group of teenagers approached from the opposite direction. They were chattering among themselves in Dutch, but as they rode past, one of them giggled and said, "Would you like to ride with us?"

I looked up, smiled and waved, the teasing invitation jitterbugging in my brain as they rounded a bend and disappeared from sight.

I applied myself to the pedals again and felt more and more elated as every turn of the wheels carried me deeper into the elemental joy that comes when all of your senses are synchronized by a simple physical activity. I was balanced, not only on the bicycle, but also on the edge of an unfolding reality that rushed to greet me, only to instantly disappear as a fresh future suddenly loomed.

On I rode as an endless pageant of time and space flashed past me, each new moment so powerful there was no thought of anything other than the here and now. The forest gave way to sandy grassland, where the shade disappeared and the early-spring sun shone hot and bright. Sweating and eager to see what lay ahead, I no longer doubled back, and about 10 minutes later the trail merged into the museum grounds, where I coasted to a halt and parked my bike.

It wasn't long before JR caught up with me and bid adieu to his two-wheel burden. Parting was not so much sweet sorrow as good riddance, but not a single complaint was uttered, not even obliquely. Flapping feet and sunken chest notwithstanding, JR is a good soldier.

The concept of having a world-class art museum smack dab in the middle of a forest blew me away. Anton and Helene didn't think of it that way of course. To them it was home, the place where they, like the rest of us, stored their treasures. It just so happened that many of their treasures were priceless works of modern art.

That Helene was one of the very first to recognize Van Gogh's genius and had the money to do something about it is one of those wonderfully serendipitous things that has benefited everybody—everybody but poor Vincent, of course, who never saw a gilder. He put a bullet in his gut back when nobody except his brother, Theo, gave a fuck.

I guess it had to be that way for the whole Van Gogh mystique to work. What good is a mad genius if he doesn't do anything crazy? It just wouldn't have been the same if he'd made a bundle and lived happily ever after. But there's no denying that cutting off a piece of his ear and giving it to a whore contributed considerably to his aura of lunacy.

What would happen if a famous artist, someone like Van Gogh or any of his destitute brethren, came back to life and demanded their share of the profits?

The art establishment would be in a total tizzy, soon various political camps would form, some advocating massive reimbursement and royalties for the artist, others desperately screaming about copyrights and possession being nine-tenths of the law. Billions would be at stake. The court battles would rage for decades. Armies of lawyers would get obscenely rich. Van Gogh would probably shoot himself again.

But at least Van Gogh had faithful Theo in his corner. Modigliani's dealer lied and told him he couldn't sell his work, when there were plenty of patrons eager to buy. Modigliani was dying of tuberculosis, you see, and his dealer was hording his paintings because he knew the price would skyrocket as soon as the artist croaked.

When you factor in the punitive damages in his case, a Modigliani zombie might end up with more money than Vinnie. What is more, he'd know how to enjoy it, for Modigliani was, as biographer June Rose called him, "the perfect bohemian," a man who took his cannabis in the form of the hashish pill cheaply available at any Parisian pharmacy during the first decade of the 20th century.

If Van Gogh did come back to life, his lawyer would have the unenviable task of going after the Netherlands government because that's whom Helene Kroller-Muller gave her entire collection to in 1935, and it was no small gift.

Just for starters, the museum that bears her and her husband's names houses the second-largest collection of Van Gogh paintings in the world. There are also works by Picasso, Mondrian, and Seurat—plus Europe's largest sculpture garden, where Dubuffet, Rodin, Moore, Giacometti, and a manicured version of Mother Nature all compete for your attention in an idyllic setting. Still, for some reason I came away from the museum thinking more about Anton and Helene than their magnificent legacy.

The individuals who create art don't really have much of a choice. Powerful forces beyond the understanding of ordinary mortals drive artists. Great artists are not really in control of their destiny; destiny is in control of them. But the Krollers were ordinary people. Yes, they were disgustingly rich but not overbearingly gifted like the artists whose creations Helene embraced. And Anton, the moneyman behind her vision, surely must have believed in what his wife was doing. After all, he was clearly very adept at making money, so perhaps he could recognize the spark of uncommon brilliance in those who worshiped at a less conventional altar.

The afternoon was still warm when we exited the museum, and after agreeing to rendezvous with JR at the gate, I raced off into the sunshine on the same bike I'd used earlier. Not that it was any better than the other bikes, which were pretty much identical, but because I already felt a bond with the machine that had provided such an exuberant inbound journey.

Instead of heading straight for the gate, I made several detours in order to explore more of the park, flying along with childlike joy as a gentle breeze dried my sweat.

It was while I was waiting for JR at the gate that, for the first and only time during my visit to the Netherlands, I actually saw somebody wearing wooden shoes. These were not the brightly painted ones you find in virtually every souvenir shop, but plain, utilitarian wood, discolored with age, stained with dirt and a bit worn down at the heels.

The man wearing them was probably around my age, with longish gray hair, dressed in a shabby chic style of a country gentleman gone slightly to seed. There was an air of understated elegance about him, but I couldn't help wondering if he wore the wooden shoes because they were comfortable or as part of a carefully cultivated image.

There are approximately 16 million people living in the Netherlands and at one time wooden shoes were ubiquitous, but today only about 5,000 people wear them. So regardless of his motives, I was lucky to see the rural eccentric wearing a pair as he went about his everyday life. And judging by the casual detachment with which he strolled along the country road, he was as at ease in his wooden shoes as I was in my Reeboks. Besides, what difference does it make whether your image is natural or contrived? If you wear it long enough, it will come to fit you.

THE POLITICS OF POT

The crystal-sharp rush of riding through an astonishing slice of Europe on such a gorgeous afternoon was intoxicating. It wasn't exactly in the same league as Hofmann's bike ride home from Sandoz, but it was righteous, nonetheless, streaked with the pure joy of being in the moment and at one with the universe.

Even before the train carried us back from Ede-Wageningen to Amsterdam, I was planning my next biking escapade. I had done okay tooling around Hoge Veluwe, but I still didn't feel ready to jump into daily rush-hour traffic along with tens of thousands of seasoned bikers, so I planned to warm up in Vondel Park before venturing into downtown traffic.

The park, Amsterdam's largest, is named after Joost van den Vondel, the so-called Shakespeare of the Netherlands. I'd never heard of him until I saw his name in a guide book, but when I Googled him, I learned that scholars have long suspected that Vondel's *Lucifer* influenced Milton's *Paradise Lost*. Apparently, not everybody agrees there's a link between the two works and yet another school of thought maintains that the Bible inspired both authors.

Personally, I don't see any reason why the competing theories should be mutually exclusive, but whatever the story, thanks to the park that bears his name, old Joost is still part of everyday life in Amsterdam even though he died in 1679. That's got to count for something.

In the morning, as JR snoozed, I ate breakfast, had a smoke, and was out on the streets by 9 a.m. There's a profusion of places to rent bicycles in Amsterdam. Toward the high end, it will cost you 12 to 13 euros to get the complete package: bike, lock, a tire-repair kit, and insurance.

There was little doubt in my mind that insurance was the way to go, considering Amsterdam's reputation as the bicycle-theft capital of Europe and all. But impatient to get started, I walked into the first rental joint I came upon after leaving the hotel, where for 7 Euros I could rent a fairly new, sturdy-looking machine with two locks. Best of all, I didn't have to bring it back until 7:30 that evening.

It seemed like a bargain, but I was still worried about getting it ripped off by some wretched junkie.

"You don't offer insurance?"

"No, it's your responsibility if the bike gets lost or stolen," said the generously pierced and tattooed bike-rental dude. "But if it's eventually found and still has both locks on it, you get a refund."

"How often does that happen?"

He smiled kindly.

I handed him my credit card.

A few minutes later, I was wheeling my cherry-red steed up the ramp onto Damrak Street and into the tail end of the rush hour. If I wanted to get to Vondel Park, which was about two miles away, I was going to have to plunge into traffic regardless of whether I was ready or not. My ill-conceived plan was already falling apart, but it was either join the masses or push the bike to the park, a la JR.

There was no hesitation. Encouraged by the amphetamine that had accompanied my morning coffee—a highly recommended way to start the day, especially when you're in your 60s and trying to do the same things you did at 30—I crossed the street, found the bike lane, and pushed off.

I was correct in assuming I'd be out of my league. (Do they even have a league for duffers such as me?) Not only was

every other rider a better cyclist than I, the blasé way some of
the women, many of them dressed for the office in high heels
and skirts, held their mobile phones in one hand and effortlessly
steered with another was a marvel to behold. I'd need another
lifetime to acquire such skills, so I aimed for what I hoped would
be survival and a minimum of embarrassment.

The stops and starts at traffic lights were the worst part. I did
okay with the stops, it was my wobbly starts that were by far the
weakest part of my game. I frequently teetered sideways before I
began to roll forward, which tilted the upper part of my body into
the lane next to me. Somehow I reached Vondel Park without
major mishap, unless you consider a cop yelling at me for riding
through a construction area "major."

There was a light rain falling when I found one of the park
gates pretty much where I though it would be. Except for a few
people on their way to work, an occasional gaggle of students,
and one or two joggers, I pretty much had the place to myself.
Maybe I could find an out-of-the-way spot to have a smoke.

L.D. Zocher designed Vondel Park, using vistas, ponds, and
winding pathways to create an illusion of nature. It was opened to
the public in 1865 and proved a success from the start. Originally
named Nieuwe Park, everybody started calling it Vondel Park
when a statue of Vondel was erected there in 1867.

In the late 1960s and early 1970s it was the camping ground
for hordes of hippies who descended on the city. Today it is
illegal to sleep there, but it is still a place where people of all
ages and social classes gather to enjoy themselves—kids with
kites, in-line skaters, lovers and jugglers, sunbathers and readers,
musicians and acrobats, teenagers playing soccer and families out
for a stroll. From June until August, there are free concerts in the
open-air theatre.

But on this damp, decidedly off-season day, it was the perfect
place for an out-of-practice cyclist to float along without worry,
free of perilous tram tracks and the disapproving looks of more
accomplished practitioners. I circled the park for about half an

hour, stopping briefly at an isolated duck pond for a quick hit of cannabis.

More than half a lifetime had past since that long-ago evening in Tangier when Terry and I smoked the cigarettes stuffed with marijuana pollen. Back then I didn't even get off, or if I did, I didn't realize it. Now I'm what they call a "drug tourist," which, by the way, I consider a perfectly legitimate label. Millions of people go to Amsterdam to get high every year, and I was delighted to be among them.

As I peddled away from Vondel Park, my strategy was simple: I would turn down any thoroughfare free of traffic. Elegant residential streets, canal-side boulevards, and bumpy cobblestone alleys all fluttered past my line of vision, zigzagging me in no particular direction other than away from all other vehicles.

I'd been riding for the better part of three hours before it suddenly occurred to me that if I wasn't careful I might have trouble finding my way back to the bike shop. I knew where it was in relationship to our hotel, but didn't have the foggiest where the shop was in relationship to where I was at that moment. I couldn't even remember the name of the rental agency. But trusting in my belief that *all* Amsterdam tram tracks eventually lead to the Centraal Station, I found some tracks and headed in what I hoped was the correct direction.

For a change, my aim was true and I soon found myself bicycling down familiar streets and recognizing landmarks, one of which was a coffee shop I'd previously frequented. I pulled up in front and padlocked the bicycle to a tree, bought a coffee, and found a seat that afforded me a half-decent view of my tethered mount.

One thing that had taken me a few days to figure out was that you don't have to buy cannabis every time you go to a coffee shop in order to smoke there. I wasn't sure of the protocol at first, so I always purchased something to smoke before sitting down for a session. But as long as you bought something to drink while you smoked, most establishments don't care too much where you scored.

Just like a bar in the U.S. where folks pop in to buy a six-pack and leave, a lot of customers just cop some cannabis and split. Some of them looked like they might be on their way home from work. Others stay a while, drinking coffee and rolling their purchases into joints, mostly fatties, stuffed with various combinations of pot, hash, and tobacco. Twenty minutes or so later, they move on, fortified and supplied, ready to experience whatever comes next with a fresh perspective.

Then there are people like me, who are there because we like getting high in a public setting, the same way that bar and pub patrons enjoy drinking in a communal setting. Deplorably, the Netherlands is one of the rare places on the planet where you can smoke herb in a public place without risk of arrest. But when you're in Amsterdam, it seems the most natural thing in the world, one of the perks of this multisided sword called civilized society.

So what if they're smoking a doobie instead of chugging a beer? It's universally acknowledged that swilling too much alcohol often leads to obnoxious behavior, but in decades of smoking I've never seen cannabis lead directly to aggression and violence.

In a way, that's another bullshit curveball. There's absolutely nothing wrong with drinking as long as it's done responsibly and the drinker is accountable for his or her actions. The same goes for potheads.

Why is it so difficult for so many people to understand (admit) that there is a world of difference between drug *use* and drug *abuse*?

It's no coincidence that many of the same people who chanted "Make Peace Not War" were also marijuana consumers. Cannabis and nonviolence go together the same way that alcohol and aggression are allied; it's a chemical reaction. And it's also not a coincidence that most governments insist their citizens choose booze over cannabis as a recreational drug.

The Netherlands is different. It decriminalized cannabis in 1976, in a manner in which the Dutch Ministry of Justice applies *gedoogbeleid*, a policy of tolerance or allowance. The decision was based on two beliefs: First, that drug use is a public health issue, not a criminal matter, and secondly, that there is a distinction between hard drugs, such as heroin and cocaine, and soft drugs, such as cannabis and psilocybin mushrooms.

The line of demarcation between "hard" and "soft" drugs is whether or not they were physically addictive or produced no worse than moderate craving when withdrawn. Another aim was to separate the market so that soft drugs were taken out of the hands of criminals.

The decriminalization is of a de facto nature and the statutes that make cannabis illegal are kept on the books, mainly due to international pressure and adherence with treaties. There is, however, institutionalized non-enforcement of statutes, an official set of guidelines telling public prosecutors under what circumstances offenders should not be prosecuted.

The well-defined limit is five grams, the maximum amount coffee shops are permitted to sell per customer. Not that anybody seems to be checking. You could go from one coffee shop to the next, compiling a huge stash if you wanted, and unless the police stop you for some unrelated reason, there is little chance of being caught. But why tempt fate when cannabis is so readily available? Take it from somebody who has been smoking pot on virtually a daily basis for more than fifty years. It's next to impossible for one person to smoke more than five grams of the high-quality weed available in Holland in one day. Even if you could, the next five grams is usually just a few blocks away at most.

The Dutch soft drug policy is pragmatic and philosophical, based on the general principle of self-determination in matters of the body. But that progressive policy didn't come without turmoil.

Like so many countries in the 1960s, the Netherlands underwent a cultural upheaval, and a band of Amsterdam anarchists known as the Provos led the way. The Provos staged street theater and various happenings, or playful "provocations," from which their name stemmed. Abbie Hoffman and Wavy

Gravy had nothing on these cats.

There was Robert Jasper Grootveld (a pot-smoking, self-proclaimed sorcerer and anti-consumerism activist), frenzied poet Johnny van Doom (aka Johnny the Selfkicker), Rob Stolk, (a working-class printer and street tactician), and my personal favorite, Bart Huges, who drilled a hole in his forehead (the so-called third eye) to attain a permanent state of expanded consciousness. Terry had told me about him back in London before the whole partial-lobotomy (the medical term is "trepanation") riff became part of hippie lore. But I'd forgotten his name until I read it in an Amsterdam guidebook decades later.

The Provos wanted to expose the evils of consumerism and the role advertising plays in the destructive spending cycle of the klootjesvolk (the narrow-minded populace). Like people engaged in similar political activities in the streets and on the college campuses in much of Western Europe and the United States, the Provos and their followers were victims of mindless and disproportionate police reprisals.

Unlike the U.S., where large segments of the population condoned police brutality as exactly what protestors deserved (regardless of their cause), the reaction in the Netherlands was different.

A favorite venue for the Provos' street theater was Spui Square, which was lined with pubs frequented by journalists, and in the summer of 1965, many wrote eyewitness accounts of the irrational violence perpetrated by the police. Their reports ignited fierce debate throughout the country, but unlike the U.S., the divisions were not sharply divided along generational lines. It had been only 20 years since the end of World War II, and older people who had lived through the German occupation were shaken by the establishment's unnecessary brutality. It reminded them too much of their Nazi oppressors.

The next year, the Provos won a seat in the municipal elections, an event that marked a significant departure from the group's anarchist ideology, but, nevertheless, gained a foothold in mainstream politics. Much of the Provos' philosophy was adopted by their successors, the kabouters, who were named after the helpful gnomes of Dutch folklore. How trippy is that?

The kabouters made additional inroads into the traditional political system by winning five seats in the Amsterdam City Council in 1970, and although the movement lost much of its old radicalism and purity of purpose, their participation in conventional politics helped lead to the current drug policies. These policies have, among other things, resulted in Holland having the lowest drug-related death rate in Europe.

None of this would have been possible if it hadn't been for the Netherlands' history of tolerance for unorthodox views, which, in the early-20th century, led to a system known as verzuiling (pillarisation). It was a compromise between the conservative establishment and liberal elements of Dutch society, wherein people of all persuasions agreed to disagree but were free to do their own thing nonetheless. These series of diverse "pillars" supported the status quo, which was in keeping with the Dutch tradition of incorporating alternative viewpoints into the structure of society. Try that in Alabama.

But why did the Netherlands come out of the cultural revolution with a relatively enlightened system while most other countries swung dramatically back to the right? Why did the seeds of change Baby Boomers felt blowing through their youth take root in Holland but not elsewhere?

A history of cultural tolerance is the foundation, but it is also significant that approximately sixty percent of the Dutch population identify themselves as agnostics or atheists. Unencumbered by the yoke of religious dogma, they are free to develop a way of life based on being reasonable to all citizens, not just to those who wield the biggest stick or have the most money, which are frequently one in the same.

In the case of soft drug consumption, even those who frown on it are willing to accept that those who disagree should have the right to indulge. After all, if those who prefer alcohol and tobacco are permitted to enjoy the worldly pleasures of their choice, why shouldn't stoners be afforded the same privileges? Take away the pervasive hypocrisy of one group trying to force its moral code of conduct on another, and such an attitude makes perfect sense.

During the early days of the Jimmy Carter administration, many of us thought there was a reasonable chance of something similar coming to pass in the United States. Several states decriminalized small amounts of marijuana in the 1970s, and even President Carter said that it was counterproductive to have drug laws that caused more harm than the drug.

But when the U.S. government's imperialistic foreign policy resulted in the seizure of the U.S. Embassy in Iran and taking of hostages, the relatively liberal Carter administration was doomed, and the country veered dramatically to the right.

As more and more countries rebelled against American dominance and the disastrous results of the corrupt regimes it supported abroad, the tighter the grip became at home. Part of it was the twisted need to maintain control, and if the military-industrial complex and right wing ideologues couldn't keep the rest of the world under their thumb, they would do their damnedest to suppress dissent among their own citizens.

As cannabis consumers are more likely to be dissenters they have quietly became a popular target of a criminal justice system. Today, there are approximately 350,000 people incarcerated in the United States for nonviolent drug crimes, which contributes greatly to clogged court and prison systems and has nothing whatsoever to do with justice. It's about money and power.

The housing and feeding of inmates, along with the never-ending War on Drugs, cost American taxpayers billions of dollars, year after year. And while neither mandatory minimum sentences nor the combined efforts of an ever-growing number of law-enforcement agencies have done anything to stop drug use, it has made a small minority rich and become a substantial part of the economy.

It's not just guards and other prison employees. The building, maintaining, and supplying of prisons alone is an enormous business, and then there's the massive drug-testing industry, another violation of civil rights turned into a money-maker that wouldn't exist without such draconian drug policies.

The genius of the establishment's master plan is the way the various elements dovetail so beautifully: First, they allowed greedy corporations to betray American workers by shipping well-paid jobs overseas, and in less than a generation, people are so desperate for a half-decent job that communities are competing with one another to have the next penitentiary built in their hometown.

I don't know who it was that first said it, but it's true: Pretty soon the only jobs left will be ones where you have to wear a uniform of some sort, a choice of either the military or McDonald's. Prison guards and prisoners, of course, both wear uniforms.

Although this is just a single component of an evil matrix, it's one of particular concern to recreational drug users, all of whom have their asses on the line, potential victims of a system designed to keep as many people behind bars as possible.

The trend toward privatization of prisons has only increased the profit motive. Just like hotels and hospitals, the last thing private prisons want is vacancies. Most of America's *klootjesvolk* don't even know they're getting played.

But I came to Amsterdam to forget all that crap. This was a holiday, time to lighten up and enjoy being where I could relax in a public establishment and enjoy a smoke break without fear of arrest. As a bonus, this particular coffee shop wasn't playing techno. Instead, a funky beat seeped into my cannabis-soaked pores and gently pulsated through my body. I couldn't resist closing my eye and twitching with guilty pleasure as the sound of Hot Chocolate took control.

"I believe in miracles, you sexy thing."

Lou Rawls kept the disco groove going with "See You When I Get There," another 1970s tour de force of commercial confection. But when the sound of Peter Tosh's "Legalize It" filled the café, everything shifted again. Here, at least, that battle had been won and Peter was preaching to the choir. I couldn't wipe the shit-eating grin off my face, and I was still smiling as I unlocked my bicycle and pushed off in what I believed was the general direction of the bike rental shop.

BLACK MAN IN THE WINDOW

The day following my solo bike ride, JR and I got an early start, joining locals for breakfast at one of several sidewalk cafés in the neighborhood. The early-spring sun went wonderfully with coffee and apple pie. This was a lifestyle I could grow used to very quickly. Even so, the disconcerting thought that we were returning to the U.S. of A. the following day kept intruding.

I'd quickly grown accustomed to not being a criminal and liked the way it felt. But I knew that the feeling was something, like cannabis itself, which I could not take home with me. I promised myself that I would return to the Netherlands as soon as I could. In the meantime, just knowing it was there, an oasis of relative sanity in an insane world, would give comfort.

We live in a society where this beneficial plant is officially treated as if it were the embodiment of evil. But what if the opposite is true and it really is the embodiment of good, a sacrament like the Rastafarians say? The notion might seem far-fetched to some, but at least in Holland you're free to believe in the magical powers of cannabis if you wish and live your life accordingly. I was already missing the place, and I hadn't left yet.

After breakfast, we went in search of gifts to take home, but, like most vacation destinations, Amsterdam's souvenir shops all sell pretty much the same junk. I managed to resist temptation, except for a marvelously vulgar beer bottle opener. It had a plastic pig dressed like a prostitute on the handle, along with the words "Amsterdam Red Light District."

This single lapse in taste turned out badly when the buddy I'd bought it for was afraid to take it home. Somebody suggested it was because the guy's wife was overweight and might not think that the piggy prostitute was funny. I'm not so sure. Surely, it's one of those things that's so over-the-top tacky, it's cool, like a glow-in-the-dark Jesus to stick on your dashboard.

Before my inappropriate sense of humor did any additional damage, we found a quiet square away from the tourist district where an outdoor art sale was taking place. I bought two little hand-colored prints from the artist—scenes of Amsterdam. They were well done, and if the style sometimes threatened to veer perilously close to cuteness, it was inevitably saved by excellent draftsmanship and sure brushwork.

I'd also promised to bring back some photos, a task I had completely neglected up until then, so I bought a cheap disposable camera at the same shop I'd purchased the bottle opener.

I took a shot of the South Church from a canal bridge reminiscent of Monet's "The Zuiderkerk: Looking Up The Groenburgwal," a postcard of which once hung in my bedroom. I suppose looking down the same canal at the same scene Claude painted in 1873 was just an everyday example of life imitating art, but it still took me a moment to realize why the view looked so familiar.

Click!

I scrambled from place to place, snapping away with my disposable camera. The results were not anything special, but the majority were composed well enough that I knew my art-school eye was still working.

JR took a shot of me, cannabis smoke bellowing out of my mouth as I lay on my hotel bed, propped up on a couple of pillows. I was in the middle of a prolonged session, steadily chipping away at the remains of my stash. The smoke drifted out the second-story window and dissolved in the same breeze that caressed my bare feet and rippled the canal water below.

I blocked all thoughts of my imminent departure and allowed

my daydreams to carry me away in a pageant of imagination and memory to that place in between the two where you don't really know which is which. Maybe that's where creativity takes place, a space where the concept of fact or fiction ceases to exist and instead coexists to form a third state of mind.

Can cannabis ease your passage to this realm and help you navigate its labyrinth of possibilities? Sometimes, but if it doesn't, you probably won't give a shit anyway.

■■■

JR and I figured a little symmetry would help bring closure to a perfectly satisfying holiday, so on our last night in Amsterdam we returned to the same Indian restaurant where we'd eaten the first night in town. The food was still mediocre, the staff still friendly, and as we lingered over our meal, I knew I wasn't anywhere near ready to go home. I tried not to allow our departure to detract from my final night in town. But it hung heavy in my mind as I sat sipping the last few drops of mango-yogurt drink, watching it grow dark outside the restaurant window.

I'd smoked up most of what was left of my stash that afternoon but had saved enough for a nightcap and a few hits to smoke in the morning, right before we checked out of the hotel and headed for the airport. I had absolutely no thoughts of trying to sneak a few buds back into the United States with me, just a wistful feeling of regret.

As JR and I walked back to the hotel, we passed a nearby coffee shop and spotted a familiar black face in the window. It was the same man we'd seen sitting there virtually every evening when we walked by. He sat Buddha-like, looking out the window, a shit-eating grin on his broad face.

Night after night he was there, same seat, same grin. If you didn't know better, you'd think he'd never left, just sat there his entire life, smoking and smiling. Judging by his coarse clothes and rough-hewn hands, he earned his daily bread via manual labor. It was hard to say how old he was, the lights of the coffee shop were behind him, and he appeared almost in silhouette, a powerful, squat figure, sagging slowly into late middle-age.

I imagined he was a working stiff who stopped off every night on his way home to get high and ended up staying until closing time. But for all I know, he could have been the owner. Whatever the story, it always made me feel good to see him sitting there, a blissed-out sentinel transmitting silent signals of tranquility into the night.

A lot of tourists think of Amsterdam as just a party town, a great place to do legally things that could get you thrown in jail back home. And while that's true, it misses the point. The real miracle is that it exists at all, that there is a nation of people confident enough in themselves to treat adults as adults. In Holland, nobody cares if you want to smoke a joint or get a blowjob, just as long as you behave yourself while indulging.

The glue that holds together what might seem at first an out-of-control situation is, believe it or not, rules and regulations. But they are rules of empowerment, not rules of restraint. The secret is that the Dutch really do believe that everybody's opinion counts. They think it reasonable. What a concept.

It would be foolish, however, to ignore recent threats to the Dutch's open-minded approach to life, most notoriously the brutal murder of controversial filmmaker Theo Van Gogh in 2004. This horrific crime has come to symbolize the crack in the dike of tolerance that the Dutch erected to hold back the tide of fanaticism and paranoia infesting most of the world. The victim was the great grandson of the art dealer of the same name, the 19th century Dutchman who was Vincent's brother and the troubled genius' closest confidant and chief benefactor.

All three men led short, troubled lives: Vincent was 37 when he committed suicide, his brother Theo was 33 when he died of syphilis in an insane asylum, and Theo's great grandson and namesake was 47 when he was murdered. A trio of talented men of the same blood, all tortured by demons of one sort or another, all cut down in their primes. Makes you wonder.

The great grandson made a short a film called *Submission* that dealt with the topic of violence against women in Islamic societies. When it was shown on Dutch television, the film provided an excuse for radical imams to incite violent action.

The latter-day Van Gogh was an iconoclastic gadfly who had already enraged most of the Netherlands' more than one million Muslims by consistently referring to them as "geitenneukers" (goat-fuckers), but who, when informed of threats to his life, said: "Who would want to kill the village idiot?"

The answer to the question is Islamist Mohammed Bouyeri, a 26-year-old Dutch citizen of Moroccan descent, who shot Van Gogh eight times as the author and filmmaker rode to work on his bicycle. Then he slit his throat, almost decapitating him, and pinned notes to his body with knives.

The exceedingly vicious nature of the slaying shone a spotlight on the Netherlands' festering problem concerning first- and second-generation immigrants, many of whom are Muslims. The Islamic Dutch feel discriminated and singled out, and not without reason.

Unemployment amongst immigrants is four times higher than the national average, and forty percent of them leave school without completing their final exams. This has helped lead to an economic situation that has forced large numbers of Muslims to the fringes of society. Immigrants and refugees are also under enormous pressure to assimilate, and have to pay for language courses and pass a test in order to be allowed to stay in the Netherlands.

There was a violet anti-Muslim backlash in the aftermath of Van Gogh's murder, including four attempted arson attack on mosques, and, in Uden, a primary Muslim school was destroyed by arson. The government used these attacks as justification for increasing the size of its police force and instituting restrictive immigration policies.

"The Netherlands has been too tolerant to intolerant people for too long," barked right-wing politician Geert Wilders, who advocated a five-year halt to "non-Western" immigrants in the wake of Van Gogh's murder.

Still, the majority of the population rejected both the murder and the antidemocratic measures of the Dutch government. The day Van Gogh was slain, 20,000 people gathered in Amsterdam to demonstrate in favor of freedom of expression and against violent means of dealing with political problems. In 2007, a piece of sculpture called De Screevw (The Scream) by Jeroen Henneman was erected near the spot where van Gogh was killed, a memorial and symbol of the freedom of speech.

Like so many other European nations, the Netherlands is reaping the bitter fruit of a harvest that was sown in its colonial past. The Dutch East Indies Company, established in 1602 (and the first-ever company to sell stock), was the personification of corporate colonialism and the world's first multinational corporation. For the next 200 years, the Dutch profited mightily from its trading posts and colonies in Indonesia, North and South America, and South Africa and the Caribbean. In the Netherlands, they still refer to it as the "Golden Age."

Sadly, the Dutch were no more enlightened than other European nations when it came to their treatment of the indigenous people they encountered on their feverish quest for capitalistic gain. In the 1620s, almost the entire native population of the Banda Islands, the source of nutmeg, was deported, driven away, starved to death, or slain in an attempt to replace them with slave labor.

At the time, a sociopath named Jan Pieterszoon Coen, a man disposed to use extreme violence bordering on genocide to obtain his ends, was the Governor-General of the Dutch East Indies. And his brutality wasn't limited to his treatment of the indigenous people. Coen once found a girl he had been entrusted to care for in the arms of a soldier. He had the girl whipped and the soldier beheaded.

The karmic wheel turns slowly at times. For centuries, though not so much today, Coen was considered a hero in Holland, a lot like Christopher Columbus in the United States. But just as Malcolm X said of the U.S. race riots in the 1960s, "the chickens have come home to roost." They just took a longer, more circuitous route before nesting in the Netherlands.

I wonder what the black man in the coffee shop window thinks about all of this. Obviously, either he or one of his close relatives came to Holland from elsewhere. Maybe he's a Muslim too. All I know is that he looked very much at ease with the world, a fatty smoldering between his thick fingers, his lips stretched over his teeth to form a broad grin, his eyes hooded slits like those of a toad.

"Hey, there's your buddy," said JR as we passed the coffee shop that final evening.

I glanced back at the black man in the window one last time, and although I can't swear to it, I think I saw him wink.

COMING TO AMERICA

As my pipe hit the bottom of the bathroom trashcan with a clunk, I exhaled the last hit of legal marijuana I would have for a while and wondered about the wisdom of abandoning a power object in such an accessible place. True, I'd only owned the pipe a little more than a week, but even so, I don't think Don Juan Matus would have approved of such careless behavior. Maybe I should have thrown it in the canal. I bet a lot of assholes do that.

JR and I paid our hotel bill, took a tram to the station, and then a train back to Schipol International Airport. This part happened way too quickly for your reluctantly departing correspondent, but we were, nonetheless, soon on our way back over the Atlantic Ocean, headed westward to the brave new world of Newark, New Jersey.

It had been very different the first time I'd crossed the Atlantic. I was ten then, and my mother and I took an ocean liner instead of a plane. The voyage lasted ten days after leaving Southampton, the last two gliding down the St. Lawrence River, first to Quebec and then Montreal.

A boy couldn't ask for a better adventure, and I remember how thrilled I was to be going. Canada was almost as good as America, and everybody wanted to go to America. But if it weren't for a bit of fortunate timing, we would have ended up in Tanganyika (now the United Republic of Tanzania) instead.

My father had waited for so long after applying that he had very nearly given up on getting a Canadian visa and had applied for a job as a construction foreman in what was then a British East African territory. The rub was that the workers he would be supervising were convicts. But the Canadian visa came through just as he was about to accept the job. I think we were all relieved. I instinctively felt sorry for those black men in chains without really knowing why.

After his visa was granted, my father went on to Canada ahead of my mother and me. The plan was to get a job and earn enough money to pay for our passages and a place for us to live. Some men in such circumstances would have kept right on going and forgotten about the wife and kid back in the old country. Maybe if it weren't for me, my father would have done something along those lines. I don't know. I do know my mother was a difficult person to live with, ultra-sensitive, easily upset, and prone to take umbrage where none was intended.

But my father was, above all else, a gentleman, and a gentleman does not desert his family, even if his wife is a ball-buster. At the time, it never even crossed my mind that my father would ditch us. I was ten and my faith in him was absolute.

It was my father who had taught me the joys of reading and then how to read. We had no television, a radio only intermittently. At that time in England, you were supposed to have a license to own a radio, and if you were caught with one and no license, you would be fined. There were actually people whose job it was to knock on doors and search homes for unlicensed radios. It seems so friggin' Orwellian. I remember that my grandmother used to hide hers under the bed.

The lack of electronic media meant that stories (mainly told by my grandfather) and books were a major source of entertainment. I can remember my father reading *The Wind in the Willows* to me before I started school, especially how we laughed together at the outrageous behavior of Mr. Toad.

When I began to have problems learning to read at school, my father struck a bargain with me: He would read to me from a book of my choice for the same amount of time I worked in my textbook. By the time we'd finished *Adventures of Huckleberry Finn*, I had a grasp on phonetics and a whole new perspective on the world.

Before he sailed for Canada, we made the rounds of various friends and family members to say goodbye. This was an exercise that I repeated with my mother a year later, and although it was relatives from the other side of the family, I experienced much the same emotions. I understood that I was seeing most of these people for the last time, but I didn't feel at all sad. Instead, I felt something akin to relief, tinged in some cases with a healthy dash of good riddance.

Part of that was because I was sick of the petty bickering and family spats, all of which are uncomfortable to a child. Another part of it was simply because I *was* a kid, still infused with a purity of being. I instinctively understood the only thing that really mattered was that I would be with my mother and father.

But looming over everything was this great adventure, a dream come true for a child who grew up playing cowboys and Indians, pretending that the bottom of the banister was the saddle of his palomino. I secretly harbored the conviction that once on the other side of the Atlantic Ocean, visiting Roy Rogers at the Double-R-Bar Ranch, wherever it might be, would be a snap.

Uncle Rex, my father's older brother, drove my mother, our luggage and me to the Cunard Line docks in Southampton, where we bade him goodbye and boarded the RMS Ascania, bound for the New World. I was so excited to be underway at last, finally going to America, that I didn't give leaving the land of my birth a second thought. My mind was on the Western horizon where my father and my future awaited. I didn't realize at the time how much of England I was taking with me.

I was so terribly alive at ten, so open to possibility—you know, a normal kid—that the voyage remains one of those seminal memories, one that never really disappears all together no matter how old I get. The days have blurred together somewhat, but certain things are indelible.

I remember crewmembers saying the ship was headed for the junkyard as soon as this, her final voyage, was finished. But I never really knew whether it was true or not, not until decades later when I found a barebones bio:

"RMS Ascania: launched 1923, maiden voyage 1925, sold for scrap in 1956."

That I was transported to my new life on a ship headed for its grave certainly has an ironic ring to it, but beyond that, it didn't amount to much. If the condemned vessel knew the score, it didn't show it. It just kept steaming westward—dead ship sailing. But the cycle of life was the last thing on my mind. Like most growing boys, food was very high on my list of priorities, especially as a Baby Boomer who remembered rationing books and food shortages.

The grub aboard the good ship Ascania was nothing short of awe-inspiring. It was like Christmas dinner every day, and when I suffered through an epic four-day bout of seasickness, the only thing that really upset me was that I couldn't partake of the bounty.

A couple of days out to sea, it became so rough that even some of the crew was queasy. Like most of the passengers, I couldn't keep a thing down for more than a few minutes, and I stopped eating for a few days. But I started again so I would have something other than bile to throw up.

I recall eating an apple very slowly, chewing each mouthful until it was a masticated mush, in the vain hope I could successfully digest it. In fact, it stayed in my stomach approximately the same amount of time—two or three minutes, maybe—as the roast beef, mashed potatoes and gravy I'd wolfed down before beginning my fast.

There was nothing anybody could do about it because we were still less than halfway across the ocean when bad weather hit. I knew it would be almost a week before we docked, and the notion that relief was nowhere in sight started to nibble at the edges of my ten-year-old optimism.

Outside of our tiny, below sea level cabin, the world was awash with vomit as passengers lurched around the rolling ship, hanging on to whatever they could, depositing the contents of their stomachs willy-nilly. It seemed like the whole world was barfing at once. The smell was indescribable.

Thankfully, the waves subsided a few days before reaching the mouth of the St. Lawrence River, and I bounced back like nothing had happened, scampering around the deck, sneaking nuts and candy from the first-class lounge, and hanging out with the crew. Like a squad of good-natured uncles, they spoiled and teased us children in equal measure, keeping us entertained so that the grownups could have their fun. I'm sure a good tip at the end of the passage was their primary motive, but most of them seemed to enjoy it well enough.

From time to time we saw icebergs in the distance, and at night in our berths, we could hear the ice complaining as the ship parted the semi-frozen sea, passing though the spring slush on its way to warmer waters. One afternoon, a steward stuck his head into the tourist-class lounge and told us that whales could be seen off the starboard bow. They were about half a mile away and to the naked eye looked like black inner tubes, but every now and then, a jet of water would squirt out of one of the rubbery-looking bumps among the waves.

You get a far greater sense of coming into a country when you arrive by ship. Instead of swooping down out of the sky, the approach is gradual and the transition easier to comprehend. You see the land in the distance get closer and closer as an outline becomes a shoreline and a then a dock. It feels more organic than air travel.

When we reached the Saint Lawrence, you could see homes and farms and people along the banks. Kids waved to us as we passed. Some of them were fishing, sitting on docks with their jeans rolled up to their knees and their feet dangling in the water. We were a long way from the Mississippi River, but I couldn't help thinking about Huckleberry Finn and Jim, and half-excepted to spot them on a raft before we disembarked in Montreal.

After we docked and finally cleared customs and immigration, my father was waiting for us. He was more tanned than I'd ever seen him before, wearing lightweight pants and a summer shirt, a straw hat pushed back off his forehead, a cigarette hanging from the corner of his smiling mouth. I don't know what my mother thought of this decidedly un-English version of my father, but I was even more overjoyed to see him than I thought I'd be.

My father would not be waiting for us in Newark when JR and I landed following our Amsterdam adventure. He'd died a few years before, suddenly and quickly at age 79. We were on vacation together, just the two of us, having a great time, when he had a heart attack. From the moment it hit him to the moment he died couldn't have been more than a few minutes, if that. Laughing one minute, dead the next. Just like that.

He lived with me the last few years of his life, and in the evenings we'd sometimes sit together at the kitchen table and talk. He'd have his glass of bourbon and I'd have my pipe, at peace with ourselves and with one another.

Often the conversation would lead back to England and our lives there. I miss it more now than ever. Or maybe it's my childhood I miss. The two are so intertwined; they've become inseparable.

■■■

Except for the cannabis lingering in my system, I was clean when JR and I cleared U.S. customs. I had triple-checked all my clothes and baggage for anything incriminating before leaving the hotel and even avoided buying any of the hundreds of dope-related souvenirs on sale in Amsterdam. I did, however, buy a Che Guevara ashtray. Actually, I would not be surprised if Che and Fidel sparked a few doobies around the campfire during their days in the Sierra Maestra Mountains, but there was nothing overtly drug-related to his image.

I have carried dope across international borders so many

times in the past, I still feel a little uneasy even when I'm clean, which these days is most of the time. I often pack a small stash in my checked luggage when I fly within the United States and have had no problems, but international flights are far too risky these days. Everybody knows it's not 1967 anymore especially us old heads who were around back then.

Still, you have to figure that a lot of boneheads try to sneak a few grams into the country after a vacation in Amsterdam. It's only human nature. So it made perfect sense for the customs agents to take a close look at what folks were bringing back with them from hedonist heaven. Why wouldn't they search my bags?

Well, they didn't. I could have had a kilo in my suitcase and got away with it. I breezed through customs and immigration with no more than a cursory glance at my papers and a snappy "Welcome to the United States." It makes you wonder. But why get greedy when you've got a joint waiting for you in the car's glove box?

When I had returned to the United States after my adventures in London and Tangier with Terry, there was no homecoming pipe waiting for me, just my parents. It was during the middle of a miserable snowstorm, but I was warmed by the knowledge that I had a few grams of Moroccan hash stashed inside my Zippo. Customs would have had to pull the lighter apart to find it, but they didn't even touch it.

Thanks to a combination of discretion, caution and good luck, I've never even come close to getting busted. Now I've got another thing going for me: I'm too old and conservative looking to fit the standard stoner profile. As my buddy Mike, another sixty-something doper, delights in telling me, "You just look like an average old guy."

While the veracity of the jibe is as undeniable as it is unflattering, all in all, it's not a bad trade-off. If avoiding detection is a fringe benefit of gray hair and wrinkles, I'll take it. I'd still have the gray hair and wrinkles if I were straight. Ironically, most of my risky border crossings took place when I did fit the profile—

young, longhaired, and slightly scruffy. Now that I've got the right look, I've lost my nerve.

Back when I would dare and did, I always found myself in the same mindset that Terry helped me find in Tangier. It is not a conscious effort; it just happens automatically whenever a customs agent looks me in the eye. It is as if the joint in my shaving kit or half-ounce rolled up in my socks did not exist. At some level, I know they do, but I temporarily sublimate that knowledge. It is kind of like yogic breathing, easy to fall into after you get the knack. You can't "try" to do it. It just happens.

Newark's veneer seemed grungier than usual after Amsterdam, where even the funk has a Continental tang. Nonetheless, it was still a relief when JR and I found his Honda Civic in the long-term parking lot and headed home. We had played a lot of CDs on the way to the airport and done a lot talking, but for the most part, we rode in silence on the final leg of our holiday.

I'm not sure about JR, but I wanted to bathe in the lingering aura of Amsterdam for as long as I could, wallow in the memory while it was fresh. But as we rode, my mind kept drifting back to an earlier fight across the Atlantic, more than 40 years earlier.

My final night with Terry in London, I made a crude pipe out of a hollow chicken bone and a piece of tinfoil, and when I dressed the next morning, I pocketed a small nugget of hash. Somewhere between Edinburgh and Reykjavik, I smoked the hash in the loo, flushed the pipe down the toilet, and lit a Woodbine. Then I sauntered back to my seat, eased it back to a semi-reclining position, and closed my eyes. Before I feel asleep, I pretended that when I woke up I'd be back at the flat.

Nonetheless, ten hours later, I was in New York, sitting in the back seat of my father's car as he squinted through the windshield and aimed the Plymouth down an icy road. The thick covering of snow and steady descent of butterfly-sized flakes gave everything an otherworldly look appropriate for my trance-like state. The 14-hour transatlantic flight had not been sufficient segue. My body was in the United States, but my head was still in London.

Now I'm an old stoner trying to keep the flickering glow of youth alive, and as JR and I drew closer to the finish line and familiar beds, I was comforted by the knowledge that a trip to Amsterdam can still provide a spark to keep that inner light burning. Whether or not the spark is an illusion or for real doesn't matter. It works either way.

PART

The Return
Of Johnnie Blanco

COCAINE KARMA

The phone call came on a sunny Sunday in May right around the
same time of year JR and I had been in Amsterdam the previous
spring. It was from Mike, a good friend and smoking buddy who
lived about half-an-hour's drive from my place.

"What are you up to?"

"Nothing. Why?"

"Come on over. I've got something I want to show you."

"What is it?"

"Something special, something you're really going to like!"

He sounded almost giddy, which was unusual for Mike. You
could tell he didn't want to come right out and tell me what it was,
so I didn't ask any more questions.

"Okay, see you in about an hour."

I had been buying marijuana from Mike for a few years. He
wasn't a dealer, just a guy with a connection who always scored
extra to sell to his friends at cost. He did the same thing with
cheese, nuts, spices, incense, pipes and wine, and I always thought
that if we had lived a hundred years ago, Mike would have run the
town store, the kind that sold everything from bullets to pickles
and doubled as the local post office.

It wasn't unusual for him to call when a new batch of weed
arrived, so I naturally assumed he'd gotten his hands on some
amazing smoke. But his tone and choice of words told me it might
be more than that. Normally, the code was "something new came
in," not "I want to show you something special, something you're

really going to like."

My guess was magic mushrooms, and as I tooled down the road towards Mike's place, I thought about a marvelously intense mushroom session we'd shared a few summers ago.

I can't remember precisely how long it had been since the last time I'd eaten shrooms before that, but it was probably five years at least, maybe more. Whatever. It had been long enough and the dose strong enough that several mirth-filled hours into the trip, I laughed at death for the first time in my life. Well, the thought of death, anyway.

I had moved about fifty feet away from the others and spread my yoga mat under an old sickle pear tree, a spot where we often saw groundhogs feasting on the fallen fruit. I lay on my back, staring up through the leaves and branches into the blue sky.

The giggles had subsided into a contented grin. Everything seemed in its proper place and exactly how it was supposed to be. I could feel the heat of the sun filtering through the shade and the ground under my body, and I was at one with both. I could smell every single plant individually the way you can separate the different instruments listening to music through earphones. At one point, I thought I felt the earth move beneath me. When I realized it was an optical illusion caused by the movement of the clouds past the gaps in the canopy, the giggles made a comeback.

As I continued to stare upward, it occurred to me that I was seeing the last thing a lot of dying men—soldiers on the battlefield, for example—see before they expire. I don't know why the thought crossed my mind, but it did. Instead of banishing the specter of my mortality as I normally would, I embraced the notion as naturally as I was embracing everything else at that moment, no thinking required.

What more could I ask for than to die outside on a beautiful day under a noble old tree, where my body could decay and fertilize the earth? It was just the next step of the ever evolving whole.

How fucking obvious! No wonder I started giggling again.

You can never replicate a trip like that. Even so, you keep trying, and if you're lucky, you might experience something totally different but equally blissful. Mike and I were always on the lookout for more mushrooms but found them difficult to score on a consistent basis.

Part of problem was our age. We're too old to hang out with the college kids, but the fact remains that college campuses are one of the easiest places to score recreational drugs, including psilocybin. The shrooms for the trip under the pear tree were obtained from a friend whose younger brother was in college.

When I was a teenager, an old rummy used to buy booze for our little gang of budding juvenile delinquents. The kindly lush was a house painter and rented a room from one of my friend's father. Since then, there's been a role reversal: Now I've got to get my psychedelics from kids 40 years younger than me. It's the kind of irony that makes you wince and smile simultaneously. But what's an old hippie to do? The wheel never stops turning, so you may as well forget finding a permanent groove.

For about five or six enchanted years, the social scene at Mike's had seemed close to idyllic, a place where aging hippies could recreate and relive their youth. But like everything else, a scene doesn't last forever, and the communal magic had been slowly slipping away for a year or so. As the gatherings became smaller, it started to feel like all the kids had gone away to college and left the adults at home alone. But the place itself remained special, and not just because Mike usually had weed for sale.

He lived in a mini-Eden, a totally improbable oasis hidden among urban sprawl, an unlikely haven where nature's embrace awaited you just a few hundred yards away from Babylon's four-lane blacktop. There was no direct entrance; you pulled off the road into a fast-food joint, headed toward the back of the parking lot and kept on going past the dumpsters until you came a to private driveway. By mid-spring, the trees, aided and abetted by wild grape vines and honeysuckle, had already formed a tunnel-like approach to the house and the fields beyond.

When I arrived the afternoon of Mike's phone call, he was on the flagstone patio, sitting in the shade of an old mulberry tree, reading the Sunday paper and sipping super-sweet iced tea. His pipe and smoking kit sat on a small table next to his lawn chair. Wasps buzzed around the grape arbor. A napping cat stirred when I closed the car door.

"So what's up?" I said, lowering myself into a lawn chair.

"You're not going to believe this. It's a once in a lifetime thing."

Mike placed something on the table in front of me. It wasn't mushrooms. It was a small brown bottle with a screw top and a white label, yellowed by age, with red lettering that read: "COCAINE SODIUM CHLORIDE."

It took a couple of heartbeats to fully comprehend what I was looking at, a time in which my preconditioned senses battled to catch up with a new reality. Then, it sunk in and my heart began to rev.

Holy shit! Sitting just an arm's length away was every coke fiend's wet dream and Holy Grail rolled into one—a bottle of pharmaceutical cocaine.

Virtually all cocaine users, regardless of whether they're sporadic dabblers, full-blown addicts, or something in between, will never sample the real deal—refined, not in some clandestine jungle lab, but under strict government guidelines by Merck & Co. of Rahway, New Jersey.

The bottle even had a one-dollar U.S. Government Tax Stamp still attached. It doesn't get any more official than that. Holy Shit! Indeed.

"Where the fuck did you get this, Mike?"

Mike shook a few tiny chunks of cocaine out of a small glass vile and onto a dark blue dinner plate, where the crystals came to rest, miniature icebergs in a ceramic sea.

Hunched over the table like an Antwerp diamond cutter, Mike first crumbled the rocks to sand-size with the flat bottom of the vile and then attacked them with a single-edged razor blade.

Chopping rapidly with surgeon-like precision, he carefully reduced the coke to a small pile of fine power. Then he divided the coke into six fat lines and sat back in his chair, taking his shadow with him and leaving the cocaine sparkling in the sunshine.

"Wait until you try this stuff," said Mike. "You're not going to believe how good it is."

My feelings about coke had always been ambiguous, partially because it seemed to bring out a side of my personality that I didn't like. It wasn't the high itself. On the rare occasions when I sampled something that hadn't been stepped on at least a half-dozen times, I found it exhilarating.

The bothersome part was that it made me selfish, more concerned with where the next line was coming from than almost anything else. Sharing with friends was secondary, especially when the stash was running low. Better to pretend you're dry and save the last few lines for yourself. I'd sensed right away that, for me anyway, coke was dangerous stuff.

If cannabis enhances life, cocaine could easily become its focal point, so I was always careful and never got in too deep. Perhaps that was because I had never had a regular source of quality product, but it's also true that I had never really searched very hard either. I came to think of it as an occasional treat, rather than a lifestyle.

Jimmie and I used to score an eight ball for the Christmas holidays, and because we both had similar misgivings, we made a pact to use it all by New Year's. There would be no squirreling it away, trying to make it last—just a spot of Christmas cheer and a few more lines for Auld Lang Syne. Ho, Ho, Ho. Laughing all the way.

Our annual ritual worked well, but not for long. After a couple of years, the quality got so poor that we eventually abandoned it by mutual consent. Nobody seemed to miss it that much.

Another guy I knew dealt blackjack at a casino and coke on the side. He seemed to have an endless supply and happily laid out line after line whenever you visited him in the house he'd purchased with the profits. He would also sell friends all they wanted at a ridiculously cheap price. There was only one problem: I don't think it was really cocaine.

I never had it analyzed, of course, but my guess is that it was some sort of bootleg meth, mixed with a mild numbing agent to give customers the impression that they scored the real thing. After a few unsatisfactory sessions, I left whatever it was alone.

Then there was an old girlfriend who worked on and off for a mid-level dealer, and sometimes she gave me a taste of something decent. But when our relationship ended, so did the perks. I missed the sex far more than the coke, anyway.

Mike, however, had been a heavy user for a number of years until something happened that convinced him to quit. It was probably just dumb luck, but I've come to think of this windfall as a sort of cosmic reward for being a dedicated head of some five-decades standing. I know it sounds farfetched, if not completely addlebrained, but maybe you will change your mind when you know the whole story.

Mike estimates that during a span of about five years in the 1970s, he spent roughly $30,000 on coke, which eventually resulted in surgery for a deviated septum. It was not, however, the money or the operation that convinced him to "let that cocaine be." It was being ripped-off by somebody he thought was his friend.

His career took Mike away from his hometown for about 20 years, but from time to time he returned to visit his parents and hang out with old friends. Knowing his homies would like nothing better than to join him in a razor party, Mike figured he'd take a nice-size stash with him.

A co-worker was his contact, a guy he'd been getting high with and scoring from for months, so Mike didn't think twice about giving him $1100, figuring he'd get the coke the following day as always. He didn't even worry when the guy wasn't at work the next morning, but when he failed to show up again the day after that, he drove over to his house to see what was up.

It turned out to be a double bummer: The fucking dirt bag had ditched his wife and taken off with Mike's money.

"His wife told me that he had done the same thing to two other regular customers, taken everybody's money and run away with his girl friend," said Mike. "I knew the girlfriend. Besides being real good-looking, she was an exhibitionist and never wore panties if she had on a skirt or a dress. Not the brightest chick in the world, but fun to be with. I never saw either of them again."

Although $1100 was a lot of money in the mid-1970s, Mike took his loss philosophically and decided it was a sign that it was time to give up cocaine. Over the next 20 years or so, he indulged a few times whenever something came his way, but never went back to buying coke on a regular basis.

Then, suddenly and completely unexpectedly, he had become the elated owner of almost 10 grams of pharmaceutical cocaine. It didn't exactly fall out of the sky into his lap but came to him through a series of circumstances almost as improbable.

"I got a call from Butch yesterday," said Mike, picking a short length of drinking straw and bending over the dinner plate again.

He inhaled two fat lines and leaned back in his chair, a faint look of surprise on his face. When he leaned forward and began to speak, I thought I saw something resembling yellow lightning flickering deep in the recesses of his eye.

"Butch knows a guy who's a veterinarian, and a friend of his, another veterinarian, retired and gave Butch's friend his vet's bag, figuring as he was still practicing, he might be able to make good use of it."

Mike passed me the straw and continued to talk as I leaned over the plate.

"All of the contents were still inside the guy's bag, including surgical instruments, and among all the other stuff was the bottle of coke. It turned out that the retired vet had specialized in eye surgery and used it as a local anesthetic. He would dissolve a small rock in water and drop it in the animal's eye. Butch said he did a lot of work with horses"

I snorted a line up my right nostril, took a breath, and then snorted another up my left—the ever popular one and one.

I relaxed, waiting for the rush to hit me. But instead of a rush, it was more like stepping off an elevator into a much higher realm. One second you were on the ground floor and the next you'd arrived. The journey between the two points so fast, it was as if it didn't exist. You're just suddenly there.

"What do you think?" said Mike, who, judging by the smile on his face, already knew the answer.

"This shit is too good for horses." I said, laughing at my own dumb joke. "I've never had anything anywhere near as good as this; it's a different high all together."

"I know. It's so clean. Wait until you see how long it lasts. There's none of that do-a-couple-of-lines-and-then-have-to-do-more-15-minutes-later crap. There's no crash either. This shit is amazing!"

Mike was right. Merck's manna and street coke were beyond comparison—two different beasts altogether, linked by a little more than a name. Street coke is hyper, chatty, and aggressive, with a jagged edge and a fatiguing crash. The pharmaceutical variety sharpens all your senses to the point that you become kind of a super version of yourself, not omnipotent or anything ridiculous like that. For me, it was more like being reborn into a better world where you were also better; the same yet better.

Mike and I explored that world over the next six or seven hours, sitting on the patio, surrounded by a hundred shades of green and sheltered by a bright blue sky. Abandoned chicken coops, overgrown with wild grape and honeysuckle vines, looked as beautiful as the ruins of antiquity. The meadow, with its clumps of roughly mowed grass turning dirty yellow in the sun, was an impressionist landscape come to life.

Beyond the abandoned vegetable garden, crows circled their home in a stand of evergreen trees, a place where an old plow lay rusting in the grass and wildflowers grew between the poison ivy.

If it had not been Sunday, we might have pulled an all-nighter, but I had to go to work the next morning, so after a mammoth session in which we shared something in the neighborhood of 16 lines, I headed back down the same road I'd traveled earlier that day.

In my pocket was a vile of coke, and in my mind the notion that the retired vet's bottle, which had found its way into our hands by such a circuitous and unlikely route, was guided by more than just unimaginably good luck. Maybe Mike had finally taken delivery of the coke he'd paid for two decades earlier, and in the meantime, it had appreciated greatly in both purity and potency.

Maybe it really was a bonus bestowed upon us by some patron saint of stoners. The circle seemed too complete to be totally random.

Then again, when you get right down to it, it doesn't really matter how or why we got it. The important thing was that we had enough of the finest cocaine known to man to keep us soaring to unprecedented heights for the foreseeable future. And best of all, our feet never had to leave the ground.

POET AT THE WHEEL

A thunderclap startled me awake. Half a heartbeat later, a lightning bolt illuminated a vehicular nightmare on the other side of the windshield, a cluster fuck of mangled machinery and large, fast-moving objects.

Two cars were smashed into the concrete highway divider, another into the side of a fourth. About 20 feet in front of us, two other cars were spinning in circles, both of them headed in our general direction.

The percussive din of the rain pelting the car's roof drowned out all other noise. There was no time to panic, nothing to do but be there and watch.

And watch I did as Dorazzo steered our rented Impala through the gauntlet like a stunt driver in a movie. He zigged when he had to zig and zagged when he had to zag. Suddenly, we were past the danger zone and out the other end, sending up a rooster tail of water that obscured the rapidly receding chaos.

I glanced over at Dorazzo. He was squinting through the windshield as the wipers struggled to clear a wedge of vision. His left hand was on the wheel, his right pushing a CD into the dashboard player.

"Why don't you fill the pipe," he said, as the sound of Miles Davis softened the rain's staccato insistence.

I stuffed some marijuana into a pipe, passed it to him, and then reached over and held the lighter over top of the bowl so he didn't have to turn his head to inhale.

"That was fucking amazing, man. You saved our ass."

Dorazzo nodded his massive head, his shaggy hair bobbing slightly in the dim light. He held the toke tightly in his chest, stifled a cough, and finally exhaled a trace of smoke.

"Why don't you fill it again?" he said, handing me back the pipe.

Later that night, after we'd checked into our downtown hotel room, we kept right on smoking, one pipe after another, as fatigue battled a lingering residue of adrenalin.

"I still can't believe how calmly you maneuvered through those cars," I said a few hours before dawn. "We're lucky I wasn't driving. I'm not sure I could have done what you did."

All my previous attempts to get Dorazzo to talk about our narrow escape had been good-naturedly rebuffed, but not this time.

"I've never been so scared in my life," he said.

Suddenly, for the first time that night, I was scared too.

Like wanderers from Ibn Battuta to Jack Kerouac, we were in search of the moment, hoping to find it, if only briefly, in the freedom of the road. But the incident had been a potent reminder of how quickly things could change and that a ticket to ride didn't always guarantee that you would reach your destination.

But our luck had held, the run from Tucson to L.A. miraculously completed. We were well supplied with a variety of controlled substances, had money in our pockets and many miles of highway ahead of us. Life was good.

Dorazzo and I were simpatico. I realized that the first time we met, more than 20 years ago. It was at Caesars Palace in Las Vegas where we chugged pina coladas at the poolside bar with a guy from Japan before going to my room to smoke some pot and snort a few lines of coke.

It was more than a mutual love of getting high that drew us together. There is a natural synergy to our relationship, a common wavelength of unspoken understanding that enhances the moment as surely as the drugs we imbibe.

It's a common enough experience but precious nonetheless. You can't create this sort of interpersonal phenomenon by taking drugs, but the right drugs (cannabis and some stimulants) can trigger the right synapses, the ones that connect a bridge of shared comprehension—a bridge that can sometimes lead us to a place where we can glimpse the bigger picture.

Either that or we're so stoned, it just seems that way. But it doesn't really matter. You can feel it right down in the core, down where it counts.

Physically, Dorazzo always reminded me of John Belushi, short and powerful, with wide shoulders and fullback calves. His longish hair and disheveled sense of style brand him a counterculture figure of undetermined caste—too energetic to be the stoner burnout his wardrobe suggests, but too sweet-natured to be the lumbering desperado his bear-like presence could invoke.

What Dorazzo really is, is a poet. And if he has not pursued his dream of writing a poem that will save the world as vigorously as he once imagined he would—so what? He moves through life with a poet's sensibilities, linking the couplets of existence into something approaching a whole.

■■■

I was the first awake the day after our freeway freak-out. Even though it had happened hours ago, the incident was still buzzing around my brain, sending me mixed signals as I brushed my teeth and took a shower.

Was it a warning, foreshadowing catastrophe further on up the road? Or was it proof of the righteousness of our cause, a signal that we were aligned with the cosmic forces and could, temporarily at least, do no wrong?

Maybe the minefield of cars parted for us the same way the Red Sea parted for Moses. You think about that shit after a close call. You can't help it.

Most likely, it was dumb luck and Dorazzo's survival instincts that saved us, not that stoner crap about being "aligned with the cosmic forces." But what is luck anyway, just random chance, an arbitrary byproduct of mathematical chaos? Or can luck be courted, perhaps controlled? Terry certainly thought so, and although it was more than 40 years ago, I have not forgotten what he taught me about magic and the power of the mind.

Just the same, as I dried myself in a thin hotel towel and took a final peek at my unshaven face, I was happy just to be alive and didn't really care why. There would be plenty of time for navel-gazing later. At that moment, more than anything else, I was hungry.

Dorazzo was sitting up in bed when I came out of the bathroom, one hand scratching his balls, the other reaching for his eyeglasses on the bedside table.

"Hungry?"

"Sure, let's go to the Standard," he said, lurching to his feet and then quickly sitting down again. "Give a minute to get my shit together."

Fifteen minutes later, we were walking up South Flower, headed toward Sixth Street and what *Playboy*, called "The Hippest Hotel in Hollywood." But, really, how long had it been since *Playboy* was hip?

True, the Standard had its trademark upside down sign going for it, a cool rooftop swimming pool, and overpriced rooms, populated by desperately trendy yuppies. For us, however, the main attractions were the delicious, reasonably priced breakfast and free pool table in the lobby.

"Want to take a ride around town and check out the scene before we head to Vegas?" asked Dorazzo between bites of Eggs Benedict.

"Sounds good. Let's go back to our room after we're finished eating, get high and hit the road."

"Okay, but let's shoot a game of pool first."

I washed down my final bites of pancakes and strawberries with my second cup of coffee and before we began playing, the five mgs of amphetamine I'd swallowed with my papaya juice kicked in. We shot three games of eight ball in what seemed like five minutes. I won the first game, Dorazzo the next two. We both sucked.

After packing everything except our stash, we got down to the serious business of getting primed for the journey. Two shared pipes of designer weed and two lines each of Mike's pharmaceutical cocaine propelled us out of the hotel and onto the highway.

I don't recall checking out or getting the car. It seemed that we were in the room one minute and the next we were rolling down the road, each moment so crammed with life that there was no room for its predecessor—just like my bicycle ride through Hoge Veluwe Park, only this time I wasn't steering.

"I'm way too high to be driving," said Dorazzo, laughing as he gunned the Impala into traffic.

"At least it isn't raining."

DINOSAUR DAZE

The luminous rush from the pharmaceutical cocaine probably had a lot to do with the way things went down. That and the complimentary buzz coming from the brain-bending sativa we'd smoked back at the hotel. But as Timothy Leary used to preach, "set" and "setting" are critical.

Dorazzo and I had both bases covered. Set and setting were virtually one in the same, two parts of the whole feeding off each other. Our immediate setting was a brand-new rented automobile, the six-cylinder magic carpet that has become the symbol of the modern American road trip. In a different place and time, the vehicle could just as well have been a wagon, camel, or ship. Feet work too.

The road itself is the larger setting, an enchanted realm whose transient nature helps creates the mindset we seek, a unique kind of freedom where the only obligation is to keep moving. We all have sand in our shoes, even those among us too numb to feel the chafe.

Mankind has been on the road since our origins as hunters and gatherers, and the urge to roam remains as much a part of our DNA as the survival instinct. Nomadic people have always understood how the journey soothes our souls and invigorates our spirits in a way no other lifestyle can. That's why they fight so hard to stay free of the shackles imposed by modern society and its constipated value system.

Like Aboriginals of the Australian Outback and the Tuareg

of the Western Sahara, we all feel that same restless stirring within us. It's just buried deep, shoved down and sublimated by centuries of worshiping the fickle gods of materialism. But we feel it nonetheless, a remote yearning bubbling below the surface that erupts, often unrecognized, when we take to the highway, an unidentified joy rising within.

"Check this out," said Dorazzo, slipping a CD into the player.

We were cruising down Wilshire Boulevard, heading for the Le Brea Tar Pits, the famous dinosaur trap, incongruously located in downtown L.A. I hoped Dorazzo didn't want to stop and get out when we got there. It felt so good just riding in the car, soaking in the sunny urban landscape, as my faithful friend steered our chariot through the City of Angels. I didn't want to do anything else. I was totally content with the way things were.

"Let's do a drive-by at the Tar Pits," I suggested.

Dorazzo laughed, and, as the melancholy sound of a peddle-steel guitar oozed out of the speakers, he turned up the volume and handed me the CD case. It was Tom Russell's *Hotwalker*, which turned out to be the key to a more expansive trip than expected.

Russell grew up in L.A. back in the 1950s and '60s, and *Hotwalker* is his homage to a time that has passed, a time that seemed, viewed through Russell's nostalgic eye, much more desirable than the dreary landscape of 21st century L.A.

Russell sings of a time when two blind sisters sang gospel songs and begged in Pershing Square, keeping beat with the change in their tin cup. A time when Charles Bukowski, America's poet laureate of skid row, and Little Jack Horton, a carnival midget, got so drunk that they stole a train. It was a time when cats like Chet Baker, Art Pepper, and Miles gave birth to Cool Jazz in beatnik clubs such as the Lighthouse in Venice Beach. Less than a hundred miles up the road, Buck Owens and Merle Haggard cranked up the electrified twang and invented the Bakersfield sound.

It was also a time when claiming races were fixed and both

the horses and the jockeys were hopped up on the same dope, a time when teenagers went to Tijuana for the girls, cheap booze, and bullfights. But most of all, it was a time, as Bukowski wrote, before the United States turned into a "nation of domesticated animals."

Listening to *Hotwalker* took us as close to being part of that world as we would ever get. The juxtaposition of what was passing before our eyes and the sound-driven images of an earlier time melted together. It was like being in two places at once, a different set of senses in different dimensions—part of us anchored in the L.A. of today, part of us flashing back to a time that evoked the outlaw lifestyle we still espouse to, if only in our hearts.

Norteno accordion music jumped out of the car's speakers and slugged it out toe-to-toe with the sounds of Saturday afternoon traffic. Outside our Detroit-built, drug-powered time machine, the scene was closer to Bukowski's L.A. than I had originally realized: Domestics with tired feet waited for buses to carry them back to the barrio, fast-food franchises peddled slow death, and an insane bum ranted at the sky, his grimy face streaked with tears.

Maybe time is like a radio dial on which you can tune in a particular frequency on the eternal continuum. All you need to do is to figure out how to turn on the radio. I guess that's what this road trip was really all about, a way to maintain a link with our past, to those long-ago summers we hold close to our hearts, lest they slip away and crumble to dust before we do.

Two relics on their way to a dinosaur graveyard, listening to the ghosts of the past and sucking on last night's roach.

PART

Five

Amsterdam Redux

LET'S NOT AND SAY WE DID

Mike opened the little drawer in the side table, the one where he keeps dozens of stories he's cut out of newspapers and magazines. He fished out a fresh clipping and handed it to me with a look of resignation.

"Here's that article I told you about."

"What article?"

"The one about the tourist chick who overdosed on mushrooms in Amsterdam and died."

"Died! How many fucking mushrooms did she eat?"

"I don't know, but they're going to stop selling them."

"Stop selling them?!"

I reluctantly took the proffered clipping, folded it in half and tucked it in my notebook. I didn't want to read it, actually see the words in print. It had only been a year or so since my first visit to Amsterdam and I was horrified at the thought that the idyllic stoners' paradise had caved in to the forces of conformity.

Besides, it was too late to change plans. JR and I had already booked our flights to Amsterdam and made a down payment on an apartment we were going to rent for two weeks. I wouldn't have turned back, anyway, not even if I could have gotten a refund on my nonrefundable ticket and apartment deposit. I'd been plotting my return since the end of my first visit. No newspaper clipping was going to change that. I needed to see for myself.

"I'll read it later. Let's do another pipe."

Mike filled his sebsi with New York Diesel, a potent high-end hybrid, and passed it to me. I took a toke and leaned back in my chair, slowly exhaling a column of sweet-smelling white smoke into the room. The distressing news from Amsterdam quickly receded as the cannabis took hold and refocused my mind on the irresistible sound of Little Walter coming out of Mike's sound system.

"Boom Boom (Out Go The Light)"

Alas, music's ability to calm the savage beast of paranoia is transitory at best, and the unread newspaper clipping in my notebook continued to gnaw at the pleasurable anticipation normally associated with an upcoming holiday. I told myself that as long as they don't close the coffee shops, everything would be okay. Don't sweat it. Just be happy there's still a place where you can get high in a public setting.

But the alarmist yin to my conciliatory yang tugged rudely at the elbow of my thoughts, demanding I listen to its contradictory point of view: *Wake up, stupid. If mushrooms have really been outlawed, it could be the thin edge of the wedge. Cannabis might be next!*

So it was with a mixture of uncertainty and optimism that I tightened my seat belt and glanced over at JR as our plane made its descent out of a cloudy morning sky—Schipol International Airport coming up fast somewhere below.

"We're getting ready to land."

JR took off his eyeglasses and rubbed his eyes with his knuckles. He looked like he was trying to pretend I wasn't there and hadn't said anything. Asleep was where he wanted to be, but his cause was helpless and he knew it.

"Okay," he said softly, pulling a comb from his pocket and rearranging his thinning strands into something that looked like a parody of a sixth-grader's hairdo on class-picture day.

"Do you want some amphetamine?" I whispered, taking my pewter pillbox from the watch pocket of my jeans.

"No, thanks. But I wouldn't say no to a cup of coffee."

"Shit, man. This stuff is ten times as good as coffee."

"That's what I'm afraid of."

I had hardly slept on the flight and had no intention of going to bed any time soon, so I popped 10 mgs of amphetamine into my mouth and washed it down with a swig of water. The Netherlands, still shrouded in early-morning fog, was beginning to stir as our plane coasted to a stop and dislodged its cargo.

We showed our passports, retrieved our bags from the carousel and cruised through the "nothing to declare" line and into the train station. We purchased two one-way tickets to Centraal Station and, twenty minutes later, we were standing once again in Amsterdam, squarely in the eye of a hedonistic hurricane, suitcases in our hands, a scrap of paper with the address to our apartment stuffed in my shirt pocket.

Following the requisite bout of directional disorientation, we got our act together and found the apartment, which was on Kloveniersburwal just a few minutes walk south of Nieuwmarkt. It was conveniently located above the Goa coffee shop, where we rendezvoused with our rental agent, Francois, a sexy-looking woman in her 30s who spoke English with a French accent. She showed us the apartment, took our money, gave us the keys, and disappeared on her bicycle.

Our third-floor apartment was quite large by Amsterdam standards: a spacious living room-kitchen combo that overlooked the canal, a bedroom, a bathroom (complete with washing machine and dryer) and shower, all fairly new and in good working condition. The TV and CD player worked too. There were even a few sodas in the refrigerator and enough pasta and tomato paste to rustle up a meal.

Sounds of the street floated up and into the apartment through an open window—snatches of conversation, shouts, laughter, bike bells, the purr of a passing motor scooter, the distant clanging of trams. Adding to the sensory smorgasbord was the musky odor of smoldering cannabis wafting skyward from the front porch of the Goa.

The sun was threatening to break through the cloud cover, and as I sank deeper into the couch, I felt strangely at home. But what is home without a pipe and a little something to smoke? It was time to go shopping.

Jet lagged JR was already snoozing when I locked the apartment door behind me and rode the painfully slow elevator to the ground floor. I strolled down Oude Hoogstrat toward the Dam and stopped at the first store that displayed pipes in the window. With such a vast selection available throughout the city, there's a temptation to buy an expensive pipe. But knowing that it would end up in a trash bin in two weeks, I settled for a midrange, wooden one and a pack of screens for 8 euros.

As I handed the clerk the money, I noticed a refrigerated glass case in back of the counter. It was filled with fresh magic mushrooms, sealed in plastic containers.

"Let me have a pack of mushrooms too," I said.

"Which ones?"

"The Colombians."

"That will be another 13 euro, please," the clerk said, adding a 35-gram pack of McSmart brand Psilocyne Colombiescenes to the bag that already held my pipe and screens.

"I thought they were going to ban mushrooms because some tourist died?"

"Nee, they just make us stop selling dried ones."

"Oh, I see. Dag."

"Tot ziens."

A few doors down the street I purchased two grams of Northern Lights (one of the first successful hybrids) at a nondescript coffee shop with a crude image of Bob Marley painted on its sign and then I headed back to the apartment. Not only did I want to cop a buzz, I now dared to read Mike's newspaper clipping.

According to Associated Press, Gaelle Caroff, a 17-year-old French student with psychological problems, had jumped from a building to her death after eating psychedelic mushrooms on a school trip. Miss Caroff's parents blamed the psilocybin, and that, along with the negative publicity and a handful of other allegedly mushroom-inspired, nonfatal incidents, was enough to get some new legislation passed. Enforcement, however, seemed a different story all together. Even so, the forces of repression were on the march, and this time the ranks of citizens who remember the Nazi occupation are considerably thinner.

BO DIDDLEY IS DEAD

It all started outside the Anne Frank House on a beautiful spring afternoon. I didn't really want to be there, but JR wanted to take the tour, so I tagged along, figuring that if I waited for him outside the negative vibe wouldn't blow my high.

Like most Boomers, I had known about Anne Frank since I was a kid, seen the Millie Perkins movie and read Anne's diary for a high school assignment. Not that I needed such a horrific tale to remind me of the evil incarnate that was Nazi Germany. My father served in the Royal Air Force throughout World War II, my mother lived through the Blitz (Uncle Wally didn't), and I played in the ruins of bombed buildings as a boy in England.

But visiting the house where doomed Anne and her family hid from the monsters who roamed the very same cobblestone streets that now carries me from coffee shop to coffee shop is not my idea of holiday fun. Bummers will occur naturally as the wheel turns. Why seek them out?

Instead, I sat on a bench, watching the line of tourists move slowly past and into the house at 263 Prinsengracht, where they paid 9 euros to see Anne's secret refuge from the same insanity that is still devouring the world. A pleasant buzz lingered from the cannabis I'd smoked before leaving the apartment. A warm breeze caressed my face.

There was a woman around my age, maybe a little older, also sitting on the same bench, and she struck up a conversation.

"Are you going in?" she said and glanced at the house.

"No, I'm waiting for a friend. It's too depressing for me."

"I know what you mean. I'm not going in either, but my daughter wanted to, so I'm waiting for her."

She paused briefly, probably trying to decide whether or not to say more, and then continued.

"I used to ride my bicycle past here all the time when I was a little girl."

"You're from Amsterdam?"

"Originally, but I moved to Michigan years and years ago. I'm just visiting."

"Were you here during the war?"

"Yes, I was a child."

"That must have been very difficult."

"Yes, the Germans came to our house one day and took my father away. They sent him to a work camp in Poland."

"Jeez, I'm sorry."

"That's okay. It was a long time ago, and besides, he survived."

"What happened?"

"It was winter and all the prisoners were either starving or freezing to death, so my father and some other men decided it would be better to die trying to get away than dying in the camp. They walked away from a work detail, hid during the day—farmers helped and fed them—and traveled at night. It took him weeks, but he finally made it back home. When my mother answered the knock at the door, she didn't recognize him at first"

The woman paused again and laughed softly.

"You know how kids are," she said. "The thing I remember the most was that he had to be deloused in the backyard before my mother would let him stay in the house. I can still see him, naked and shivering as she washed him down with some sort of special soap."

I chuckled with her at the mental picture she had held on to for so long, a moment of humor amid fearful circumstances. But our mirth ended when a woman in her late 30s approached, dabbing at her mascara-smeared eyes with a tissue.

"It's so sad," she said, glancing at me as her mother stood and wrapped her arms around her.

"I know, honey. I know. Let's go and get the kids."

The mother looked over her shoulder as they slowly walked away and mouthed the words "good bye." I waved and smiled weakly.

What a mind fuck! Instead of visiting a ghost house, I'd had an encounter with a living witness to the Nazi occupation of Amsterdam. I felt mildly disoriented, and it was good to see JR heading my way a few minutes later, the same deadpan expression on his face as when he went into the house.

"How was it?" I asked.

It was a stupid question but it was the best I could come up with.

"It was okay."

As we walked back to the apartment, I told JR about the woman, but he was no help in sorting out my feelings.

"How about that?" was all he said.

The freaky thing was that, even though the woman spoke of a terrible time when unthinkable things happened, talking to her was a warm, pleasurable experience. It made me feel happy, sad, and guilty at the same time, an unfamiliar jumble of emotions that was hard to pin down.

A dark mood had descended, certainly, but not without occasional flashes of insight to help light the way. The woman's story was one such beacon, the gift of hope passed down from her father, through her, to me—a random beneficiary who just happened to be sitting on the same bench.

The next sensory mind fuck was much more belligerent and lay in ambush, waiting for us to step out of the elevator and onto the hallway outside our third-floor apartment.

"It smells like a dead body!" I gasped, as the revolting stench washed over us like an olfactory tsunami.

"Gag me with a maggot," said JR, sounding like the world's oldest third-grader, as I held my breath and fumbled with the key and lock.

Quickly—well, as quickly as an old stoner and his procrastinating pal could manage—we scurried inside. Thankfully, the appalling stink was held at bay by the tight-fitting door and the breeze blowing in the partially open windows. Safe in the bosom of our rented sanctuary, the stink bomb in the hallway was temporarily forgotten.

I dug out my pipe and stash and put on a Hank Crawford/ Jimmy McGriff CD. A couple of pipes of Northern Lights later, I was gazing out the windows, feeling the groove, and digging the scene on the street below. JR sat at the table, editing the manuscript that would eventually become the first half of this book.

Northern Lights is an early hybrid, approximately two-thirds sativa and one-third indica, first developed in the 1970s. Some locals, spoiled by the profusion of products available in the Netherlands, look down on this venerable strain of weed, but the Northern Light #5 that I was smoking was a former Cannabis Cup winner and a very spacey high.

Even so, what I saw taking place outside my window was not a hallucination. Northern Lights isn't that good. What I saw was really taking place.

A young woman dressed in a white wedding gown was being hung from a tree growing next to the canal. It took me a second or two to realize what was going on, but I needed confirmation.

"Hey, get a look at this. They're hanging some chick from a tree."

JR rose reluctantly from his chair, a semi-disgusted expression on his face. That's the way he reacts to seemingly ridiculous situations, as if they're an insult to his intelligence, some sort of childish prank. But it's only a front, a defensive maneuver to give him time to think. He's all too aware of the likelihood of the unlikely.

"I think it must be a photo shoot of some sort," I said when JR reached the window.

Sure enough, there was a group of people scurrying around the girl in the tree like worker bees servicing a doomed queen—fixing her hair, rearranging her gown, and, most vitally, supporting her weight, so she didn't actually hang. But what if the ladder or somebody's hand slipped?

"Good grief!" said JR

He gave the mock hanging a perfunctory once-over and returned to his task without further comment, leaving me alone at the window, trying to ward off an uninvited and deepening funk.

Apparently, the clowns behind the photo project hadn't figured out a way to get a full-body shot without breaking the model's neck. I felt sorry for her. She deserved better. Still, that did not stop me from fantasizing about fucking her while she was wearing the wedding dress and matching white pumps.

When the CD ended, I turned on the TV. A second later I wished I hadn't. CNN was broadcasting a mini-tribute to Bo Diddley, who had just died at his home in Archer, Florida.

I had hoped to watch *SpongeBob*, which is fall-down funny in Dutch, especially when you're whacked out on high-grade nederweit. But instead, I ended up with another blister on my heart. Even JR seemed genuinely disconcerted.

"Oh, no!" he wailed, his face twisting into a pantomime mask of agony.

It's his stock response to bad news, and when he does it, he screws his eyes shut and dips his head down and sideways.

"Yeah, it's a fucking bummer," I said. "He was a true American Master. Did you ever see him live?"

JR shook his head sadly and made the face again.

I was lucky. I had seen Bo three times over the years, and each performance was better than the last. The final time was outdoors at night, about nine or ten years prior; Mike was with me, and we'd eaten some pot brownies. There was a big crowd of around 6,000 wildly cheering Bo on, and he responded with a powerhouse performance.

I can still see him standing in the orange spotlight, linebacker legs spread wide and planted, hollering into the night sky and thrashing his rectangular guitar loud enough to be heard on Mars. The sound came up through the ground he was standing on, from the earth itself, passed through his body, and was transformed into a something as primeval as it was irresistible.

"Bo Diddley was the fucking King Kong of guitar players!"

"Hey, that's a good line," said JR, without looking up. "You should use it."

I made a dismissive sound and reached for my stash.

"Want to get high?"

"No, thanks. I want to finish this."

I turned off the TV, slid a Jimmy Smith CD into the player and took my time rolling a fatty. I used a cocktail of Northern Lights, Amnesia, and Ice (a Skunk/Northern Lights/Shiva hybrid) and twisted it up in a couple of Spanish King Size Slim Papers.

The joint wasn't perfect, not like the machine-rolled ones Mike makes. Shit, Mike's joints looked like Camels. But mine was fat and firm, packed with well-manicured weed and tailored for a clean draw.

When I'd finished the joint and the spit had dried, I fired it up with the bootleg Marley lighter I'd bought at a souvenir shop near the Dam. I knew better, but I was hoping a massive infusion of cannabis would chase away the shadow of the Reaper. A half hour later, the CD was over and I still hadn't finished the joint— lost in the music, temporarily transported to a place where only the music and my body existed.

But when the music stopped, the magical barrier evaporated and other worlds flooded back, including a faint whiff of the abomination in the hallway.

FINDING THE GROOVE AGAIN

The girl behind the counter at Coffee Shop Ben had short hair and wore an even shorter denim miniskirt. She was in her twenties, Moroccan maybe and sexy in her way. A North African Betty Boop, complete with kiss curls and a bow-tie lips, but with a normal voice—kind of husky, actually.

She took a Tupperware container and a small electronic scale from under the counter and weighed the dope, three grams of nicely manicured buds of Amnesia (a cross of Skunk, Cinderella 99 and Jack Herer). She handed over the weed, took my money, and gave me my change, which I threw in the little metal tip basket.

Coffee Shop Ben was pretty much a dump, with a real bog of a shithouse. But I was drawn to the dark, den-like atmosphere, and if you looked closely, you could still see dusty reminders of the original decor concept—a Moroccan café, minus the dancing boy.

A dusty, old kif bag and a couple of ancient drums hung on a wall, and some of the tables were still recognizable as Moroccan after decades of abuse. The Ben also featured uncomfortable Moroccan-style seats, the type that are built into the wall like a ledge.

That the seats might discourage customers from lingering too long was probably coincidental. As far as I could tell, as long as you're consuming something they'd sold you—cannabis, drinks, snacks—it was cool to stay there as long as you wanted. I sat there for more than an hour writing postcards and smoking Amnesia in the semidarkness.

The room was enclosed in glass and from certain angles you could see a kaleidoscope of images, reflections of images, and reflections of reflections. They all interacted and merged with one another to create an endless chain of reflections, seemingly stretching into infinity.

The neon-splashed funhouse-mirror effect reached out the front door and into the street. It looked like a portal to another dimension. Maybe it was. All I know is that when I finally left the Ben, I was so stoned I forgot my reading glasses, left them lying on the table along with the empty mango-juice bottle and dirty ashtray.

When I went back to get them half an hour later, Betty Boop saw me come in and had my glasses in her hand by the time I reached the counter. She smiled and held them out to me.

"Thanks. No wonder they called it Amnesia."

She laughed.

I wandered outside again, full of cannabis and the giddy rush of making a sexy young woman laugh. Before I took another step, the yummy aroma drifting out of the Wok and Walk next door ambushed me. Thai women who work there will cook any kind of stir-fry you want. It's almost worth the price of a meal to watch them wield their woks and spatulas. They worked quickly and efficiently amid a great chaos of heat, steam and sizzling, turning out one delicious, made-to-order meal after another.

I scarfed down my spicy noodles and veggies almost as quickly as they had cooked it, and headed back toward the Dam, stopping at Rene's on Damstraat for raspberry tarts. I bought two and ate one before I got back to the apartment. The Amsterdam munchies are a bitch.

JR had just got out of the shower and was putting on his baggy slacks when I opened the door.

"Hey, you're finally awake. Do you want this tart before I eat it?"

"No thanks. I was about to go get some lunch."

"I just ate, but I'll come with you and get some coffee."

JR nodded and began the ritualistic-like fiddle fucking around that inevitably accompanies his departure from virtually anywhere. His friends tease him about it, but I would not be surprised if he actually exaggerates the old-lady routine on purpose. JR has been known to keep a running gag going for decades, even if he's the only one laughing.

While I waited for my friend to get his shit together, I had a couple of tokes of Amnesia over by the window and watched the passing parade—the usual mix of locals going about their daily business, freaks freaking and tourists dragging their wheeled suitcases over the cobbles.

About five minutes later I turned around and was surprised to see JR standing in front of the door, staring at it like a dog waiting to be taken for a walk. He hadn't said a word, just walked over to the door and waited until I noticed he was ready to go. Goodness knows how long he'd been there. I've known JR half my life, and there are plenty of times when I'm not sure whether he's joking or not. Maybe he doesn't know either.

"Okay," I said. "Let's go."

We turned left outside the apartment gate, walked past the Goa and down Kloveniersburwal toward the row of cafes that lined our side of the canal near Nieuwmarket Square. De Waag (Weight House), a chunky castle-like building that dates back to the late-15th century, dominates the square.

Originally, De Waag was part of the city's fortifications, known as St Anthoniespoort, but 100 years later it became the city's weight house, with various guilds occupying the upper floor. By the 19th century, it was the site of public executions, an eerie foreshadowing of the German occupation, when Jews were assembled outside the Waag prior to being deported to Nazi concentration camps.

Today, the Waag is a fancy restaurant. Across the square sits the Jolly Joker, one of several coffee shops nestled among the bars and cafes. They seem the ultimate rebuke to totalitarianism and tyranny, but I know their existence is transitory. As, indeed, were the Nazis'.

Like Evelyn Waugh, I was just lucky to be there when "the going was good." Ironically, considering who I am and where I was, I had trouble letting go. It takes me a while, even in Amsterdam, before I realize my best course of action is total surrender. Amsterdam will take care of the rest.

BRUNCH IN BRUGES

The green and soggy Netherlands flicked past outside the train windows like a chain of slightly out-of-focus frames from a movie reel. The friendly women who sold us our tickets said it would be a long ride. An hour outside of Amsterdam, I wondered if it was going to be too long.

JR and I needed a change of pace and neither of us had ever been to Belgium, so we took the 9:56 a.m. train from Amsterdam to Antwerp, where we had to switch trains to reach Bruges by mid-afternoon.

There was, however, a faded Belgium link for me. My father had been there during World War II. I have a photograph of him standing outside a Belgian pub, wearing his Royal Air Force uniform and smoking a pipe. All he ever said about his time there was that he had to eat "bloody dog biscuits" for weeks on end. Occasionally, it seems, washed down with Belgium beer.

I didn't know what would happen, if anything, when the train crossed the border into Belgium, so after a morning smoke, I had left my stash back at the apartment. I did, however, have 5 mgs of amphetamine in my system and 15 mgs more in my pewter pillbox. Gradually, the stimulant began to take hold: The weariness and years faded, replaced by a relaxed alertness and an urge to talk.

"We've only got 15 minutes to change trains in Antwerp," I said.

JR appeared to be either asleep or in a trance. But I knew

better.

"Good grief," he said, suddenly sitting erect and looking at his watch. He screwed his face into his patented pained expression and looked at his watch again. The conductor passed, swaying with the train the way a sailor sways with a ship. Before I could stop myself, I was off on another riff.

"Did I ever tell you about the couple I knew who got robbed on a train in India?"

JR looked at me the way Squidward looks at SpongeBob.

"Go on."

"It was Dave and Nancy. You probably met them at one of Mike's Halloween party's. Anyway, they took the old hippie hash-trail back in the late '60s, started in Morocco and kept going all the way to Afghanistan and beyond.

One night in India, when they were asleep in their berth, somebody slit open their sleeping bags and took everything— money, traveler's checks, passports. They didn't feel a thing or know it had happened until they woke up the next morning."

"Well, they obviously survived the ordeal if they were at Mike's parties."

"Yeah, but they're both dead now."

"They are! What happened?"

"Nancy had some sort of heart problem. She had surgery a few years before she died, but they did a half-assed job. She was supposed to get another operation but never did. And she never stopped doing crystal meth, which certainly didn't help."

"Jeez. What happened to Dave?"

"I'm not sure. He and Nancy blew their money and lost their house, so they were living up the mountains in a trailer when she died. Less than a year later, somebody stopped by to visit Dave and found him face down on the floor."

"Was he doing meth too?"

"No, Dave was a beer drinker. The booze might have acerbated whatever was wrong with him, but I don't think it killed him. Maybe he was still on painkillers for his bum knees and took too many. He'd had both knees replaced about five years before he croaked and was pretty heavy into painkillers for years before he finally got his double-knee job."

Another amphetamine rush kicked me into verbal overdrive.

"The ironic thing was that natural gas had been discovered on the property where Dave had his trailer and he'd just signed a deal that would bring him about $100,000 a year in royalties. His money worries were finally over.

JR was mute.

"It's always like that," I babbled on "You're the most vulnerable when you think you've got it made. Remember the end of the *Sands Of Iwo Jima*? The battle had been won and Old Glory was waving on top of a hill of dead bodies. John Wayne finally relaxes and says something along the lines of, 'I've never felt so good in my life.' *Bam!* No sooner are the words out of his mouth, and a dying Japanese soldier shoots him dead."

I paused to take a breath and a soft voice over the public address system informed us that Antwerp was next.

The pharmaceutical-grade amphetamine I had ingested gave me a clear edge changing trains. It wasn't as if I felt like Superman or anything like that. I just did what needed to be done without hesitation and found my body responding accordingly. I'm always surprised at times like this by how nimble I feel. There were several steep flights of stairs to climb before we reached the main level, and I rushed ahead of JR, scanning platform signboards for information as I jogged up the stairs.

The speed coursing through my system was the real thing, not some junk cooked up in a bathtub by a biker gang. If the only stuff I could score was the shit Nancy used to snort, I would happily go without, as has been the case far more often than not.

But when available, the pill-form factory brand delivers every time. Strong. Clean. No crash. The U.S. Air Force gives it to fighter pilots.

I reached the main level and glanced back at JR, more than half a flight below, headed slowly in my general direction, a slightly baffled look on his face. We had about 10 minutes to make the train for Bruges, and I didn't want to waste time going in the wrong direction.

Fortunately, deliverance was less than 10 yards away, standing next to a large ornate clock—a storybook stationmaster, complete with rosy-cheeks, handlebar mustache, and a gold watch fob adorning his vest. His English turned out to be as impeccable as his blue uniform, and with the help of this remarkable-looking man, we found our train with five minutes to spare and were soon rolling toward our destination.

Bruges' historic city center is a UNESCO World Heritage Site, an enchanting slice of yesterday existing on the margins of industrial society, a place that somehow manages to be part of both yesterday and today at the same time. There's generally a hint of that virtually anywhere you go in Western Europe, but Bruges specializes in that vibe and has the bones to back it up.

Unlike Amsterdam, Bruges' train station is not located in the heart of the old city. It's a few miles away, a utilitarian transportation hub totally lacking in charm, more 1950s industrial than 15th-century Gothic. Fortunately, there is a bus station out front, where you can catch the bus to a veritable fairyland.

We got off the bus at Market Square, which is surrounded by inns and restaurants, many dating back 500 or 600 years. Most of them have large outdoor seating sections stretching out onto the square, with menus tacked to some part of the low wooden partitions that mark the entrances and boundaries of each establishment.

The sun had been popping in and out of the clouds ever since we got off the train but was shining brightly when we sat down at the Café Sint-Joris (same guy as St. George the Dragon Slayer). We took an outdoor table near the front and ordered beers and vegetable lasagna, then waited, absorbing the view and vibe as the wind rustled the paper napkins under the cutlery.

The medieval belfry tower (13th-15th century) demands your attention with an in-your-face intensity. Still standing where it has

always stood, this majestic time machine has been the heartbeat
of Bruges for centuries and still soars impressively above every
other building within the moat that surrounds the egg-shaped old
city.

The tower houses a four-faced clock and an elaborate 47-bell
carillon, capable of many complicated chimes and peals. As if on
cue, the clock struck three as our food was served. In the old days,
it might have sounded an alarm that a house was on fire or the
French were attacking.

After the waitress retreated, I placed another 5 mgs of
amphetamine on my tongue and washed it down with a swig of
summer beer before tucking into my grub. The lasagna was a bit
rubbery, but I ate every bit, pausing regularly for a gulp of beer
or a bite of salad.

Sharing the square with the tower is a statue, erected in 1887,
of Jan Breydel (a butcher) and Pieter de Coninck (a weaver), a
pair of Flemish patriots who led violent uprisings against Philip
the Fair of France in 1302 and 1309. They stand close to one
another, looking in the same direction, each with their right hand
on a huge broadsword stuck in something at Breydel's feet—a
dead Frenchman perhaps.

Breydel, the larger of the two, is wearing chain mail armor and
holding a spear with a flag attached. His thighs and calves bulge
like a superhero's beneath his mail. No wonder the local soccer
stadium is named after him. The older De Coninck, remembered
as an eloquent speaker and rabble-rouser, is wrapped in a robe,
holding a scroll in his left hand. Both have what appeared to be
Mick Jagger hairdos.

The same year we visited, a movie called *In Bruges*, starring
Colin Farrell and Brendan Gleeson, was released. It's hard to
know how different our perceptions of the medieval city would
have been if we had seen the movie before going. We weren't
there long enough to enjoy the sex, drugs and Bacchanalian
festival featured in the film, but if we'd seen the movie we might
have booked a room and taken our chances.

But as it was, we were newbies fumbling for context. Still, there's no denying that, in hindsight, the movie added more than just a thin sheen of cultish glamour to the visit. It also transformed the fleeting glances of a couple of day-trippers into something tangible. What I only vaguely sensed as a possibility had been taken by the filmmakers and emphasized until Bruges itself became one of the movie's leading characters.

"Let's check out the clock tower," I suggested. "The view must be breathtaking."

"Okay."

We paid the bill, left a tip, and ambled across the square to the belfry. There are 366 steps leading to the observatory, from which Gleeson fell to his death in one of *In Bruges'* gorier scenes. Nobody took the plunge when we were there, but, as was the case in the movie when one of the bad guys attempted to visit the observatory, the fucking tower was closed.

Unlike the movie villain, we didn't administer a vicious beating to the tower attendant, just shrugged and walked away in search of other medieval curiosities.

Like Amsterdam, Bruges is a canal city, much smaller, less commercial, and more picturesque. There's a certain power in the history-soaked pores of the buildings and cobblestones that infiltrates your senses. It gave me a curious storybook feeling, almost as if I'd wandered onto a movie set, which is probably the reason they don't film more movies here. The city itself could easily dominate a film in lesser hands than those of Martin McDonagh, who wrote and directed *In Bruges*.

Ten minutes of semi-aimless wandering brought us to the St. Bonifacius Bridge on the Groenerei canal. There was an enchanting-looking old house on the other side, with an arched recess leading to an open door that beckoned like a magic portal. JR and I automatically yielded to temptation, crossed over to the other side, and entered a world even weirder that the one from which we had come.

The inside of the house, which appeared to be empty at

first, reminded me of castles I'd visited as a kid in England. The sunlight coming through the leaded widows lent scant warmth to the cold masonry interior and sparse furnishings. Displayed on the walls of this austere interior were a series of paintings, all by the same artist.

They were not 16th century, but they certainly shared something in common with Hieronymus Bosch, the Dutch painter whose "Garden of Earthly Delight" triptych has been freaking out viewers since he painted it somewhere between 1500 and 1505.

The virtually monochromatic paintings on the walls were delicately rendered apparitions of beauty and horror, executed with a firm command of draftsmanship and composition. The splendor of the human form was counterbalanced with surreal glimpses of the blood and bone beneath the façade of flesh. The juxtaposition of the exquisite and the grotesque takes the viewer by surprise at first, but as one monstrous apparition follows another, revulsion quickly overtakes a sense of wonder at the technical mastery of the work.

"Whoever painted these is one sick motherfucker," said JR, crudely but succinctly putting into words my very thoughts.

Then, in one of those monumental moments of embarrassment you never forget, we rounded a corner and were suddenly in the same room as the man who had created the paintings.

His back was toward us as he labored over a canvas and, thankfully, he did not turn when we entered. Perhaps the hiss of the airbrush he wielded had obscured JR's unvarnished evaluation of his art. Whatever the case, we turned on our heels and quickly exited the building I later learned was called Nuit Blanche, which roughly translates into "white" or "sleepless night."

It turns out that the artist, David De Graef, owns the house, which serves as his studio, gallery, and a five-star guesthouse. He looks the part—a graying hipster, lean and alert as he spray-painted along a line that wavered between fine art and surfboard decoration.

His Web site describes De Graef's work as "visionary creations" that "invite you to the depths of an obsessing world where no moral value is absolute … melt(ing) power and finesse to reflect our joy and unease." It goes on to say that he "draws inspiration from physical and mental decay, always put in perspective by a certain optimism and sense of humor."

Optimism? Humor? Perhaps I would have noticed these subtleties had we lingered longer, but at the time JR's words rang truer than the blurb I read months later on De Graef's Web site. But who gives a shit what I think? His airbrushed nightmares must be popular with the moneyed set. How else could he afford to own such a staggeringly beautiful piece of history?

Very much like *In Bruges*, Nuit Blanche taps the convoluted soul of this ancient and once violent city; its very preservation a constant reminder that rot will eventually claim all.

As we boarded the train and headed into the rainy darkness, I looked forward to the comforting distractions of Amsterdam.

FRESH MINT TEA

The Green House coffee shop at OudeziJay Ds Vourbugwal 191 not only sells some of the finest cannabis in Amsterdam, it also serves fresh mint tea Moroccan style. The best I've had since I was in Tangier with Terry, more than 40 years ago.

There is a small collection of tables and chairs flanking the entrance, and I got lucky. I copped a primo seat at an outside table under the awning. It was a sunny but chilly afternoon, and I was glad I'd worn a lightweight jacket over my hoodie.

My first glass of tea was turning lukewarm by the time I got my pipe going and took a drink. It was delicious just the same, and I ordered another, promising myself to drink it scalding hot with lots of sugar, just like at the Dancing Boy Cafe.

The table next to me was occupied by three young Moroccan men, smoking blunts and chatting excitedly. They were well groomed and fashionably dressed in western garb, either the idle rich or successful gangsters. One of them glanced at me but quickly looked away again. Like the mint tea, their presence reinforced the faint echo of the past. I don't dream that I'm back in Morocco anymore. Those nocturnal flashbacks faded as the decades slipped away.

It also probably has a lot of do with smoking cannabis. Smoking in the evening doesn't stop you dreaming; it stops you from remembering your dreams. That's the way it works with me anyway. Who knows? Maybe the cannabis acts as a filter, allowing only the most profound dreams to disturb your rest. Still, if you're lucky, every now and then there's a dream so full of mystery and wonder that it shines through even the thickest cloud of cannabis.

Like most of us, there are a handful of dreams that have never left me. One of them, however, stands out because it gave me a taste of something I had never had before or since and probably never will again. The most powerful aspect of the dream was not what I saw and did, although they were freaky enough by themselves. It was the way it made me feel. I can't say for sure, but it sure tasted like a slice of paradise.

In the beginning of the vision, I found myself in a rural setting—grass, bushes, trees, and hills in the distance. It was a pleasant summer's day and I was with a group of friendly strangers. There was, however, somebody accompanying me who I knew, most likely my daughter, but I'm not sure. You know how things are in dreams.

We were apparently gathered together to go hiking or maybe camping. I felt like I knew what I was doing but couldn't for the life of me tell you what it was.

There was also the matter of the bags we all had. I don't remember where we got them just that everybody had one. At first, I thought they were promotional items, tote bags imprinted with a company logo or some such crap. But I was wrong.

It was a magic bag, which changed size and shape to fit whatever you wanted to put in it, from your stash to your sleeping bag. It simply became whatever size you needed. But that was minor shit compared to what happened soon.

Seemingly out of nowhere, there was a voice speaking to us. It sounded as if it was being broadcast over an invisible public address system. The voice was male, authoritative, reassuring—Gregory Peck, maybe?

The voice said, "Some of you will go ahead and prepare the way for the rest."

At that, a dozen or so people separated themselves and began to head slowly in the direction of the hills, leaving the rest of us at the staging grounds. Not long after they were out of sight, the rest of us began to follow. Don't ask me how much time elapsed between the departures of the two groups. We were operating on dreamtime, and that is all anybody needs to know.

The going was moderately taxing, and I remember working up a sweat as we reached the foot of the hills and began to climb. By that point, my magical bag had transformed itself into a little gris-gris sack, hanging around my neck.

As we climbed higher, the vegetation began to turn patchy, and in the distance, the mountains were brown, except for an occasional streak of red when the sun struck at a certain angle.

A barely visible footpath led us to the crest of a steep hill, which looked across the valley to the mountains on the other side. Fear tickled my apprehension as I peered over the edge.

It was then that the voice told us to sit on the other side of the hill, just below the beginning of the descent. We were to sit down, put our rolled up bags behind our necks like pillows, and lean back on the side of the hill as if we were sitting in reclining lounge chairs.

The bag became the appropriate size, and after a bit of shifting and fidgeting, I settled into position and immediately felt very comfortable and more at ease. Then the voice spoke for what was to be the final time (for me, at least).

"Before we begin, let us give thanks to those who have gone ahead to help us."

As we all sat staring across the valley, "those who had gone ahead" began to slowly rise up out of the valley floor. They had their backs to us, but I could still recognize them as the people from our group, despite the fact they were now the color of the mountains and actually seemed to be carved out of the earth.

They grew larger and larger right before our eyes until they were the size of skyscrapers. The figures pushed upward until they loomed above the mountains and us, almost blotting out the sky. But before that happened, they stopped growing and left a thin line of light across the very top of the world.

The instant the monolithic earth figures and the line in the sky met, a feeling of breathtaking ecstasy filled my entire being, body, mind and soul. Words are inadequate to describe how it felt, but that having been said, here are a few clichéd phrases from the notes I took a couple of weeks after the dream:

Better than any drug, better than sex … I was filled with the wonder and joy of life … everything was as it should be … I had achieved nirvana … I had not seen the light; I was a part of the light …

"Shit!"

I woke up with bitter realization that my bladder was screaming at me. I lay there for few seconds, utterly crushed that my euphoria had disappeared the instant I awoke. I reluctantly got up and sat on the toilet with the lights out, hoping I could stay half-asleep and that the dream would return once I was safely back in the warm embrace of my bed.

It didn't work. I was so overwhelmed with disappointment and excitement that sleep was impossible. When morning came and I got up to go to work, there was a tangible afterglow that took a week or so to gradually dim and expire. Before it did, I had an almost evangelic need to tell people about the dream.

Most folks just indulged me and listened politely, but even those who were actually paying attention must have been puzzled to hear a confessed atheist blabbing about what seemed to be some sort of religious experience.

For me, it is a bit more complicated. I chose to think of the dream as a special treat, which I was extremely lucky to experience. It was a strange and magnificent occasion on which the veil parted and allowed me to experience the whole. If only fleetingly.

If there's a connection between Tangier in the 1960s and Amsterdam in the 2000s, maybe it's the fresh mint tea and good smoke. Still, I can't help but wonder if I would even have known there was a veil, let alone an unseen whole, if I'd never gone to Morocco with Terry.

The waitress came outside to clean a nearby table and I ordered another fresh mint tea. Two of the three Moroccan's sitting at the next table had split, leaving just the guy who had looked my way a few times. At first, I didn't realize that he was talking to me.

"Sir, I hope you don't mind me asking," he said, "but I was wondering how long you have been smoking."

I turned sideways to look at him. He had an intelligent face, an expensive haircut, and hash under his fingernails.

"It's been more than 40 years," I said, trying to sound taciturn but not entirely unfriendly.

"Forty years! That's a long time. Do you ever smoke it with tobacco or do you just smoke it pure?"

"Usually pure."

"I see," he said, nodding slowly. "Well, enjoy your smoke."

"You too."

The waitress arriving with my tea interrupted our conversation. I got the sense he regarded me as somewhat of an oddity, an antique left over from bygone days that he'd read and heard about but had never before encountered in the flesh.

Have I really reached the relic stage when my main worth is the fact that I'd lived through a certain time in history? Step right up and see the last living hippie! I flatter myself, of course. There are plenty more like me out there, just nowhere near as many as before.

I finished another pipe of Amnesia, drained my last glass of tea, and left a five-euro tip in the saucer. As I rose from my chair, I muttered goodbye to the Moroccan who had been curious about my smoking habits. His two friends had since returned, and he was deep in conversation. He was momentarily puzzled until he realized who had spoken to him.

"Ah, yes," he said, glancing up. "Good day to you too, sir."

Maybe I should have been more talkative, told him I'd been to Morocco years ago and asked him where he was from. Who knows? Maybe he knew Blue Hat or, more likely, his barefoot son. Maybe he knew the barefoot son's son. Maybe *he* was the son of the barefoot son. A lot of time had passed, a lot of babies born.

THE WHITE MAN IN THE WINDOW

It was around 9:30 when JR and I emerged from the apartment and into the morning light, a couple of cadavers in shorts and sneakers, bent on a spot of exercise before a day of debauchery.

The respectable folks were already at work; the Red Light District was beginning to stir. The only people who paid attention to the pair of creaky joggers ambling along the cobbles were a couple of whores occupying side-street windows, who laughed at us as we passed.

Our route took us up and down alleyways and then around De Waag and back toward the apartment. The Goa was still closed when we got back, but an employee was unlocking the roll-up metal door that covered the entire front of the shop when it was closed. Soon the aroma of cannabis, tobacco and coffee would be drifting up toward the apartment.

Thankfully, the vile smell in the hallway was gone and the black mood that had borne down on me the day before had lifted. There remained a vague residue of uneasiness, the kind that accompanies the knowledge that you have a dental appointment in two weeks, but right then everything was cool.

"I'm going to take a shower. Do you want to go first?"

"No, you go ahead," said JR.

It was a large, well-appointed shower, with black tiles, plenty of hot water and good pressure. There was also a squeegee, which we figured must have been to clean the tiles because it really didn't work that well on any body part. I know because I tried as many as I could think of.

When I got out of the shower, JR was asleep on the waterbed, still in his shorts and sweat socks, looking borderline decrepit but at peace with the world. I didn't have the heart to wake him, so I got dressed, left a note, and locked the door behind me.

There were a few more people in the streets by then, including a couple of backpacking lesbians sitting at one of the Goa's outside tables, enjoying morning coffee and a smoke. I turned left and headed for the Bulldog.

The Bulldog franchise is the McDonalds of coffee shops, a mini-empire built on a foundation of cannabis consumption. Henk de Vries opened the original Bulldog, at Oudzids Voorburgwal 90, in 1972, the same year Wernard Bruining opened Mellow Yellow, another early cannabis venue.

Both were pioneers who put their butts on the line in the fight for cannabis freedom. De Vries got his start selling matchboxes of pot at a pop festival in 1970. By '72 he was in the thick of the battle, running both the Bulldog (named after his dog Joris) and fighting a seemingly never-ending legal battle.

De Vries was arrested many times but never gave up. He was more than a stoner trying to run an illegal business; he was a figurehead in a movement whose moment had come. It was the early '70s, and yes, the times they were changing. As tough as it was at first, old Henk was in exactly the right place (liberal, tolerant Amsterdam) at exactly the right time—when the light of the counterculture was still boring new holes in people's heads.

As De Vries persisted, the police eventually came to the realization that the Bulldog and its clientele were causing no trouble. They were just sitting around drinking coffee, smoking cannabis, and socializing. It was a practical attitude and a significant part of a scene that eventually helped lead to the current official policy of non-enforcement.

Finally free of legal hassles, De Vries expanded, and in the mid-1980s purchased the old police station at Leidseplein 15, where, ironically, he'd been booked on countless occasions.

Fittingly, the Leidseplein Bulldog was opened on April Fool's Day 1985, giving every pothead in Amsterdam the last laugh.

Since then, the Bulldog empire has expanded to include hotels in Amsterdam and British Colombia, bike rentals, and a line of products ranging from rolling papers to caps and T-shirts. The Bulldog Energy Drink sponsors all kinds of events, including auto racing, paintball contests, and my personal favorite, high altitude paragliding in Pakistan.

There is also an esoteric group of charitable organizations for which the Bulldog raises money: the Sid Yogtong Kick Boxer Camp, the Pattaya Orphange, and the Pattaya Retirement Home, all located in Thailand. There is also Bulldog online, which finds homes for abandoned or mistreated English bulldogs.

I've read a fistful of coffee shop reviews and travel blogs that rip the Bulldog for being too commercial, too mainstream. They also complain it doesn't sell the best pot in town, which is true. But they don't sell the worst either. And while it is commercial compared to a lot of other coffee shops, the Bulldog isn't exactly Starbucks with cannabis. The tripped-out mural on the outside wall that greets customers is clearly not the work of corporate America.

I ordered a coffee with milk at the counter and watched the muffin man make his morning delivery, a basket full of cannabis-infused baked goods. I don't really recommend them to an experienced stoner. They're not very potent (I had to eat three before I got a buzz) but they're just right for the tourist day-tripper.

When my coffee was ready, I selected the table closest to the open double-window, the shop's primo seat, which gave me an unobstructed view of the canal and the street on both sides. I took a sip of coffee and plucked a fairly large bud of Northern Lights from my stash. It was sticky with resin and too fresh to crumble, so I cut it into small pieces with my Leatherman Squirt and filled my pipe.

I took a deep hit, sat back, and slowly blew the smoke out

the window into the morning air where it was dispersed by the breeze. All stoners soon discover that the first high of the day is frequently the best, especially if you're going to be smoking the same grade of weed all day. As the THC filtered into my system, it brought the familiar feeling of wellbeing and enhanced sensory perception that are the foundation of cannabis' appeal.

I no longer experience the golden rays of those early intoxications—not on a regular basis anyway. After four decades, it's more like a reliable groove, a place where I want to be—a place that nurtures my soul. I took another toke and another sip of coffee and settled back in my seat and gazed out the window.

Amsterdam is a people watcher's paradise, the passing parade, an eclectic mélange of humanity—and it's not just stoners and backpackers. There are drunken soccer hooligans, as well as old heads and neo-hippies. White kids in dreadlocks, grumpy old women careening around in electronic wheelchairs, Indonesian gigolos with their ugly white girlfriends. You name it. There are panhandlers and pickpockets, and platoons of similarly dressed, hopelessly straight Asian tourists who are seemingly oblivious to anyone not in their group. A guy carrying a small flag often leads them.

There was one guy who kept walking past the window every few minutes, casting furtive glances in my direction, clearly some sort of hustler hoping to catch my eye. The angle from where I was sitting allowed me to see him coming and gave me time to look away. After four unsuccessful passes, he gave up and moved on.

Over the years, my brain has developed a way to enjoy being high and still have an antenna up for possible trouble. It's very handy, even in Amsterdam. Stoner multitasking.

As I filled my third pipe, customers started to drift in, a young tourist couple, preppy in a shabby-chic kind of way, purchased some cannabis and left. Another couple bought some weed and stayed, drinking coffee and rolling spleefs. I turned away and looked out the window again, an unlit pipe in my hand.

Across the canal, a whore sat in a window. She was brown-skinned, a Latina maybe, probably in her 30s, neither attractive nor ugly—just a semi-respectable body for rent. She wore a tight white dress that complemented her completion. I watched her, on and off, for more than an hour, and although she wrapped on the window whenever a man passed, I only saw one guy stop and talk and, after a few minutes, he walked on.

Besides providing sexual services for money, the whores are as much a part of the Amsterdam tourist scene as the Eiffel Tower is in Paris or Buckingham Palace in London. While all my data is anecdotal, I don't think it would be exaggerating to say that for every customer a whore services, there are hundreds (maybe thousands) who walk by just to look.

There are also dozens of cheap Red Light District souvenirs, ranging from ballpoint pens and coffee mugs to T-shirts and pornographic playing cards, all bearing the image of a prostitute. None of this junk would sell if real-life whores weren't just across the street or around the next corner.

It's the same thing with coffee shops. Even the terminally straight, who would never dream of going inside, get a cheap thrill walking past a coffee shop. A whiff of the forbidden as they scurry by.

To a lesser but still noticeable degree, the coffee shop patron is, like the whore, a curiosity, part of what the travel agencies and vacation packagers refer to as the "Amsterdam Experience." The same way the gawkers wonder about what kind of people the prostitutes are, they also wonder about the dope fiends who patronize the coffee shops.

Those who walked past the Bulldog window that morning were probably disappointed by the old white guy they saw in the window. He wasn't at all eccentric looking, just medium-sized with close-cropped gray hair, creased face, and bags under his eyes that made him sadder looking than he was.

Actually, I was happy to do my bit for the tourist industry. It was good to feel a part of something, even if I was just a human prop in a world of sin and laughter. I knew I belonged.

NOBODY'S PLACE

My mother used to curse every time she saw a Volkswagen.

Having lived through the Blitz and knowing firsthand the horror of war, she had a perfect right to feel the way she did. But by the 1960s, these impromptu outbursts seemed inappropriately funny, especially as they were usually aimed at the American drivers who probably had no clue that the lovable Beetle was a Nazi invention. Even my father, who was in the RAF and survived several cross-channel bombing-raids, thought her rants were amusing.

Mother's lifelong grudge against the VW notwithstanding, growing up in England in the shadow of World War II automatically gave me a built-in prejudice against Germany. As time passed, it was easy to dismiss this bias on an intellectual level but not in the gut, not completely anyway. Old fears frequently endure decades past their shelf life, so visiting Deutschland was never on my bucket list.

But that changed when Dorazzo and his family moved to suburban Düsseldorf after attending an overseas-job convention in New York City. Their transatlantic shift made it possible for us to rendezvous in Europe, and we had spent ten days together in Germany and the Netherlands a month or so before a serendipitous business trip carried me back to Germany much sooner than expected.

Dorazzo was waiting for me at the airport, standing on the fringe of the small crowd gathered to greet disembarking passengers. Instead of holding one of those signs bearing people's names or corporate affiliations, he proffered what looked like a credit card with a plain white face.

If anyone else noticed him, they probably thought he was a bit slow on the uptake, but I knew what it was: his membership card to Nobody's Place, a Dutch coffee shop in Venlo, just across the border from Germany, where we had become members in good standing earlier that year.

After checking my bags at the hotel, we were once again rolling down the autobahn en route to Venlo, memories of my first visit coming back to me in greater detail the closer we got to the border, which was less than an hour's drive from Dorazzo's apartment.

On that first trip to Venlo, we'd arrived at Nobody's Place before it was open for business and had time to enjoy a leisurely alfresco breakfast at a café in the square outside of the 16th-century town hall. Willem van Bommell designed the original structure, but when it was restored in the 19th century, none other than Pierre Cuypers, the architect who built the Rijksmuseum and Centraal Station in Amsterdam, was given the commission. Cuypers added two towers to the original pair and enough gingerbread to leave his distinctive imprint.

We were sitting perhaps a mile away from the German border, but Cuypers handiwork announced that it was definitely Dutch territory. Such a distinction was in grave peril when Germany invaded neutral Netherlands in 1940. The Germans occupied Venlo until the Allied forces liberated it at the end of the war, and by then, most of the town's historic buildings had been destroyed. Somehow, the massive town hall survived relatively unscathed and still dominates the square, which is now furnished with a replica throne for tourists to sit on and pose for photographs.

Nobody's Place is at the corner of Rodesrtraat and Sloterbeekstrat, a short walk from town hall, near the railroad station. From a distance, it looks like a working-class restaurant, but the moment you open the door and enter, the coffee shop ambiance and aroma are unmistakable.

"Can I help you?" asked the smiling young woman behind the counter.

"We'd like to join and purchase something to smoke."

"Do you have your passports with you?"

We handed over our passports and paid the five euros membership fee, which reverts back to cardholders in the form of a five-Euro discount upon a second visit. Along with our white-faced cards, we were given a piece of paper listing a mind-boggling forty-two rules that members must observe.

None of the coffee shops I visited in Amsterdam required a membership or handed out a printed list of regulations, but in the late 1990s, Nobody's Place was forced to install its own rules in response to the local government's anti-coffee shop initiatives known as Q-4 Project and Tango. Unable to rid the town of coffee shops solely because they sold cannabis, the authorities claimed the shops and their customers were a "nuisance" and a "disturbance."

Although exaggerated, there was a measure of truth to the claim, driven to a large degree by the sheer number of Germans crossing the border to replenish their stashes on a daily basis. This time, instead of jackbooted storm troopers, it was stoners invading Venlo in search of a plant deemed illegal in the fatherland.

The purge succeeded in reducing the number of coffee shops in Venlo and pushed the few survivors to the edge of the city. The staggeringly detailed nature of Nobody's Palace's rules and regulations is a telling indicator of the nerve-wracking tightrope it navigates to stay in business. Rule number forty-one spoke directly to the reason for this seemingly officious catalog of do's and don'ts:

"If these rules are not abided to, we could be charged with disturbance and the attraction of criminal behavior. We want to prevent this at all cost. It is about the reputation of us all and therefore we don't want to give anyone reason to complain."

Not only was behavior inside Nobody's Place carefully

monitored, the rules extended outside to include the general vicinity: "Do not stand in front of the shop or in your car." "Make sure that you do not cause a disturbance in the neighborhood," "Do not throw litter on the street." Then there was this howler: "Do not leave with a joint in your mouth," which could easily be construed as an endorsement of the products sold inside.

To a large extent, the rules were common sense requests that should go unspoken. Other rules, however, were peculiar, number twenty-four for example: "No aggression. No tough tales."

I get the "no aggression" part, but what exactly qualifies as a "tough tale"? Rule number twenty-eight also uses the term: "It is only allowed to communicate in Dutch, German, or English in Nobody's Place, so that staff is able to intervene in case of an argument or if rules are disobeyed (for example tough tales)." Regardless of what, exactly, the expression implied, it sure sounded as if the customer demographic was not as blissed-out as one might have imagined.

Then there was my favorite, rule twenty-seven: "If you do not date a girl, then do not try to find one here. Even good-looking girls and boys should be able to peacefully smoke a joint with us."

While neither Dorazzo nor I qualified as "good-looking," after purchasing some dynamite weed, we sat at one of the wooden table in a sunlit part of the shop and enjoyed a peaceful, mind-bending smoke. Still, I must admit that a group of young men at a nearby table, one of whom was chopping up marijuana and tobacco with what appeared to be a small meat cleaver, appeared capable of tough tales or worse.

Besides a stash of primo herb, I also pocketed a Nobody's Place drink coaster before we left as a souvenir. I believe it captures the true spirit of the shop far better than a lengthy list of rules and a smattering of dubious customers.

The image on the coaster is of a female Buddha sitting on a nest of cannabis rather than the traditional lily pad. She has a garland of marijuana leaves around her head and a water pipe on her lap, the mouthpiece of which she holds in her left hand. The inscription read: "Thank You For 27 Years. We Couldn't Do It Without You."

■■■

"We'll be crossing the border in a few minutes," said Dorazzo, jolting me out of my jet-lagged recollections and into the present.

"I'm going to get my five-euro discount sooner than I figured."

"We're not going to Nobody's Place this time. We're going to that place I told you about, the one that used to be a rest stop."

The entrance to the former rest stop is easy to miss. It's shockingly close to the border and the building itself is difficult to see from the road, but Dorazzo steered his car into the parking lot like the regular customer he had became since my previous visit to Venlo. The unusual location was part of the same cleanup that forced all coffee shops, including Nobody's Place, to move out of the town's primary commercial area.

The rest stop was actually two coffee shops in one: The top layer is called Oasis, a large, airy space, furnished in a semi-upscale manner, and Roots, which is fittingly situated below and has a cave-like atmosphere. Both establishments sell the same high-quality cannabis.

Although you have to be a member, the Oasis/Roots complex was more laid back than Nobody's Place, probably because it's even further away from other businesses and less likely to offend the sensibilities of the straight citizens of Venlo. There was even a whacked-out tout hovering near the sales window at the Oasis, singing stoned-out praises of the products for sale. I smiled, walked past him, and approached the counter.

"Hi. What's the most potent sativa you have?"

"We just got a shipment of Jack Haze. It's expensive but very strong."

"How much?"

"Twenty-five euros a two-gram bag."

"I'll take two bags," I said and handed him a fifty-euro bill.

Upon hearing this, the tout ambled closer, his dancing gait a tad unsteady, his eyes rolling wildly in their sockets. He looked like a burnt-out rodeo clown.

"You're going to need more than that," he said. "That stuff is amazing! You should get another bag."

Dorazzo laughed and I forked over another twenty-five euros.

We found a table to our liking, and I rolled a large joint of the luxurious weed. Forty-five minutes later, we were still sitting there, a third of the joint unfinished in the ashtray. The tout was correct. Jack Haze was perhaps the best marijuana I had ever smoked, a super-strong sativa that exploded like a Roman candle, setting off a euphoric firestorm of perception and insight.

"Maybe we'd better start to head back," said Dorazzo.

"Well, we could, but I really don't feel like moving right now."

"Okay. Let's finish that joint."

Finally, more than an hour after we had fired up the joint, we returned to the car, eased onto the highway and headed east. On our prior visit to Venlo, Dorazzo had been worried about being stopped by the German authorities after crossing back into Deutschland, but he didn't mention it this time. While it would be easy to bust nearly every customer departing the Oasis/ Roots rest stop as soon as they crossed the border, there were only occasional spot checks and the flow of cannabis from the Netherlands to Germany went virtually unchecked.

Dorazzo steered us safely back to my hotel, where we smoked Jack Haze and talked into the early morning hours. At the time, neither of us realized that a change in the Dutch political climate would soon cast a pall over the entire scene, one that would make the forty-two rules at Nobody's Place seem entirely benign. Maybe if we had listened closely, we might have heard the faint sound of jackboots on the march again. But we were too much in the moment to notice.

SINTERKLAAS AND GANJA GIRL

Although the autobahn was covered with leaves, the branches of nearby trees were still full of multi-colored foliage. Among the greens, soft browns and oranges, the yellow leaves shone the brightest as the sunlight turned them into iridescent splashes of gold. But despite Mother Nature's beautiful backdrop, Dorazzo felt decidedly edgy as he headed to Venlo again. It was the first day of November 2011, and for him, November was a "shitty month when people die."

It was not, however, the demise of a fellow human being that troubled him as he drove west toward the border. It was the possible death of the Netherlands' coffee shop scene. The political pendulum had continued to swing to the right in the October elections, resulting in a center-right coalition government that seemed bent on rolling back the Netherlands' liberal approach to life in general and recreational drug use in particular. An anti-cannabis crusade was part of an overall erosion of tolerance that also included attitudes toward Muslims, immigration, and legalized prostitution.

While the same old "disturbance" and "nuisance" canards were tendered by those who wished to curtail cannabis consumption, Dirk Korf, professor of criminology at the University of Amsterdam, was closer to the mark when he said: "There's clearly a shift in the moral debate. It's all about the culture of control."

As Dorazzo approached the roundabout where drivers have to decide whether they want go toward Amsterdam, Belgium or central Venlo, he was struggling to maintain his sense of optimism. He had half expected to find Roots/Oasis closed. The Netherlands citizens to whom he had recently spoken were split roughly fifty-fifty on whether or not the new law banning the sale of cannabis to tourists would spread beyond the area of Maastricht. He had been gathering a stash against that possibility and, as the summer drew to a close, increased the frequency of his Venlo runs.

If the Christian Democrats, one of the larger junior parties in the Netherlands' fragmented coalition, has its way, soft-drugs tourism would be terminated and all coffee shops would eventually shut down. As a stopgap measure, the forces of repression want coffee shops to become citizen-only private clubs. Moreover, the THC content of the cannabis would be limited to fifteen percent, which would be weaker than most of the marijuana sold in pre-crackdown coffee shops.

A significant part of the problem stems from the fact that large-scale production of cannabis has remained illegal although selling and consuming cannabis at coffee shops (and growing a maximum of five plants for personal use) has been tolerated for decades. Considering the political climate, it's not surprising that raiding so-called cannabis plantations has become a priority for law enforcement, complete with "sniffer helicopters" and all the latest crime-fighting paraphernalia.

Rumors of the pending crackdown had been floating for years, but except for banning foreigners from coffee shops in the southeastern border-city of Maastricht, the status quo had basically been maintained. It was difficult to know what to expect because even the psychedelic mushroom ban, which was eventually enforced, was masterly circumvented.

Instead of traditional magic mushrooms, the smart shops switched to selling schlerotia (termed as "truffles"), mushroom spores, and active mycelium cultures, all of which remained legal. Dorazzo and I shared some of these delightful psilocybin-packed delicacies at the 2010 North Sea Jazz festival in Rotterdam, and I found them just as potent as the best mushrooms I've eaten and much easier to digest.

The best solution as far as stoners and progressive citizens of the Netherlands are concerned would be to legalize cannabis. Tax revenue from coffee shops already generate approximately 400-million euros a year, and an additional 400- to 800-million euros in revenue could be generated by taxing growers. Furthermore, if drug tourism ends, the loss of ancillary revenue—accommodations, food, entertainment, etc.—would be astronomical.

Perhaps that's one of the reasons the mayor of Amsterdam, Eberhard van der Laan, spoke out against the crackdown, telling Reuters that restricting the activities of coffee shops would lead to greater health risks, nuisance, and drug dealing on the streets. As mayor, he could simply choose not to enforce the weed pass regulations. "At the moment the mayor is in conference with the minister to convince him that the measures regarding coffee shops will be counterproductive for Amsterdam," the mayor's office said in a November 2011 statement.

Roots/Oasis had become Dorazzo's refuge from the lockstep mentality of Germany and the general madness of the world; so partly out of concern for his haven and source of cannabis and partly to gather information on my behalf, he tried to get a sense of what the proprietors knew that we didn't.

It would have been a breach of coffee-shop etiquette to ask too many pointed questions. Still, he'd been a regular customer for several years and the young woman behind the counter, whom Dorazzo called Ganja Girl, had always been friendly. So over the last few visits, he had expressed his concerns in the oblique manner for which the situation called.

"In case things change, it was nice to meet you," he said after paying his bill and stuffing the cannabis into his pants pocket.

Ganja Girl had laughed and said, "I'll see you."

But despite the laugher and assurances, Dorazzo's concern mounted in late October when the scene at Roots/Oasis resembled a fire sale. Both levels were open on a non-holiday Tuesday, which was rare, and doing brisk business. Had the spoiled local stoners, used to having the finest cannabis easily available, finally gotten a sense of urgency? Did they know something he didn't? Was the end imminent?

Regardless of the crush of customers, the cheerfulness behind the counter and the "Don't worry" mantra remained unchanged, as did the excellent dope they sold. But that was in October. This was November, past the supposed deadline for the start of the crackdown. You never know. Things could have changed and there was only one way to find out for sure.

Dorazzo felt a little flushed as he swung the car into the circular route that led to the parking lot. Although it was sometimes tough to find the disposable income to pay for it, he had gotten used to having primo pot readily available less than an hour away from home. No cannabis user would ever want to lose a sweet deal like that.

He felt a little better after driving past the small wooden security hut and back to where a neon-highlighted statue of a ganja smoker occupied a sizeable portion of the parking area. Then the anxiety vanished. The stoners' sanctuary was indeed open for business. Better yet, there was a sign on the door that read:

25th ANNIVERSARY ROOTS/OASE
November 19, 10-2200
Special Discounts, Live Music
2 DJS, SINGERS
GRILL FREE HAMBURGERS (cheese)

Inside, it was a normal weekend morning with the wooden tables slowly filling up. The National Geographic Channel was showing an HD scene of a big animal eating a smaller one and the sound system was set at morning levels for rap/reggae mixes. Prices and goods were the same. Nothing had changed. Everything was cool for now.

■■■

A little more than two weeks later, the cold, crisp morning air provided a brief blast of invigoration like the oxygen inhalers they used to sell in old Vegas steam rooms for two bucks a pop. At Oasis, pops cost about 12 euros for a gram of prime smoke. It was November 19—the height of St. Nicholas Days, the Netherlands' Sinterklaas on which the mythical figure of the Santa Claus is based.

There was already activity on the outside patio as a barbecue station for free hamburgers was prepared. A few bundled groups were taking advantage of the calm weather to smoke large spliffs on the patio, where leafless trees were decorated with shiny orange holiday ornaments.

Dorazzo was happy to see Ganja Girl, the angel of "polm" (strong hash, of cloudy national origin) and his best chance for garnering inside info. Although she had been providing him progressively fatter bags of cannabis as the weeks and months rolled by, he remained cautious and, as had become his habit of late, approached the counter as if it might be the last time.

"I'm glad to see everything is still here."

"I am glad too that everything is still here," said Ganja Girl, cutting a two-gram chunk off a baseball-sized hunk of hash.

"I hope I can still come in after New Year."

"We are still selling," she said with a shrug.

"Will you get any sort of warning?"

"They warn us (not to sell) already."

"I keep hearing different things about if and when the law might change."

"I just keep hoping."

Ganja Girl held up crossed fingers on each hand, fluorescent green fingernails flashing. Then she handed Dorazzo a leaf-inscribed commemorative keychain: "Roots/Oase 25 Yeers."

"Thanks. I hope you have another twenty-five years, but right now I'll be happy to see the Christmas tree."

"You will see a great tree. We might just put up a giant plant or a giant bud and hang things on that."

"I want to see the tree next year too."

"The politicians can't make up their minds so they just keep talking," she replied with an exaggerated sigh. "It's been this way for nine or ten years that I can remember."

"I hope I can get in next year."

"I'll see you. Don't worry."

"I'm worried!" said Dorazzo, pouting.

Ganja Girl laughed, as citizens of the Netherlands often tend to do when discussing politics or the future.

As Dorazzo left the party, he could have sworn he heard the faint sound of sleigh bells somewhere in the distance. He patted the stash in his pocket and gave thanks.

Epilogue: Sadly, the Oasis did close, but cannabis is still available in many parts of the Netherlands. The rightwing lost a lot of seats in the next election, which resulted in each municipality being allowed to decide whether or not to keep coffee shops open. Amsterdam remains the same as ever.

PART

Six

South Of The Border

SEARCHING FOR QUETZALCOATL

Cops with pump action shotguns slung over their shoulders were checking vehicles as they exited Guadalajara's Don Miguel Hidalgo y Costilla International Airport. Just ahead of my taxi a young couple on a motor scooter were being questioned. The couple was still there when another cop waved us on and we lurched into afternoon traffic.

It was good to be somewhere I'd never been before, where each moment unfolds anew and the sense of adventure is keen. Like any adventure worthy of its name, there was also a hint of danger to keep the senses sharp. More than a hint, actually.

It wasn't until I'd purchased my plane ticket and the departure date drew near, that I began to fret. Still, I was so determined to take this journey, negative thoughts were temporarily shunted aside. The one thing I knew for sure was that if I didn't go, I would regret it for the rest of my life.

Even so, when the weeks turned into days, it was impossible not to think about the insane narco violence that had gripped Mexico in an escalating dance of the dead. There's nothing quite like worrying about being kidnapped, tortured and decapitated to keep you awake at night.

But there was no turning back, and as the cab glided along the highway with the windows down, I eased into a relaxed state of optimistic fatalism. Whatever was going to happen was going to happen. As Randolph Scott used to say in the old cowboy movies, "there are some things a man can't ride around." But the truth was that I didn't want to ride around. I was doing exactly what I wanted to do.

The sunny breeze carried the smell of the taco stands and the shouts of men working at a roadside garage. Traffic was busy but not chaotic, and about fifteen minutes after we left the airport we turned right off the main highway and on to a secondary road. The green foothills of the Sierra Madre soon rose above us as we gradually descended toward Lake Chapala.

Legend has it that Lake Chapala is possibly the body of water from which the Mesoamerican deity Quetzalcoatl (aka the Plumed Serpent) arose. In the earliest depictions, Quetzalcoatl is portrayed as a fully zoomorphic being, an actual snake, with dragon-like fangs. It must have been a real freak-out for the locals who lived in tiny fishing villages along the banks when he showed up unannounced.

Despite his ferocious appearance, Quetzalcoatl had only the best of intentions and is credited with introducing maize, the arts, crafts and science to the indigenous people. He also represented the forces of good and light against those of evil and darkness. In other words, a multitasking, intergalactic reptile sent to Earth to give us wretched humans some acutely needed assistance.

I had read H. D. Lawrence's novel, *The Plumed Serpent*, years ago and thought it would be a good idea to reread it before embarking on my expedition. Lawrence had spent time at Lake Chapala when he was writing the book in the 1920s, which made it even more relevant. The book was even better than I remembered, but I set it aside after about a hundred pages, when I got to the part where bandits hack a guy to death with machetes after robbing him of one thousand gold pesos. I didn't want to exhaust my supply of Clonazepam before leaving.

As we got closer to the lakeside village where I would be staying, there were homes perched on the steep hills on either side of the road. High walls, giving them the appearance of fort-like compounds, surrounded most. Around these parts your home was literally your castle—the only thing missing was a moat.

When we neared the village, the driver confirmed the address and then took a sharp turn onto a narrow cobblestone street that led to the plaza. The driver pulled over to the side of the road, where a couple of other taxis were parked, and pointed across the street to my hotel. It didn't look much different than the stores on either side of it, just a gray stucco front and a dark interior beyond the open double-door.

The receptionist didn't speak English, but another employee did, and he explained to her who I was and that I had paid in advance. She flashed a professional smile, handed me the key and gestured over her shoulder at the open door that led to a long, sun-dappled courtyard.

A extravagant display of flowering plants—orange, purple, yellow and white—overhung the courtyard and mingled with the other vegetation growing out of large pots on both sides of the path. The lush florae created a pleasant jungle-like ambiance, enhanced by the chirping of birds and the trickle of water from a small fountain.

The accommodations, shamelessly advertised as "suites," were on either side of a walkway that led to a bar-restaurant at the far end. Each suite was named after a bird, the likeness of which was crudely painted on the outside wall. I had the Heron suite, complete with an image of a disheveled bird that looked like it hadn't eaten in a week.

The suite consisted of two fairly large rooms and a bathroom that reminded me of the one in the Nuevo Laredo whorehouse where I took a couple of showers so many years ago. It was pleasantly cool inside, thanks to the windows being strategically located in order to maximize the cross drafts. The walls were painted yellow, black and red, and the worn linoleum floors smelled of Lysol.

Most of the utilitarian fixtures seemed to be made of poured concrete. The bed was concrete, as were the bedside tables and the base of the couch. The bedside lamp was a metal bust of an Indian woman with a bright yellow shawl over her head. Her face was painted a reddish brown and her eyes were closed. The light bulb looked like it was growing out of the top of her head. The joint definitely had a funky charm, enhanced considerably by the lush vegetation outside the door.

I unpacked, took a piss, brushed my teeth and headed out, making sure I had the key in my pocket. All my valuables we tucked snugly in a money belt strapped underneath my shirt. The amphetamine I'd swallowed just before my plane landed was still cranking. I felt intensely alive, tingling with anticipation.

I walked out of the front door of the hotel and came face to face with Terry. It had been almost half a century since we parted, but the years in between suddenly seemed inconsequential. The past had caught up with the future, and I was free to be in the now.

SEMTIMENTAL JOURNEY

We've all lost contact with friends over the years. It is part of the human condition, and that's probably how it's supposed to be. But I've always been sentimental and still feel a sweet nostalgia tinged with sadness when I think of certain folks I've lost along the way, especially those I was particularly fond of. When they cross my mind, there's usually a flashback that lasts a nanosecond, a snapshot from the past that vanishes the moment I think about it.

There's Steve, a high school buddy who made me listen to Hank Ballard's version of the "Twist," instead of Chubby Checker's. He also turned me on to country music by playing Hank William's "Love Sick Blues" and Patsy Cline's "Back In Baby's Arms." At night we would drive around in his souped-up Plymouth, trying to find a location, usually at the top of a hill, where the car's AM radio would pick up a country station in Wheeling, West Virginia. Sometimes we'd get drunk together on bourbon I had siphoned from my Dad's basement bar.

We were the two cool kids in *Stand By Me*, but like the characters played by Wil Wheaton and River Phoenix, not too cool to hang out with social rejects we'd known since we were in sixth grade. I only saw Steve a couple of times after we graduated. Somebody said he'd joined the Navy. At least he didn't get killed trying to break up a knife fight.

Then there was Michael, a former schoolteacher from Texas who quit teaching to follow his bliss. He lived with his girlfriend,

Ginger, in the apartment below mine, and almost every evening, he'd would steal a few crumbs of hashish from another girl who lived with him and Ginger.

The chick with the hash worked in a nightclub, where guys trying to get in her pants gave her all kinds of goodies. Her stash was so bountiful, she never missed the hash Michael pinched and shared with me.

We'd sit for hours, smoking, listening to blues records and shooting the shit—a pastime I still enjoy. In a way it was a shame Michael stopped teaching. He was a natural and had the gift of imparting constructive criticism without making the recipient feel bad. A few casual comments he made about my writing turned out to be extremely helpful, subtle tips that guide me still.

One summer, I returned from an extended vacation and Michael was no longer living downstairs. There was a note saying he was going to California and would send me his new address when he got settled. He didn't, and that was that.

There are a handful of others: Curtis and Jay-D from my Army days, art school buddy Harvey, and Chris, another Texan who lived off a stipend he inherited when both his parents died in a head-on car accident. We used to loll around his place smoking weed and watching *The Galloping Gourmet* on TV. Then we'd go out and buy the ingredients and try to replicate the meal. I recall doing a bang-up job with a large grouper, stuffed with celery and baked in tinfoil.

I miss them all and would love to see them again. But they don't haunt me the way Terry did. He was different and finding him grew into an obsession. It just didn't seem right that a person who had influenced me so profoundly should completely disappear from my life.

I knew the odds were against ever seeing him again, and on a superficial day-to-day level I was okay with it. But I couldn't let go, not entirely.

The advent of the Internet gave me fresh hope of finding him, and I spent a lot of time typing his name into search engines and scouring the results. It seemed that as far as the Internet was concerned, he didn't exist. I'd stop for months and then have another go. I got nowhere until I had a brainstorm that was so obvious that I felt like a dumb ass for not thinking of it years ago.

Instead of looking for Terry, I looked for Susan.

I found her website within minutes and sent her an email asking if she was indeed the Susan I once knew, and if she was, could she help me find Terry? She replied the very same evening.

Yes, she was the same Susan and, yes, she remembered me. Terry was fine and living in Mexico, but he didn't have a phone and wasn't on the Internet. She was, however, able to give me his address.

I wrote straightaway, hoping for the best, even though I knew Terry wasn't the letter-writing type. Susan had suggested that I include my phone number so he could call me the next time he was in the States, which I did. A couple of months passed and nothing happened, so I wrote again and enclosed an international phone card. Still nothing.

I thought about going to Mexico and trying to find him. The address Susan gave me was for a post-office box, but it included the name of the village. In the end I decided it was a fool's errand. A gringo who couldn't speak Spanish poking around might have led to all sorts of problems.

I emailed Susan again, and she answered, saying that months go by without hearing from Terry and she didn't know what to suggest. Then my luck turned, or so it seemed.

It was Thanksgiving Day, and I was just sitting down to eat with my family when my mobile phone rang. Not wanting to interrupt the festivities, I ignored the call. After diner was over, I listened to the voice mail. Shit! It was Terry.

I was in a state of high anxiety for the next couple of weeks. Terry said he'd call me back in a few days, so I kept my phone turned on and within easy reach day and night. The call never came, but I didn't give up. Encouraged by the friendly tone of his voice mail, I sent him a Christmas card, asking him to try again.

The silence that followed convinced me that the phone message was as close to Terry as I would ever get. Besides I was eager to finish this book. I wrote the final chapter around that voice mail and figured I was done. I shopped the book to a couple of literary agents and half a dozen publishers without any luck. One made an offer, but the terms were so lopsided in the publisher's favor that I passed.

Another Thanksgiving came and went. The book languished, a tale without an ending. I tried to talk myself into believing that was the way it was meant to be, but knew how unsatisfying an unsolved mystery would be to potential readers.

Then the cosmic roulette wheel spun again and my lucky number came up. I had just finished smoking some primo pot and was laying down listening to an old Waylon Jennings CD when the phone rang. I let it ring three or four times before deciding to answer. At first I didn't realize who it was.

"Who?" I asked.

"It's Terry."

Holy shit! My mind swirled, my pulse raced and I began to sweat—all the normal stuff people do when life gets serious.

It had finally happened: I was actually talking to Terry. His voice was much deeper than I remembered—age and cigarettes, I suppose—and only the slightest hint of a Spanish accent remained.

The conversation flowed easily and we talked for almost an hour, sharing enough snatches of our lives to give a rough idea of what had gone down since those youthful days we shared in London and Morocco. Several times Terry mentioned he was "stuck" in Mexico, which surprised me; I thought he was there by choice. It had something to do with a stalled business deal and a missing partner, and it didn't sound like he would be leaving anytime soon, so I reiterated that I wanted to come and see him. We just had to figure out when. Terry said he'd call me back in a couple of days.

He didn't.

I couldn't figure it out and kept circling back to the same conundrum: Why did Terry finally call after such a long time if he didn't want to see me? It just didn't add up. Did I consider giving up and leaving him alone? Hell, no! I was more determined than ever, so I waited a month and then called him again.

Gradually, over the course of several more calls, I learned that Terry had fallen on financially hard times, mainly due, I gathered, to the aforementioned business deal. His house had serious plumbing problems and he didn't have the money to get it fixed. When I said that I would stay in a hotel and pay for anything we did, he seemed relieved and offered to find an inexpensive place for me to stay, close to his house. I wired him more money than was needed for the hotel and told him to keep what was left over and do what ever he liked with it.

"I'd pick you up at the airport," said Terry during the final call prior to my departure, "but the tires on my 25-year-old car are bad and I might not make it."

"How much does a cab cost?"

"It's pretty cheap, around $35 dollars."

"Sounds good. How shall I contact you when I get there?"

"I'll be sitting on a bench across from the hotel when you arrive."

He wasn't, of course, but I wasn't worried. Terry was generally late. I knew he'd show up.

DREAMS AND REALITY

Almost colliding with Terry as I left the hotel was not how I'd imagined our reunion, but I have to admit the timing was exquisite. A split second, one way or the other, would have changed the entire dynamic. As it was, the sudden in-your-face nature of our meeting triggered a sensory overload that popped and sizzled like an old-fashioned flashbulb.

Terry, dressed in jeans and a short-sleeved shirt, was as lean as ever, his face wrinkled but recognizable, his eyes now closer to gray than blue. He still had a mustache, but it was trimmed straight across and gave him a more severe look than the droopy hippie version he loved to stroke back in the day.

More than anything else, my immediate impression was that he looked older than I thought he would. But what the hell did I expect? The sapling of his early manhood was nothing more than a memory, and it was too soon to know how much of his youthful chi remained inside the mortal shell.

I don't remember exactly what happened next, whether we hugged or just shook hands. I know I said, "I can't believe this is really happening," more than once. Giddy with excitement, a boyish exuberance had taken over and carried me to a place that I'd almost forgotten—a place of unlimited possibilities where dreams and reality came together as naturally as the sea meets the shore.

"Let's go over to the plaza and sit down," said Terry. "We can talk there."

Everything seemed real and unreal at the same time. There I was, sitting on a wooden bench in Mexico, talking to a long lost friend who I hadn't seen in 46 years. It was the culmination of a decades' long search for a man I'd only known for three or four months. It was one of those circumstances when the light of reality is so bright it almost blinds you.

It was impossible to soak it all in at once, and the specifics of our first conversation escape me. I know I must have babbled on, doing most of the talking and bombarding Terry with questions. The unique circumstances seemed to have intensified the amphetamine, and I wanted to know everything at once, but managed to restrain myself enough to salvage a modicum of decorum.

Before I left for Mexico, a friend asked what I would do if Terry had changed so much that we didn't have anything in common anymore. I said I was ready to accept whatever happened, and I was. But it was never an issue. There was still a chemistry between us, not like it was the last time I'd seen him, of course, but similar. We were comfortable together, and that says a lot. If there was a lull in the conversation, it came when Terry was pondering one of my questions.

It was a pleasantly warm evening, and most of the crowd had already left the plaza, the vendors were packing up and heading home. Except for our voices, the only sounds were the occasional shrill laugher of a child somewhere in the distance and the *thump, thump, thump* of an occasional car rolling slowly over the cobblestones.

"Let's go back to the house," said Terry. "I have some pot if you want to smoke."

"Cool. How is the weed around here?"

"It's okay, but it's not the really good stuff. You have to drive about 300 miles and it's dangerous."

As we left the plaza, I wanted to ask what kind of danger he was talking about, but decided against it. I'd already asked too many questions and didn't want to sound pushy. Besides, there was already enough sensory stimulation taking place. Here I was, for the first time in almost five decades, walking and talking with Terry, a new adventure afoot.

Although it was long ago and far away, walking together felt precisely the same as it did in Tangier and London. It's funny how you can remember a feeling much better than a fact. There was something comforting and fulfilling about being with Terry. It was probably what I had craved the most, the thing that drove my fixation to find him as much as anything. A simple need to be in his presence.

I'd thought of him as my daemon—Max Demian to my Emil Sinclair. And in some ways he was. But that romantic notion was of the intellect, what I was experiencing came from a different place. It came from my core, the very essence of who I was and why I was there. Terry had been my guide and mentor, the guy who set me on a journey that had finally led me back to him.

The streets were paved with rocks from Lake Chapala, hammered into the earth by local masons many years ago and worn semi-smooth by time and traffic. The sidewalks were narrow with barely enough room for one person to pass, so we walked in the street most of the way, ducking between parked cars when a vehicle clattered and bumped its way past.

We stopped at a tiny store to pick up something to drink. Behind the counter, sat a chunky, middle-age man with a bored look on his pock-marked face. He was clearly the proprietor and probably lived above the store with his family. He glanced our way when we entered and then looked away, satisfied were we harmless gringos who were going to spend a few pesos.

"I wouldn't get that if I were you," said Terry, as I reach for a bottle of Corona in refrigerator. "The Corona they sell in Mexico is not the same as the Corona they sell in the States. It tastes bad."

"What do you recommend?"

"Try Modelo; it's much better."

I bought a can of Modelo and a bottle of orange soda; Terry didn't want anything. I held out a handful of pesos, and the owner picked out the correct amount as I stood there looking like an idiot.

"Gracias, senior."

"You're welcome" was not one of the six Spanish phrases I had practiced prior to my visit, so I settled for "buenas noches" and a smile.

I knew that good manners and respect were fundamental to getting by in Mexico, and during my stay I made a point of saying hello to almost everybody I encountered. They replied in kind every single time, and I soon grew to like these cordial formalities. The ritual of acknowledging and being acknowledged was somehow comforting and quite unlike back home, where people were too busy using their mobile devices to bother about the actual world around them.

A few minutes after leaving the store we turned left at the next intersection and then left again a block later. There was a high wall that started at the corner and extended down the block. Terry stopped at the second door in the wall, pulled a key out of his pocket and inserted it into the lock.

"Be careful around the inside latch," said Terry, as he closed the metal door behind us. "A Black Widow spider lives there. We don't want to disturb her."

THE SPIDER'S HOUSE

The door opened onto a patio paved with six-sided tiles, over which an ancient plum tree spread its gnarled limbs. The twisted branches reached out for support wherever they could find it. One rested on top of the outer wall and another on the roof of the house.

Once inside the house two things were instantly obvious: It was both splendid and falling into disrepair. The spacious living room, where I was to spend much of my time over the next week, was covered in a layer of dust and infused with sunlight. There were six large, full-length windows, two on each of the three outside walls, and as the sun made its journey through the sky, there was always daylight coming through at least one of the windows.

There was a fireplace at one end of the room with a pen-and-ink drawing of three charras on the mantelpiece. During the Mexican revolution, these women, dressed in traditional charro clothing and riding sidesaddle, were used a decoys. They would gallop off to raise a cloud of dust so that the Federales would think an attack would come from that direction. Then the revolutionaries would attack from the rear. Today, they compete in a precision equestrian event called the escaramuza.

Small terracotta statues of Hindu deities flanked the drawing and larger clay figures of a bird and a dog guarded the hearth. A couple of bookshelves, built into one of the outside walls, held a scattering of dusty books and decorative pieces of sculpture, seemingly abandoned like treasures in an Pharaoh's tomb.

The green-drenched view from the windows overlooked an unkempt but beautiful garden. Plants spilled over the tops of their containers, untrimmed fruit trees were bursting with leaves and what looked like bamboo reached for the sun from a giant earthenware pot.

All the greenery created a shady oasis, and where the sunlight penetrated, the foliage was splashed with incandescent yellow. It was magnificently unkempt and reminded me of Frances Hodgson Burnett's novel, *The Secret Garden*, although, as I would later discover, it did not have the transformative healing power of the walled garden as fictional Misselthwaite Manor.

"This place is beautiful."

"Thank you. My father built it for me. Well, I gave him $40,000, and he designed it and had it built."

"He did a wonderful job. Was he an architect?"

"By training, yes, but he worked at a Madison Avenue advertising agency."

I was about to sit on the large leather couch that faced the fireplace, when Terry said, "Let's go up to my bedroom to smoke, just in case my sister stops by. I'm going outside to take a piss. I'll be right back."

Terry's sister, Cassandra, lived in another house on the same property, which was where he apparently spent most of his time, returning to his own house to sleep. I'd spoken to her briefly over the phone, but we'd never met. Terry had always smoked openly in the company of Susan, and it struck me odd that Cassandra obviously disapproved. I didn't know he had another sister until Susan mentioned her in an email.

While Terry was urinating, I had a quick look around. The kitchen was in a sad state: What had once been a handsome room had been turned into an indoor junkyard. The tables, counters, stovetop, sink, and every other available surface were cluttered with tools, plumbing fixtures, cooking utensils, cutlery, old shopping bags, empty bottles, and other household miscellanea—

all of it covered with an even thicker layer of dust than the living room. It had been months, probably years, since a meal had been prepared there.

I jogged up the stairway a few steps to a mezzanine that housed a large bedroom. There were two single beds, completed with blankets and pillows, covered, not only with dust but also paint and plaster flakes that had fallen from the ceiling. The enjoining bathroom still had a few dusty towels hanging on a rack. What a sad and lonely place, deserted and waiting for the roof to cave in.

Terry returned from the garden and we walked up the stairs another level to his bedroom. It was dark inside, with only the bed and the immediate area around it illuminated, the rest of the room was in shadow and indistinguishable.

"I've got some rolling papers somewhere. Let's see if I can find them," said Terry, leaving the room.

There was a small amount of marijuana on the bedside table, along with a collection of personal items, including a tiny passport-size photo of a man, which I guessed was his father.

A Lady of Guadalupe prayer card was propped against the base of the lamp, which was a bit of a surprise. I don't recall much talk, if any, of Catholicism, when we roomed together in London. That's probably because Terry didn't have a care in the world back then, but it was already clear to me that life had worn him down. You could hear it in his voice and see it in his eyes.

"Here you go," said Terry, interrupting my reverie and handing me a couple of papers. "I don't smoke much anymore, just a few puffs when I go to bed."

"But you're going to smoke with me tonight, right?"

"A little."

The role reversal was a mild shock at first: My mentor, the guy who "opened the world of Hip" to me had lapsed into a state of near-abstinence. This time I was the smiling advocate of the stoner lifestyle, winging my way through an incredible day, feeling twenty years younger than I should and very much alive.

At first glance, the pot didn't look very promising. Dirt weed is usually brown, and besides, this stuff looked dried up, unlike anything I'd smoked in decades. But when I began to clean it, I discovered that the tiny buds were still moist inside, and the fatty I rolled got both of us wrecked.

As we sat across from each other in that dim circle of light, talking and smoking the joint, the rest of the world disappeared. Nothing existed in the darkness beyond. We had shared the sacrament together again, a ritual renewed between us. At that moment, we could just as well have been in the London flat as Terry's bedroom in Jalisco.

It was impossible to know what Terry was thinking, of course, but at one point he laughed and said, apropos nothing in particular, "I'm really wasted."

He had clearly exceeded the "few puffs before bed" stage, and I wondered how long it had been since he'd been so high.

Was it just my stubborn persistence that had brought us to that moment or was something larger in play? I thought about London and how much the new scene resembled the old one. Was there something to all this beyond my obsessive search for my old smuggling buddy? Does it even matter?

Terry told me about the death of his mother and father and brother Kit, a series of events that had a profound effect on him. Back in London, Susan had told me that Kit, who had apparently drank himself to death, was Terry's boyhood hero, but he spoke more about his father's demise than the others.

"My father had been sick for some time, and I tried to convince him to go back to the States to see a specialist. At first he refused to go and was treated here by a local doctor. When he finally went, he was diagnosed with cancer. The treatments were very painful and toward the end, he wore a medicated mask over his face. But nothing worked."

Terry stopped for a few seconds, gathering himself in the semi-darkness of his most private space. This was some heavy shit he was laying on me.

"After his last trip to the States, he asked me if I would mind driving back by the old route, the way we used to go when we first staring coming to Mexico. It took longer, but he knew he was dying and wanted to see it one last time."

I visualized the two of them, cruising down a rural Mexico road, old memories gliding by one last time. It was heartbreaking stuff, but there was nothing I could say or do that would ease his grief—nothing I could think of, anyway—so I just listened.

"It's funny when I think about all the plans my mother and father made … and then how everything fell apart."

I tried to change the subject by talking about the things we'd done together, asking if he remembered this or that. He said he did but never added much, so I wondered if he really did recall or was just pretending for my sake. Then I mentioned Susan's old boyfriend, Carlos.

"I'm surprised you remember him," he said, a smiling again. "He was a real asshole."

"Yeah, I never really understood what she saw in him. Remember the stories he used to tell about how he'd been some sort of revolutionary back in Argentina and showed everybody the scars he had around his wrists? Claimed they were from the handcuffs he'd worn."

"That was a load of shit."

"What ever happened to him?"

"I don't know. Susan dumped him."

We must have talked for at least two hours, and no matter how many times I tried to change the topic, Terry always returned to the death of his family members. After a while, I gave up trying to get away from the subject and went with the flow.

"I also watched my father die. We were on vacation when he had a heart attack and collapsed on the sidewalk. He was literally laughing one second and dead the next. It was an extraordinary moment, and in a way it was like watching my own death as well as his. That was around ten years ago, but I miss him more now than when he died, especially when I do or see things I know he would have enjoyed."

Terry nodded but didn't say anything and the silence hung in the air like an invisible curtain of black crepe. Death was all around us, but we were still alive in a world of endless possibilities. That was more than enough for me, but I had an eerie feeling that Terry didn't care much one way or another.

I lit the roach, took a puff and held it out to him.

"No thanks, that's enough for me. It's getting late. I'll walk you back to your hotel."

It was a lovely night, the air fresh and warm, the sky a deep blue, speckled with yellow stars. Except for the noise of an out-of-tune mariachi band rehearsing somewhere down the street, it was quiet outside of Terry's gate. I glanced round, looking for some sort of landmark that would help me find the house again, and settled on a sign for some sort of repair shop on the opposite corner.

As we ambled over the cobbles toward my hotel I noticed how different everything looked. The afternoon sunlight had been replaced by long stretches of darkness, broken occasionally by a pool of dim light that only served to emphasized the stark contrast between the two. The picturesque had turned vaguely menacing. It wasn't long, however, before we were in front of the hotel, the orangey glow of the lobby a reassuring welcome.

"What are your plans for tomorrow?"

"I'll stop by the hotel around noon."

"Cool. See you then."

Terry turned and walked away, and I continued up the stone pathway to the lavish embrace of the Heron suite. It had been quite a day, the end of a protracted pursuit for my past; there was no mission-accomplished moment, and as I fell asleep all I could think about was what tomorrow might bring.

THE PLAZA

Around six in the morning, I was jarred awake by a rooster crowing. Any thought of dozing off again evaporated when, about five minutes later, a loud metallic banging noise knocked the last vestiges of sleep out of my brain. I guessed it was coming from the old, mission-style church across the street from my hotel. But it didn't sound like any church bell I'd ever heard. It sounded more a clunk than a chime, as if somebody was hitting an anvil with a crowbar.

I took a piss and crawled back into bed for an hour or so, where I divided my time between scribbling in my notebook, flicking through the TV channels, and watching a horde of pencil-point size bugs attack a few crumbs on the table left over from my bedtime snack.

By the time I finally got up, taken a twenty-second shower (that's how long the hot water lasted) and shaved, I could hear the maids happily chattering outside. I peeked out the window and saw them on the flat roof of the row of rooms across the path from mine. They were hanging the laundry out to dry and gossiping, just like they do in Morocco.

I pulled on my jeans and a fresh T-shirt and headed for the plaza in search of breakfast.

The plaza has been a central part of Mexican culture for at least 4,000 years. Originally it was a sacred space used for religious ceremonies and represented the primordial sea from which the earth emerged. Over the ensuing centuries it evolved into the heart of the community, a kind of public living room-cum-marketplace where friends meet, ritual and celebrations take place, and tourists buy handicrafts made by local artisans.

In an ironic twist of imperialistic infringement, European invaders who sought to eradicate native culture actually preserved it as they covered the Mesoamerican plazas with Renaissance-style orthogonal grids with a central open space. I'm sure old Quetzalcoatl had a good laugh about it.

The first person I encountered was an old lady wearing plastic sandals sweeping the plaza with a handmade broom fashioned from broomcom, a variety of sorghum cultivated for its stiff stems. A little girl, most likely her granddaughter, accompanied her. The toddler's job was to carry the plastic bucket in which the old woman deposited the litter.

"Buenos días."

The old lady glanced my way, smiled shyly and replied. I was to see her every morning on my way to breakfast, but that was the only day the little girl was with her.

Later that week, I saw the woman actually making a broom. Her brown hands were large and her fingers thick, but she tied the broomcom around a wooden shaft with commendable dexterity. I admired the dignity with which she went about her daily task and wondered what her life had been like when she was young.

I found a perfect breakfast spot, at the far end of the plaza, a restaurant with a large patio that accommodated a number of umbrella-covered tables. Three or four of the tables were already occupied by English-speaking expats, who, despite their age, looked bright-eyed and full of life. I liked the vibe and settled into a wicker chair at an unoccupied table that afforded me an unobstructed view of the plaza.

Getting a decent vegetarian meal can be a pain in the ass in a lot of restaurants, but after a quick scan of the menu, I settled on molletes rancheros—a fresh bolio from the bakery across the plaza, smeared with a layer of refried beans covered in cheese. It's popped in the oven until the cheese melts, and served with a side order of salsa and lime wedges. The salsa, fresh and pungent, was probably made that very morning from veggies not long removed from the earth.

A few drops of lime juice, squeezed on top of the salsa, was the catalyst that released a surprisingly complex combination of tastes—light and zesty, dark and warm, all at the same time. I was instantly hooked and ordered the same thing every freakin' morning but one. The waffles and fruit were very good, but for this gringo, molletes rancheros were a culinary revelation.

Although it was fairly early in the morning, the plaza was already awake, the ageless rhythm and patterns of village life beginning to stir. Vendors wandered in and out of the restaurant, selling fresh strawberries and green beans. They were not at all intrusive, politely showing their wares and silently moving on if no interest was shown. At the table to my right, a shoeshine guy was polishing a burly gringo's motorcycle boots.

A doe-eyed young girl carried a tray of small hand-carved and painted bobble-head turtles for sale. She moved almost by rote, her face a docile mask, her eyes remote. I beckoned her closer and she held out the tray so I could better see the selection of wooden reptiles on display.

I picked a purple one. It had a green head with saucer eyes that looked up at you as it bobbed this way and that. I can't recall how much it cost, but the fact she had made a sale didn't seem to move the child one way or another. The turtle girl simply thanked me and continued on her route, only to return the next morning and every morning thereafter, wandering through the restaurant with her tray—another player in the daily cycle of life in the plaza.

A couple of young musicians, one with a guitar and the other with a flute, were regulars. Their music was folksy and sweet, and most of the patrons tipped them after they'd finished their mini-concert. They might have had to kick back a few pesos to the proprietor, but I doubt it. The village plaza belonged to nobody and to everybody.

After wolfing down the molletes rancheros, I lingered over

my third cup of coffee. It was excellent, but not quite as good as the brew at the roadside restaurant where Curtis, D-Jay and I stopped on our way to Nuevo Laredo. Along with some primo Jamaican Blue Mountain, the coffee in that obscure roadside joint was the best I've ever tasted.

That first trip to Mexico was about a craving for freedom and adventure, sex and drugs, a temporary diversion from the rigid limitation of army life and an uncertain future. This trip was a search for the past, a circle back to the beginning of a stoner journey and the person who set my compass. But instead of a smiling, reassuring guru, I had found a man wounded by circumstances, who seemed to lack the strength to escape the limbo in which he was trapped. And yet I still felt drawn to him and eagerly awaited our meeting later that day.

THE LIGHT OF DAY

I poured some of the cocaine onto the glass top of the coffee table, chopped it up with a credit card and carved out two fat lines. Then I rolled a twenty-dollar bill into a cylinder and bent over the table, ready to take my first taste in three or four years.

"Here, use this," said Terry, handing me a three-inch section of a plastic drinking straw. "Old bills have lots of germs."

"Thanks. Want a bump?"

"No thanks, I'm going to have lunch with Cassandra. See you in a while."

If Mike's pharmaceutical windfall was an A plus, the stuff Terry procured for me was a B. A note in my journal read, "very enjoyable ... very enjoyable," and indeed it was, so much so that the remainder of my stay was flavored by the reunion with Mama Coca.

I rolled a joint, smoked half, did another line, and soon found myself enveloped in a cocaine and cannabis cocoon. Time slowed down and I became enamored by the beauty of sunlight coming through the windows and how its qualities changed as the afternoon progressed. It was reminiscent of that sunny winter day in London when I stood at the window staring at a tree in a neighboring backyard, waiting for my first dose of acid to kick in.

By the time the light began to fade, I'd finished the joint and snorted several more lines. Two or three hours had past since Terry left, but I was totally satisfied to simply exist in the here and now, cruising along in a cozy trance-like state where perception infiltrated my mind as surely and gradually as the sun moved slowly through the sky.

Mankind's connection to nature has always been a very meaningful part of my mindset. We're all born that way, but can easily lose the thread amid the struggles of day-to-day living and the false promise of materialism. But I was lucky to have a grandfather, born and raised in the country, who showed me where to find birds' nests in the bushes and where the best blackberries and wild raspberries grew.

He told me about rescuing lambs in the snow and climbing the greasy pole at the village fair. Every night before he went to bed, he stepped outside to look at the sky and predicted the next day's weather. His blood still runs in me.

The importance of man's relationship with nature is often reinforced when I'm high, reminding me that I'm part of the whole, an infinitesimal part to be sure, but a part nonetheless. The concept is simultaneously enhancing and terrifying, as eternal as the sky and as absolute as the final heartbeat.

Being at peace with the whole is to become one with it, and during that first afternoon in Terry's living room, the light of day shone so brightly that the truth sparkled in its reflection. And its beauty mesmerized me.

As darkness approached, I saw Terry's wisp-like figure coming through the garden, moving slowly but fluidly toward the house. Then I heard the front door open and close.

"Hey, how's it going?" Terry said, folding himself into the armchair next to the fireplace.

"Fine. The coke is pretty good. Want some?"

"No, no. Thanks all the same."

He did, however, take a drag on the new joint I'd just rolled, and conversation soon flowed freely. We talked about Quetzalcoatl and whether or not he was an extra-terrestrial, and about Terry's mother buying him an Aston Martin, which had since been totaled. He told me about a woman friend who had gotten high on acid in the woods and freaked out. I told him about Amsterdam.

Bits and pieces of Terry's life surfaced, never in much detail but enough to at least help fill in some of the gaps. At one time he had a thriving business as an agent for Mexican artists. He showed me a portfolio containing 10 lithographs by Marcus Huerta.

The prints were of strange figures, a blend of human and animal—men with swan necks and fishes growing out the back of their heads. Not the sort of thing I would want hanging in my home, but the draftsmanship was excellent and the compositions first-rate.

"What happened to your art business?"

"Well, it sort of dried up."

I didn't know what to make of such a noncommittal reply, other than it was a topic Terry really didn't want to talk about. But if that was the case, why did he show me the portfolio in the first place?

I didn't push too hard in pursuit of any topic. After all, what was I to Terry? A guy he hadn't seen in almost fifty years, who suddenly parachutes into his life, acting like they were bosom buddies. If it was a strange circumstance for me, and it was, it must have been even stranger for him. In a way, I don't think he really knew what to do with me.

My presence seemed to have fostered a gentle, almost imperceptible tug-of-war between the melancholic Terry of today and the exuberant young man I met in London. Back then Terry had a untamed enthusiasm for life, now he describes himself as a "hermit," which wasn't accurate in the strictest sense of the word but dishearteningly close.

I couldn't help trying to invoke the person I had held in my heart for so long. I wanted to make him laugh, see him smile— fuel his sense of adventure. I felt, and still feel, that the former Terry still dwelled somewhere inside him, buried beneath the layers of grief and worry.

There were a few lighthearted moments, one of which I managed to capture with my phone camera. One gorgeous afternoon, I was in the garden when Terry returned from having lunch with Cassandra. The path between the two houses was almost overgrown, a green tunnel of foliage, flecked with sunlight. He was still partly in the shadows when I asked him to stop so I could take a photo.

"Say vagina."

Caught off-guard, Terry laughed, and I pressed the button at the precise instant required to freeze the moment. Despite the shadows playing across his face, you could clearly see the smile on his lips and in his eyes. Surprise had momentarily overridden all other emotions and the Terry of my youth suddenly shone through. The image seemed almost magical, especially when compared to a handful of others I took that day and later, in which he appears to be unsuccessfully attempting to conjure up a smile.

Most encouraging was the tone of our conversation. I plunged headlong into whatever subject came to mind, and while Terry was nowhere near as talkative as me, he seemed happy enough to participate. I suppose it was the first time in a long time that anybody had shown such interest in him and asked so many questions.

Despite my intrusion into his life, Terry was unfailingly polite and considerate, two of his most admirable traits. Much of his courtly manner I attribute to breeding. His family was affluent, well educated, and led a charmed life as part of the artsy expat community in an idyllic Mexican village. They were, in a sense, part of the new American aristocracy, but not the conventional country club type. They were of a bohemian subset, the adventurous couple that went off on a great adventure and never came back.

Then rot set in. Cancer slowly killed his father and mother, and as Terry said, "everything fell apart." Clearly, his parents were the lynchpin that held everything together, and without the emotional and financial safety net they provided, my old smuggling buddy had lost his way.

That's my theory, anyway.

"Are you sure you won't change your mind?" I asked as I cut out another line.

"No, that's okay. If it wasn't for all these financial problems, I'd party more, but not the way things are now. There's a lot of stress."

Finally, there was a far more legit reason than the crap about people he knew getting ruined by drugs. It was a situation with which I could easily empathize. A few years back, I was so depressed about losing my job and didn't smoke weed for about three weeks.

"I know how you feel. I don't like to get high when I'm bummed out. Who needs enhanced reality at times like that? Do you think you are going to have to sell this house?"

"I don't want to, but it might come down to that. I've got about three acres of land I'd rather sell, but with the real-estate market being so bad, it's tough to find a buyer."

"You remind me of the penniless aristocracy in England after World War II—asset rich, cash poor. You know, the landed gentry living on big estates who couldn't even pay their taxes."

Terry chuckled and nodded his head, apparently appreciating the analogy.

"It would be great if you could sell the land and use the money to fix this place. It's such a beautiful house, it would be a sin to let it fall to pieces."

"That's what I'd like to do. I hope I can hang on until the real-estate market improves."

As the sun dipped below the rooftops and the sky darkened, our chitchat faded and a tranquil silence filled the room. Terry was sitting bent over, with both elbows resting on his knees, his chin in his hands. He looked like Van Gogh's painting of an old man sitting in the same position called, "On The Threshold of Eternity."

"Hey, Terry. You look tired. I think I'll head back to the hotel."

"Okay, I'll walk you to the corner."

We stopped at the corner and breathed in the warn night air. Terry lit a cigarette and looked up and down the street, as if he was checking to see if the coast was clear.

"When do you want to get together tomorrow?"

"Stop by around one in the afternoon."

"Okay."

As I walked away, I glanced back over my shoulder and was struck by the forlorn expression on my friend's face. He looked so frail and unhappy I spoke without really thinking about what I was saying.

"Don't worry so much, I believe in supporting the penniless aristocracy."

"In that case," Terry said, "come around 12 noon."

When I slipped Terry some money the next day, he headed straight to the grocery store.

SPINNING WHEEL

I threw my backpack onto the rear seat of the cab and hugged Terry goodbye. I didn't look back as the cab pulled away from the plaza. Looking back was what drew me to this Mexican village in the first place. Yes, it was the end of one journey and the beginning of another. But the past is forever.

I had found the living ghost of the Terry I'd known so long ago. In many ways that was enough. But as the cab's tires rippled over the cobbles one final time and carried me away from my old friend, I was still in his grip, still searching for answers and still looking for the lad I used to know—and, by extension, my own youth.

The past and the present can't coexist, but that doesn't stop you from wishing they could. Maybe if I had found Terry before his world fell apart things would have been different. Who knows?

On the most elementary level, it's simple: Time passes. Shit happens. People change. Even so, I felt like I was coming down from a mediocre acid trip—knowing I'd been somewhere but not sure where or what it meant—if anything.

How are you supposed to feel when you've accomplished something that you've wanted to do for more than half your life? All the years of searching and wondering and hoping had been rewarded the instant Terry and I almost collided at the hotel door. It was a once-in-a-lifetime jackpot, made all the sweeter because the wheel of life had spun around so many times before my number came up.

But the euphoria that took possession of me that first evening faded, leaving me with a confusing muddle of emotions. One thing, however, soon became apparent: My mission shifted from finding Terry to saving him.

I couldn't, of course, and it was naïve and pretentious of me to have such an idiotic thought in the first place. At best my visit might have temporarily lifted his spirits, but rebooting his soul was way beyond my reach.

I also couldn't solve his financial dilemma, but I could lessen the pain a little. A few days before I left, I calculated how much money I needed to get home and gave him what was left. A week or so later, I found 1500 pesos tucked away in my backpack and mailed it to his post office box.

I deposit a couple of hundred bucks in his account every now and then, partly because it feels good to help him and partly to maintain the relationship. Whatever the reason, I don't want Terry to fade away again. He was my guru, partner in crime, and for a brief period, especially in Morocco, we were a team.

Seeing Terry again fulfilled a need that had been my companion for decades. The moment we met at the hotel door it felt like I'd been shot out of a carnival cannon. My mind raced ahead of my feet and I almost walked into the path of a vehicle crossing the street to the plaza. If Terry hadn't said, "Watch your step" and plucked the back of my T-shirt at precisely the moment he did, a raggedy-ass pickup truck would have nailed me flush.

I had forgotten about the incident until I returned home and started to process what had taken place in Mexico. Tying together the string of events that took place wasn't enough, and it wasn't until I looked at things in a larger context that I started to recognize the connections. In retrospect, the incident at the curb outside my hotel took on a greater meaning.

It was the second time that Terry had changed the course of my life. Decades ago he introduced me to the boundless possibilities the world has to offer, first through a reckless adventure and then with the help of mind-expanding substances.

Within seconds of our reunion, he saved me from serious injury and possible death by uttering three words and reflexively tugging my T-shirt.

When I turned to thank him, Terry was smiling. It was the familiar half-amused, half-benevolent grin I'd seen so often in the past, the one I hadn't seen in almost 50 years. For a few seconds I was the eager young fool again, Terry my guide, if not through life, at least safely across the street.

Just who is The Old Head? Some say The Old Head is an urban legend. Others say he's a coffee shop marketing ploy. The truth, as in most great things in life, probably lies somewhere in between.

Actually, The Old Head is an internationally renowned journalist who insists on anonymity in order to protect the guilty. Although the names of many individuals have been changed, the narrative is entirely true. Those who wish to learn more about The Old Head can gain all there is to know by reading this book.

*Since you obviously enjoy
a lively and offbeat travelogue,
check out these other great books from*
The Corregidor Peace Institute Press

Ted Lerner's Timeless Classic

"Hilarious…the must read."
—Asia Pacific Business Traveller Magazine

"Exceedingly enjoyable and laugh out loud funny"
—Asia Times Online

"Lerner seems equipped with extra sensitive senses making for very entertaining and articulate writing."
—Manila Times

"Hey, Joe, you like snake?"
"Hey, Joe, welcome to Tondo!"
"Hey, Joe, what's your name?"
It's the phrase that greets every foreign guy in the Philippines on a daily basis. And perhaps nobody personifies the meaning of this moniker better than Ted Lerner, an American writer whose popular, freewheeling column, "Hey, Joe," has been entertaining readers in the Philippines and overseas for nearly 20 years.

In "Hey, Joe," Ted presents a collection of his best Manila stories, a kaleidoscope of funny and bizarre incidents, offbeat characters and keen observations dished up by a wide-eyed foreigner living in a city exploding with life, unfathomable urban chaos and a story around every corner.

From his run ins with mangy Filipino mutts, to everyone asking him "Where's my Christmas?," to the characters who peddle every product under the sun through his neighborhood, the author captures perfectly the ups and downs of everyday life experienced by the foreigner living in one of the world's largest and most chaotic cities.

"Hey, Joe" paints a multi-colored portrait of this imposing Asian metropolis, a third world, urban travel adventure as told not only through a foreigner's eyes, but also through his ears, nose, fingers and mouth. Indeed, like the city of Manila itself, Ted Lerner's "Hey, Joe," is a full body experience.

Made in the USA
Las Vegas, NV
08 December 2020